5.00 fine
N BO

1971

1972 2ranstated from
German

Colorado
Collection
2015

D0955428

Collectors
Item

CHALLENGING THE DEEP

CHALLENGING THE LEFT

CHALLENGING THE DEEP

by Hans Hass

translated by Ewald Osers

WILLIAM MORROW AND COMPANY, INC.
NEW YORK

Translation published in the United States in 1973.
Copyright © 1972 by George G. Harrap & Co. Ltd.
Published in Great Britain in 1972 under the title:
To Unplumbed Depths.

German edition published by Verlag Fritz Molden under
the title: *In unberührte Tiefen*. Copyright © 1971 by
Verlag Fritz Molden, Vienna-Munich-Zurich.

All rights reserved. No part of this book may be
reproduced or utilized in any form or by any means,
electronic or mechanical, including photocopying,
recording or by any information storage and
retrieval system, without permission in writing
from the Publisher. Inquiries should be addressed
to William Morrow and Company, Inc., 105 Madison
Ave., New York, N.Y. 10016.

Printed in Great Britain.

. . . .

Hass, Hans.
   Challenging the deep.

   Translation of In unberührte Tiefen.
   Autobiographical.
   1. Diving, Submarine.   2.   Skin diving.
I. Title.
GV840.S78H3313   797.2'3'0924 [B]   72-8443
ISBN 0-688-00140-8

Corrigendum

Please note that due to a binding error text page
captions (pages 48, 112, 128, 145, 161, 193)
appear two pages after the relevant set of
illustrations.

PUBLISHER'S PREFACE

Astronauts apart, one would think that these days there was no longer anyone who could maintain that he had conquered an unknown land or opened up a new continent. Yet Dr Hans Hass, whose intellectual curiosity remains undimmed, can claim precisely this. He pioneered man's penetration of nature's vast, unexplored seas.

He was the first to venture with spear and camera into the shark-infested waters of the Caribbean (1939), and he was the first to do the same in the Red Sea (1949), on Australia's Great Barrier Reef (1952), off the Galapagos Islands (1953), and in the Indian Ocean (1957). Since he proved it was possible, countless people have followed him, a whole avalanche of explorers and sportsmen; following his example, biologists transferred their studies to the ocean bed; and a whole industry supplying diving and underwater gear, underwater cameras and other specialist equipment for diving enthusiasts began to build up.

In 1960 Hans Hass sold his famous ship and gave up diving. What had spurred him on in his daring ventures had basically been that which was hidden and puzzling in nature, and it became clear to him that the answer to this puzzle was not only to be found in the sea. For more than ten years, little was heard of him. In the meantime more underwater books appeared every year; in many of them the name of Hass was barely mentioned. In fact, what Hass had done and told of decades before was often presented as something new and sensational.

The time seems ripe, therefore, to make available a complete perspective of the achievements of Hans Hass to show both the unique blend of sense of adventure and scientific curiosity, and the motives of the man behind them. This book is a linking of the best of his previous books, most of them long out of print or unavailable in English, together with an account of his most recent activities.

Hass has recently returned from his biological-philosophical 'marine researches on dry land' to the sea again, for although he continues his work in that field, he has been seized again by a longing for the sea. With his family, now grown up, and his wife, Lotte, who is as keen on diving now as ever, he is off on his remarkable adventures again, and is making new films.

Hans Hass is the founder of modern underwater research; at once a scientist and a popularizer.

CONTENTS

INTRODUCTION

I am flicking through the pages of my old manuscripts, and the past is coming to life again before my mind's eye. Everything was different then. The vast seas were still untouched. Fish and sharks swam about undisturbed, through mysterious abysses which no human eye had ever seen. Man still confined himself to sailing his boats over the 'sky' of the submarine continents, among the 'clouds' which we call waves. But Man was cunning. He hooked tasty morsels to the end of long thin lines and lowered them into the sea. And woe to the fish that devoured them. Man also cast out nets and fish traps. But he himself remained on the surface. He was not yet gripped by any sporting zeal to roam the depths himself or to molest the fish in their own realm. The sports enthusiasts were still busy conquering the mountains. With strips of wood on their feet they climbed up the wintry slopes and glaciers—and slid down the way they had just come up. Then they climbed up once more and once more skied down. There were no ski-lifts then to save them the trouble of climbing. Nor were there any skindiving devices which would enable Man to turn himself into a fish for an hour. There were no schnorkels, no fins, no masks. There were no luxury hotels with skindivers' launches, compressors and diving instructors. There were no diving clubs, no underwater spear-fishing competitions, no underwater photography, no specialized journals for the submarine sportsman. Man had not yet conquered the sea. The confrontation between Man and the ocean was still taking place on the sky of the submarine continents. It was a struggle against the rolling cloud banks of waves which grew to gigantic size in a storm. Only professional divers in clumsy diving suits, dangling from a long hose and emitting air bubbles, were seen from time to time. Otherwise the world below water was undisturbed.

As for myself, I was keen on sport and a bit of a daredevil—like a lot of other young people. If there was anything at all that distinguished me from my school-friends it was perhaps my predilection for doing something that others were not doing. But there was really nothing then to justify or predict the road I was to take. I was living a long way from the nearest sea—in Vienna. I was particularly far away from the tropical seas which I was subsequently to explore. It would have been far more likely for some young people in the Caribbean or off the coasts of the South Sea islands to take up the sport of spear fishing and skindiving, to build a watertight case for a photographic or cine-camera and take pictures among the coral reefs. But oddly enough no one there seems to have conceived the idea—perhaps because of the sharks, about which terrible tales were told. In the course of my expeditions I have never once come to a new spot where the natives have not regarded me as a lunatic and a suicide. Now that countless people have followed in my tracks, the fear of sharks may not have greatly diminished but at least a breakthrough has been made. Today the world of fish has been invaded everywhere by swarms of skindiving fish-men.

I was not the first underwater spear fisherman nor do I hold myself solely responsible for the turn which skindiving and submarine research have since taken. But in the tropical seas I was the first nearly everywhere, and my books and films have played a major part in promoting this development which must certainly be unpleasant for the creatures of the sea. I have antagonized a great many wives whose husbands, inspired by my accounts, have taken up an activity which to them, the wives, seems highly dangerous and unwise. And there are no doubt quite a few parents in whose bad books I am. I even fear that I may be indirectly responsible for the deaths of some people I have never seen or spoken to. I myself have frequently staked my life rather thoughtlessly. But in the oceans I eventually discovered a huge as yet untouched field of activity, a gigantic realm which 'normal' people have passed by without a second thought.

In the last chapter of my first book—the chapter entitled 'A Look into the Future'—I wrote:

The world has been so thoroughly explored that there is little left for young discoverers. The wastes of eternal ice, the zones of infernal heat, the most jagged gigantic mountain, the darkest primeval forest—into all these Man has forced his way, on all these has he left his footprints. In the years to come I shall try to explore more closely the coral reefs of the tropical seas and to record their landscapes and colourful denizens in colour photographs and colour films. With greatly improved equipment I shall venture to stand up to the great predators of the sea and—if possible—go hunting under water at night with a searchlight on my head. To what extent I shall succeed in this I cannot possibly tell today.

Well, I did succeed. And it may not be quite without interest to turn back to the days when all this began, to my first attempts in the Mediterranean. My moment of truth came on a sunny day in July 1937. I was eighteen, I had passed

9

my school-leaving exam, and my parents had sent me to France on my own. I was to have my corners knocked off. I had them knocked off all right—first in Paris, then at Juan-les-Pins. Then I met a girl and things did not work out right. I was irritable, unhappy, depressed. I rode out alone to the Cap d'Antibes. There I clambered about the rocks and let the wind blow through my hair. . . .

And here I shall go on to what I experienced and wrote down at the time.

HUNTING UNDER WATER

A New Sport

A brilliant hot day had lured me out into the romantic wilderness of the coast beyond Juan-les-Pins. There was not a breath of wind, the air was shimmering, the waves were lapping lazily against the rocks. Except for their regular splash all was silent: the sea was lazy and gentle, and only now and then came the muffled rumble of a wave which had lost itself in one of the coast's many caverns and was now angrily seeking its way out.

As I was clambering over a large boulder I caught sight of a man swimming among the rocks, his face under water, as if searching for something in the greenish-blue depths. In his right hand was a long pole, and as he raised his head to breathe I noticed that he was wearing a curious pair of goggles. But the strangest thing about him was the way in which, from time to time, he would vanish in the water. He did not dive in the usual manner, but instead sank soundlessly, without even a ripple betraying his disappearance. After an astonishingly long time he would reappear unexpectedly in a total different spot; just as soundlessly as he had vanished.

What was he diving for? As a passionate swimmer and diver I was consumed with curiosity. Was he looking for shells or sponges? Curiously I clambered on to a rock which projected far out into the sea and from there watched the strange diver at close range.

Almost within arm's reach the sun-tanned body swam past. Then it dived, and I was able to observe it closely in the calm clear water. His long spear poised in his right hand, he swam past, below my vantage point, just like a large light-coloured predatory fish. He hardly seemed to move his arms and legs, yet his progress was very fast. Cautiously he approached a tangle of coloured seaweed, visible deep down near a dark crevice.

In one of those rare moments when the waves seem to stand still and the sea acquires an almost unreal clarity I saw a large fish hovering near the sea bed by the clump of seaweed. And then the unexpected happened. The hunter in the depths suddenly shot forward like an arrow, I saw a sudden bright flash, and then he surfaced again with the large fish wriggling on his spear, pierced through the middle.

I was thunderstruck. I should not have believed this possible.

The man now climbed out of the water, put down his harpoon and rubber goggles and killed the fish with a knife he wore on his belt. I opened the conversation with a polite inquiry.

The underwater hunter, as I soon learned, was an American. His skin seemed tanned by sun and water, his hair was bleached pale like straw. In my curiosity I fired at him all those countless questions which were to be fired at me so often in the future. How did he manage to stay so long under water? How did he stop the fish from swimming away? Were these strange goggles indispensable?

The American replied courteously and readily. He told me about the beauty of the sea bed, about the many fish which lived there, and about the harpoon with which he hunted them. He conjured up before me, for the first time, that new world that was to become so familiar to me later. But Guy Gilpatrik—that was his name—imparted to me not only his enthusiasm as an underwater hunter but also advised me how I might conquer this world for myself.

'But don't ever forget the dangers,' he concluded, pointing to a long knife which he wore on a small leather belt on his left hip. 'There are sharks here, too.'

'Sharks?'

The friendly American also warned me against the giant octopus. 'You've got to be very careful,' he said. 'Never dive too close to steep rocks, because that's where the enormous specimens frequently hide in crevices and caves. Such an octopus will quite suddenly shoot out his long tentacles, embrace anything that swims past too close, and pull it into its hole with incredible force. And never try to strike an octopus with your harpoon—it won't retreat like other fish but, on the contrary, will grip the harpoon and climb up on it. And that could be quite dangerous!'

He finally warned me against poisonous moray eels and sting-rays, wished me success in my attempts and once more disappeared under the waves, soundlessly and suddenly as he had appeared.

No doubt everybody experiences a moment in his life when he feels that he has met his own good fortune and must grasp it and hold on to it. That is how I felt that day. Without much reflection I set off at once, in spite of the noon-day heat, to get some underwater hunting equipment as quickly as possible.

The goggles were soon found, but I had to wait a few days for my harpoon since its manufacture required a good deal of metal-working. So it came about that for the first few days I set out with nothing more than my goggles to make my first acquaintance with that strange realm that was to become so familiar to me.

The Skindiver's Goggles

When I held my first underwater goggles in my hands that day in Antibes, that little contraption of glass and rubber, I little suspected how many wonderful hours it would give me. I experienced some magnificent calm summer days under a brilliant sky and with a motionless sea. The depths of the ocean revealed to me their wonders and the romantic ideas of my youth were coming true.

Precipitous rocks dropped sheer into the sea, riven by crevices disappearing far below in the strange blue of the depths. Delicately coloured seaweed and other flora covered the rocks, continually changing their hue in the tremulous light filtering in from above.

And this fairy-tale world was populated by fishes—scintillating in all colours, swarming in all sizes and shapes in the crevices and among the brilliant seaweed, the bolder ones approaching so close that one felt like catching them with one's hands—but then one had a surprise. One's vision was distorted and one's arms suddenly seemed very short. Everything in fact seemed much larger and closer than it was in reality—the light was refracted by the air enclosed in the goggles.

It is a bit of a disappointment when one has speared one's first fish and has proudly dragged it to the shore to discover that on dry land it seems to have shrunk quite considerably.

At no time in my life have I been so utterly happy as in those early days when all these strange impressions were borne in on me for the first time. I spent hours swimming along the coast of Antibes, diving, never tiring of all the new things I saw. Even without a harpoon I tried to creep up on all those beautiful fishes the American had described to me—the flat, silvery sheepsheads whose favourite spot is just outside the crevices, the plump, greedy bogues which feed in shoals off the forests of seaweed, the slim, broad-mouthed grey mullet which flit past the rock faces, and many others.

Frequently I also dived to admire the magnificent colours of a delicate sea anemone at close quarters.

Apprenticeship and First Attempts

My harpoon was ready! I remember very well how proudly I set out on my first spear-fishing expedition, and I must admit that I was sadly disappointed. I had intended to come home in the evening laden with fish, but I soon discovered that it was by no means so easy to get within spearing distance of a fish. It seemed to me as though the fish had all been far more trusting when I had visited them without a harpoon. Now they seemed to guess my intentions and made off the moment I dived.

At last I got close to a fairly large fish. I had to get that one—it was positioned perfectly just off a rock, clearly outlined and motionless. Very slowly and carefully I crept up on my quarry. I took aim and flung my harpoon with all my strength—against the rock. The fish moved away, mockingly as it seemed to me, and not even in too much of a hurry. And the point of my beautiful harpoon was broken.

I was not very lucky with my new point either. On the very first day I ran it through my own hand while swimming. The pain and shock made me drop it, and it fell to a depth of over sixty feet. After several hours of laborious work I eventually succeeded in recovering it with a noose. But my hand was still bleeding. I began to realize that it would be both wiser and more profitable to go hunting with a companion.

As chance had it, I ran into my old friend Viktor Marischka in Juan-les-Pins. I told him about my adventures on the bottom of the sea and he was so excited at the idea that he immediately went to buy a pair of goggles. From that day onwards I had a faithful companion and indefatigable comrade.

Near Cannes is the pearl of the Mediterranean, the island of Ste Marguerite; its small sister, the island of St Honorat, is much lonelier but incomparably richer in fish, especially at its eastern point. St Honorat is not uninhabited. Hidden behind tall bramble hedges, in the shady pine wood which covers the whole island, is an ancient monastery, and on the southern beach a fortress towers defiantly skywards, testimony to a long history.

That was where we were advised to try our luck. And the rocks off the beach were in fact swarming with fish.

Viktor had spotted the strange flat fish, a slow, lazy fellow. I speared it and with triumphant shouts we swam back to the beach to show it to our friends. I was about to touch it when I received an electric shock. I had caught an electric ray, that strange fish which renders other fish senseless by giving them electric shocks.

A few days passed; gradually we became more successful and brought home some nice specimens. Then one day, by a cliff, I saw my first big fish. It was lying quite still with dark green scales, a broad head, and long fins now scarcely moving in the calm water. That was how we saw it a little over thirty feet down, in front of a crevice. Viktor and I, both of us terribly excited, held a council of war on a rock. What should we do? Dive down and try to spear the monster? But how were we to raise it, seeing that it was probably much stronger than either of us?

Viktor had an idea. We swam back to the island and bought a long rope from some fishermen. We tied the harpoon point to one end and 'secured' the other end round Viktor. I was to dive down and spear the fish while Viktor was to remain sitting on the rock—the rest would work out somehow.

Meanwhile the wind had freshened and was driving high waves in front of it. Viktor was cold on his rock and wanted to get into the water, so we both swam to the spot where we supposed the fish to be.

To begin with we had quite a game with the waves which lifted us up and deposited us on the sharp, urchin-covered rocks, only to sweep us down again into the water. To make things worse, our rope was caught in the rock. While we were trying to free it it twisted around our legs and we were helplessly at the mercy of the waves.

After a great deal of trouble we succeeded in freeing ourselves. By then the water was rather murky and opaque. Close to the rocks were thousands of minute fish which always adopt that kind of spot in bad weather. That is why, even during a gale, one can see fishermen sitting on the rocks and catching nothing but tiny little fish—these then go into *bouillabaisse*.

At last we sighted our fish again—it was still in the same place. I filled my lungs with air and dived. Forty feet is a long way when one has only one hand free for swimming. The fish spotted me at once and watched me closely. It was a large grouper. I arched my body, took careful aim and thrust my harpoon—or rather, I was about to thrust it when it was abruptly snatched from my hand from above. Furiously I surfaced and was about to berate Viktor—but he was innocent. An enormous wave had caught him and carried him away, and with him the rope and harpoon.

We decided to call it a day. Bruised and shivering with cold we climbed ashore. Menacing dark clouds were covering the sun, a heavy thunderstorm was approaching. Then came the first heavy drops of rain and all hell broke loose.

However, we soon felt that St Honorat was offering us too little variety and we tried our luck near the small village of Théoule, beyond Cannes.

The seabed at Théoule is flat and stony and abruptly drops to considerable depths. At this shelf edge there are numerous grey mullet. These mullet are invariably found in shallow water, mostly in small shoals. They seem even-tempered; they swim placidly along the bottom, burrowing with their heads among the moss and seaweed or brushing their wide mouths along the rocks. From time to time they stop for a few moments and chew peacefully and with relish.

These were the fish I was then hunting. I soon succeeded in spearing two of them. Then I spotted a shoal of particularly large ones. I picked on the fattest of them and pounced, but unfortunately my aim was short and I only wounded its gill. It bled heavily and escaped towards the shore. I pursued it for a while but was then held up by a fishing boat and lost sight of it.

'What rotten luck! A huge grey mullet has just got away from me!' I angrily called out to Viktor who was busily searching for shells on the beach. I had no idea that a grey mullet with a gill wound invariably swims close inshore and there drifts rather helplessly, just under the surface.

To the infinite amazement of our many spectators the following scene then took place. Viktor, his eyes fixed straight ahead of him, suddenly began to creep cautiously through the water and then with a shout hurled himself forward; there was a big splash and with his hands Viktor pulled a huge struggling fish from the waves. The people were delighted; no one realized that this was the very fish I had wounded. Instead they firmly believed that Viktor had caught it with his bare hands. More and more fishermen came running up to gape at this unusual sight and to ask the strangest questions.

With a casual gesture Viktor remarked, 'Catching fish with one's hands? What's so special about that? In Austria any child will do it for you!'

The History of Underwater Hunting

If we examine the many methods which man, over the centuries, has devised for catching fish then we may well find it surprising that in spite of his inventiveness he has only rarely tried to attack aquatic creatures in their own element. The South Sea islanders are the only ones reported in ancient records as penetrating into this submarine world in order to hunt there. Wyatt Gill gives an account of how giant turtles are caught with bare hands in the Penrhyn Islands:

When there is no wind at all and the surface of the sea is like a mirror the islanders go out in their craft at daybreak. They move in a long file, straining their eyes to spot a turtle on the coral sea floor. From time to time a call is heard across the water: 'There's a turtle running!' The boats now quickly form a circle above their quarry, and the natives vigorously tap the sides of their boats in order, as they believe, to confuse the turtle. When they think they have achieved their purpose a man with a rope under his armpits dives down to the seabed in order to grab the turtle. Others follow him, to encircle the quarry and to assist the first man whose special task it is to seize the legs of the huge creature and to have himself pulled up to the surface together with it. Occasionally his companions try to help him by pulling him up by his hair.

More difficult still is fishing with a noose, as observed by Dr Krämer in the Gilbert Islands and on Nauro:

Special mention should be made of a strange device, the eel catcher. With it the fisherman proceeds to the leeward side of the reef and dives down to the spot where he has seen moray eels or conger eels peeping out from holes along the edge of the reef. Quickly he places a juicy bait in front of the hole and arranges the noose of the eel catcher around the opening. As soon as the eel pushes its head out he tightens the sling and surfaces with the beast. It is said that these fishermen can spend many minutes under water and on Nauro I was shown old people who had gone deaf from prolonged stay under water.

According to Wyatt Gill, a noose is used even for catching sharks.

The Nauro islanders also hunt fish under water with a pointed club. According to Dr Hambruch, the natives describe it as follows: 'If one takes a pointed stick, swims with it in the sea and spots a fish one can spear it. One gets into the water, allows oneself to float, closes one eye and when one sees a squid one spears it.'

Even more skilful and courageous are the natives of Hawaii. They too spear fish under water, but will take on even the terrifying predators of the oceans.

Another expert has this to say of the Kanakas: 'They love the sea above everything else; there are scarcely more skilful or more intrepid swimmers and divers than those islanders whose perseverance in fighting the dangers of the sea is unrivalled.' Elsewhere the report continues:

The Kanakas had a great variety of methods of fishing. They used spears, baskets, rods and lines, or nets. The spears were used as a rule by divers under water, and also in shallow water at night with the light of torches. Sharks were killed in single combat by the intrepid and skilful Kanaka divers in deeper water, although the natives not infrequently returned from these encounters as mutilated cripples. In order to attract these dangerous marine

17

predators, human sacrifices, especially from among the slaves, were occasionally made and the decaying corpses lashed to the canoes on special boards and towed out to sea until the sharks gathered near the boat. Then the Kanakas, armed only with daggers, would dive down to engage their dangerous opponents in combat.

Should not this kind of underwater hunting by these death-defying children of the tropics be assessed, from a purely sporting point of view, far higher than all our methods of fishing? We regard angling as the most elegant and noble form of fishing—yet essentially it is based on a very mean trick. Underwater hunting on the other hand, is fair in every respect. The spear-hunter himself dives down into the realm of his opponent, engages him, and offers him a chance of escape. The fish has nearly all the advantages on its side—it can swim considerably faster and more skilfully, and above all is not dependent on air from the world above. The hunter's advantage lies in his weapon and his human intelligence. There are, of course, also fish which have at their disposal far more dangerous weapons than the hunter. Against them man has one advantage only—his intelligence.

It seems probable that underwater hunting became more widespread only with the development of watertight face masks, replacing our early goggles. How and by whom the knowledge of underwater hunting reached America, I do not know. But it probably happened fairly recently. My American mentor Gilpatrik had learnt the sport from an American naval officer who, I was told, had speared fish weighing up to eighteen pounds.

It is worth noting that the new sport, in spite of its novelty, has already begun to degenerate. There are people who go to all kinds of lengths to make underwater hunting easier for themselves. They use diving apparatus which enables them to stroll about the seabed for longish periods, and they shoot the fish with catapults and crossbows. In France they even have regular underwater rifles and pistols from which small harpoons may be fired over considerable distances.

Walking about in a diver's helmet and letting fly at the fish all around one makes no particular demands on the physical prowess of the hunter. No matter how profitable this method may be, to me it seems neither fair nor particularly interesting. To stalk a fish, to lie in wait and guess what it will do next—that to me is the attraction of spear-fishing.

Whereas the spear of the South Sea islanders was equipped only with a barb, the weapon I had made at Antibes on Gilpatrik's advice was shaped as a harpoon. It had a length of 2·8 metres (just over nine feet) and consisted of a wooden shaft, a steel headpiece and the harpoon head.

The wooden shaft had a length of two metres (about six feet six inches) and a diameter of twenty-seven millimetres (just over one inch); it consisted of two parts which were screwed together. Screwed on top of this shaft was a steel rod roughly seventy centimetres (about twenty-eight inches) long and one centimetre (about 0·4 inch) thick; at its upper end it was so shaped that the harpoon head proper fitted firmly onto it. The head was so constructed that it would detach itself from the steel shaft as soon as it entered a fish and was lodged in it. The link between the hunter and the speared fish was provided by a cord roughly three metres (about ten feet) in length which was fastened both to the head itself and to the harpoon shaft; until the moment of spearing it was held to the shaft by a rubber band.

Technique is Vital

Just as with fishing with a rod, the first prerequisite for underwater spearing is an eye for a good spot. Limestone rocks, which lack a submarine flora of sea-weed and mosses, are totally unsuitable. The herbivorous fish avoid these spots and so, in consequence, do the predators.

We soon discovered that broken reefs and romantic rocky headlands provide the richest hunting grounds. The favourite spots of fish are the clefts and crevices, among seaweed and boulders; here they are safe also from man's rods and nets. What angler would risk his equipment in this maze of jagged and sharp-edged rock?

This is precisely why this kind of broken coast is particularly suitable for spear-fishing. The hunter simply dives down among the caves and crevices and spears the fish all the more easily as they consider themselves safe in their hide-outs.

A flat coast is suitable for spear-fishing only when seaweeds and boulders alternate with sandy patches on the sea floor. A sandy beach or extensive weed forests, on the other hand, are exceedingly dull and unprofitable since large fish are only rarely encountered there.

To my mind the rocky cliffs—apart from off-shore reefs—are the most interesting. True, one usually catches less there than one does off rocky coasts dropping less steeply into the sea, but on the other hand one can often observe gigantic fish lying at great depths or, though generally keeping further out to sea, occasionally coming within the hunter's range.

There is not much more one can say—anyone fishing for a little while will soon develop an acute instinct for discovering the best spots.

At first we used to dive headlong into the water. But spectacular though this was it brought us little profit. For one thing, one's goggles would slip off one's nose and a good deal of salt water would get into one's curiously opened eyes, and, for another, the fish would scatter and we would be left with an empty submarine landscape. We soon discovered that the best way was to make the slowest and the most stately movements possible. So we stepped into the water rather like corpulent elderly ladies entering a swimming pool. To move cautiously and soundlessly is always the ideal technique for the spear fisher.

One's new hunting ground is then reconnoitred soundlessly by lying on the water, eyes downwards.

One other thing: underwater hunting is a strenuous business. Anyone bitten by the bug, therefore, anyone abandoning the hunt only when forced to do so by the cold, must be in really good shape—especially where heart and lungs are concerned. And he must also have steady nerves because there are frequent incidents and surprises that have to be coped with.

As soon as a likely fish is spotted one dives and tries to approach within striking distance of it. But diving with the long harpoon is quite an art and needs practice. It is what beginners find most difficult.

The hunter with the harpoon must dive under the surface in absolute silence. The best thing is to let oneself sink vertically to about three feet below the surface; only then, using one's left hand, does one turn over so that one swims downwards head first. On no account must one's feet emerge above water in this manoeuvre, otherwise the splashing will drive the fish away.

Caution is needed not only in diving but also in all underwater swimming movements. In order not to scare the fish away one must creep up on them with quite small, smooth movements. In this respect they are just like land animals—they take fright only if something moves. So long as one remains motionless or moves only cautiously they are aware of one's approach but do not take fright.

As I have said, fish are highly sensitive. They feel and hear the slightest movements in the water. I say 'hear' as it is almost unimaginable how acute a fish's hearing must be for it to identify, against the roar of breaking waves, the faint sounds of a cautious approach at a range of up to a hundred feet. Of course, whether they *hear* in our sense of the word or perhaps *sense* is still the subject of argument among scientists. Certainly the water is set in vibration by any fast movement and these vibrations can be perceived as a noise even by the human ear which is by no means adapted to underwater life. The beating of the fins of alarmed fish is a case in point.

When one has approached a fish closely enough one takes careful aim and tries to pierce it. The beginner had best aim at the middle of the fish and be glad if he hits it at all. But the experienced underwater marksman aims at the rear end of the gills, which is where the vital organs are located. A fish hit in the gills bleeds fast, whereas it bleeds only slightly or not at all if hit in the belly. Fish wounded in the belly frequently escape with considerable vigour whereas a fish wounded in the gills is frequently so helpless that it can be caught by hand.

To spear a fish the hunter's whole body must lunge forward like a steel spring—otherwise one strikes short or too late. And never spear a fish hovering in front of a rock. You will certainly strike the rock and damage your harpoon head.

When a fish is hit one clearly feels a resistance; but not until the cord has detached itself can one be sure whether it is truly caught. Strange as it may seem, one only rarely sees the fish detaching the point from the shaft. Usually its reflex movements are incredibly rapid and escape observation.

Occasionally one may pierce a fish so forcefully that it wriggles on the steel shaft. In that case the fish should be pushed down far enough for the harpoon head to detach itself and the quarry to hang on the cord—otherwise too large a wound will be opened on the struggling fish. The fish is next killed by striking its head. It should be gutted and placed in the shade so it does not spoil. But it is by no means always easy to get one's quarry ashore, especially if it is a large fish. We shall hear more about this later. One should also be careful to avoid the fin spikes; with many fish they are poisonous.

Exciting Adventure

One morning Viktor shook me awake impatiently: 'Wake up! Big news! I've been told that an old cutter ran aground some years ago not far from here. It's said to be in quite shallow water!'

Rarely have I been so excited as on that morning. The dreams of my earliest youth were about to come true—I was to see a real wreck!

At last we reached the spot and inspected the wreckage of an impressive two-master lying in twenty-five to thirty feet of water. It was an eerie sight—the ship had broken up and was covered with a thick growth of seaweed. We swam around excitedly—there was the smoke-stack, with a coating of green moss, over there were the bows, everywhere there were twisted rusty chunks of metal. As I dived down quite low I gazed through an open door—it made me shiver.

A moment later a frightening thing happened. Out of a crack came a huge octopus and clumsily stalked over the deck on its long tentacles. I had to bag it!

21

But I had to act fast. Viktor was a long way off. I am not normally foolhardy, but the excitement of the hunt had made me careless and I forgot my American friend's warning never to spear an octopus with a harpoon. I dived once more and ran my harpoon point right through the beast's revolting head. I immediately snatched the shaft back to make sure the point came off. Then everything happened at once. The octopus squirted out a pitch-black fluid and the water turned opaque. Dragging my quarry behind me I hastily swam towards the surface.

But no sooner had I filled my lungs with air again than, with chilling horror, I felt the octopus's revolting tentacles encircling my legs and sucking themselves on to them. I desperately tried to keep above water but the beast hung on my legs like lead. How could I defend myself? I needed my hand for swimming and I could not have stabbed at the animal with my knife in the blackened water anyway for fear of slashing myself.

I wildly screamed for help. Fortunately Viktor was near by. He dragged me ashore together with the octopus and there we tore it off my legs with all our combined strength and killed it. Only then did I see that each of its tentacles was over five foot long.

In later years I frequently speared smaller octopuses and even caught them in my hand. The most difficult thing always is to get them out of their holes, where they hang on powerfully with their suckers. The native fishermen have their own methods of dealing with this. They will tie angler's hooks and strips of white and red material to the end of a willow switch and with it poke about in the holes and crevices. The octopus seems to react to these colours: it will grip the switch and allow itself to be pulled out of its hole. It is also claimed that you can get an octopus out by means of a mirror lowered on a line, allegedly because it will be tempted into fighting its own mirror image. But I have never tried this myself. The best and quickest way of killing an octopus is to reach with both hands into its sack-shaped head and with a jerk turn it inside out.

Sickening as the appearance of a live octopus is, suitably prepared it is a very popular delicacy. The younger creatures in particular have a soft, juicy and tasty flesh. For an elderly octopus, on the other hand, you need a particularly strong set of dentures.

Each Species must be treated differently

My technique was improving every day but I felt that something important was lacking. One day, suddenly, I realized what it was. Technique alone was not enough. My fish were not just quarries to be speared. I had to study their character and peculiarities, and the more I succeeded in doing so the more interesting my pursuit became.

Take the sheepshead—a somewhat stately fish, but always on the move, swimming among the seaweed, from crevice to crevice, picking up a tasty morsel here and another there, looking about curiously, or swimming alongside a companion in what looks very much like animated conversation. Sheepsheads are very sensitive fish and the moment they become aware of danger they escape with almost exaggerated alarm. They are not easily outwitted.

The easiest way is to surprise them in their holes, because there they believe themselves safe. It is far more difficult to get anywhere near them in the open—except by exploiting their curiosity and indecision. You dive down and cautiously pursue the fish—but this must be done really soundlessly or else it will sense danger. But if you move softly the fish will turn its head, first one way then another, to look curiously at its strange pursuer. That is the right moment. You strike with lightning speed just as it is stationary for a moment, broadside on. If disturbed during a meal they look most indignant.

The sea bass, on the other hand, a bold predator, shows no fear at all and will even swim straight at your harpoon head in a challenging mood. It is difficult, especially for a beginner, to get at this fish—since obviously you cannot spear it head-on. It took me some time to discover the right method of coming to grips with it. You make a feint with your spear; the fish instinctively dodges and escapes but presently returns in an elegant turn and, fins quivering, stares at the harpoon before making off again. That is when you should strike.

The beautifully coloured bogues are much more harmless as a species. They usually appear in shoals and look exceedingly comical. Often they are so stuffed with food that you almost expect them to burst. But then they spend all day long feeding, their heads browsing among the seaweed. Single fish, straggling behind the shoal, are relatively easy to spear, but it is very difficult to creep up on a shoal. No matter how cautiously you move, one of these shy creatures is certain to sense the danger and all of a sudden they are all gone. You can clearly hear a dull thud in the water.

There is only one way to outwit a shoal of bogues. You choose a fish feeding some distance away from the rest, then you dive down as far away from it as possible and creep up on it like a Red Indian, between seaweeds and the rocks, keeping close to the bottom. If you are lucky it will be feeding at a particularly tempting spot, and unless you are noticed by its friends you may get within striking distance.

Umbrines are particularly beautiful peaceful creatures and are always found in the same spot. They seem absent-minded and dreamy; they avoid other fish but enjoy the company of their own species. They are frequently encountered in quite large shoals, still and almost motionless. They are rarely seen feeding, and when they do feed they are less greedy than other fish. Gently they brush over the moss and only here and there do they dreamily pick up a morsel, without seeming to experience any particular pleasure in doing so. Whatever they do, their movements are invariably smooth and harmonious. When approached they do not escape but calmly withdraw into their cracks to avoid any unpleasant disturbance. They are found near rock faces, on mossy boulder-strewn sea beds, and in shallow water where seaweeds, sand and rocks alternate. They are most difficult to catch near a rock face because there they can escape downward. It is easier to spear them among the seaweeds, and easiest of all to surprise them in their holes. Their flesh is exceedingly hard and you have to strike vigorously.

Each kind of fish, therefore, has its own peculiar character and has to be treated differently. It is this that makes spear-fishing so fascinating. Each fish is a new problem demanding a new solution.

When I had realized all this I also knew that my old dream had come true—I saw the way to combine sport with science. Until then, scientists had hardly ever been able to encounter fish in their natural habitat. The underwater hunter does just that.

Successful Days which nearly ended in Tragedy

As I was learning to interpret correctly the behaviour of different species success followed success. Soon we did not know what to do with the quantities of fish we caught; in the end we sold them and lived on the proceeds.

Our hunting fever drove us into the water every morning and frequently, in spite of the cold and strain, we would stay in the sea for up to five hours. At night we just dropped into bed. Nevertheless, I was often unable to go to sleep for several hours, my mind being busy with thoughts of bigger fish and better harpoons.

It was about that time that I had my first encounter with tunnies. This was off Cape Miramar, where we had hoped for miracles but at first experienced bitter disappointments. All we encountered were a few small bream, and even these were strangely shy. Later we discovered the reason: this area was the haunt of a man with diving equipment and an underwater rifle. With this rifle he could fire small harpoons complete with line and cork over a distance of several yards. The man had practised his 'hunting' near Cape Miramar the previous day, so it was small wonder that the fish were still nervous.

Irritably we swam around the cape when suddenly I heard a gurgling scream, turned my head and saw Viktor gesticulating wildly.

'Tunnies, tunnies!' he yelled.

I shall never forget the sight. The water below me, a moment before a yawning void, was now flashing with the bodies of thirty huge fish—and their number was still growing.

I filled my lungs with air, swallowed some water in my excitement, came up once more to spit out the water and then went down to some sixteen feet. The fish took no notice of my presence but calmly carried on. I thrust my harpoon into the side of one of these glistening giants. At once I felt a strong tug, and I had no sooner struggled to the surface than the tunny pulled me down again. It was pulling very powerfully at my short rope and a moment later, after a fierce struggle, I was holding my harpoon in my hand with a chunk of flesh at the point. I had not only lost my quarry but the whole shoal had disappeared. Angry and disappointed we swam ashore, sat down on a boulder and reflected. It would have been wonderful to return to Juan-les-Pins with the huge tunny. It was a great pity.

'And it was all because of the short line,' Viktor observed. 'With a longer line we would certainly have tired it out and landed it.'

We had experienced the drawbacks of a long line in the recent storm and therefore decided to try something different. We bought about fifty feet of thin cord. I coiled it up and wound it round my body; to prevent premature release I held it together by an elaborate knot designed to open automatically in case of need. But my own clever invention very nearly cost me my life a few days later.

We were fishing near Trayas, off Cape Roux, near Anthéor, and finally near Agay. A wonderful spot. We kept to the most distant promontory, among the most romantic rocks of the whole coast, a spot swarming with the most varied kind of fish.

At the very outset I speared a number of bogues and a brightly coloured wrasse. Suddenly I saw two enormous sea bass, the biggest I had seen for some time. To my mortification I just had a small bogue on my harpoon which, therefore, was not ready for action. I hastily clambered up on a rock and called out to Viktor that two splendid sea bass were close by. With trembling fingers I detached the speared fish, chucked it over to my startled companion, readied my harpoon and slipped back into the water.

The sea bass were still there. They were much too engrossed in their love play to notice me. I struck. It was a perfect hit and the struck fish immediately pulled hard on the line. My joy and excitement were indescribable. I gave it all fifty feet of my line and climbed up on a rock.

'Quick, Viktor, over here! I've got him!'

Slowly and cautiously I hauled on the line; the fish weighed a good seven pounds, a real prize specimen. But it was also a devilishly wild beast. It tugged the line first one way then another, and I had a desperate time trying to hold it. It was too fat to catch hold of; time and again it slipped through my hands.

Just as Viktor was arriving to secure our quarry the fish performed a bold leap and was gone. It had jerked free. I nearly exploded with rage.

After a short sulky silence I climbed back into the water and swam around aimlessly. Unexpectedly I caught sight of my lost prize. About twenty feet down in a trough in the rock the huge sea bass was lying, evidently badly wounded. I got as close as possible and struck—at the rock. The fish had skilfully dodged my thrust and suddenly slipped deep down. I swam up to the surface, filled my lungs and went down once more, with the determination of despair. I could see it in the distance, at a depth of at least forty feet, a depth I had never yet ventured down to. I believe at that moment I would have dived down to fifty feet. I had a pain in my nose and ears and my goggles were pressing so heavily against my eyes that I was scarcely able to see. I struck instinctively and scored a hit. A few seconds later the fish was landed.

My mood was restored. After fifteen minutes' rest I was back at work, this time alone. I was lucky—I speared one fish after another. I surprised two giant red steenbras engaged in love play and one of these splendid creatures was pierced by my harpoon a moment later.

I wanted to uncoil my line to land this particularly large fish but the knot did not open. Things were getting exceedingly uncomfortable: instead of me pulling the fish towards the shore it was pulling me down towards the seabed. I tried to undo the knot, but this was hopeless. Water got into my nose and my goggles; I was coughing, swallowing water and thrashing about me. At the last moment I calmed down, realized my danger, whipped out my knife from its sheath and tried to cut the fatal cord. At that moment the fish turned sharply and came off the harpoon point. I was free again, but so was the fish.

How I got back to the surface after these seemingly endless dangerous minutes I do not remember. When I came round from my semi-conscious state I was lying on a rock with Viktor desperately wanting to know what had kept me below water so long.

A few days later we had to return to Vienna. But we knew that this was no final farewell. I was dreaming about a great summer expedition, about a sailing cutter that would take me with a few friends down the coast of Dalmatia, from one underwater fishing spot to another.

Preparations and new Experiences

When, on my return from the Mediterranean, I told my friends and acquaintances of my new sport and my exciting adventures, I found that no one would believe me. Most of them accused me of an excessively lively imagination. This annoyed me so much that I conceived the idea of taking photographs under water. Thus all the photographs I was to take in later years ultimately sprang from my injured vanity.

I must confess that I knew very little about photography but I never doubted for a moment that I would be successful. After all, I knew how much light and sunshine there was under water.

The experts to whom I disclosed my plans were unable to help me. I therefore had to begin by ploughing my way through photographic literature. But to my great chagrin I did not find a single word about my favourite subject —underwater photography. This was hardly surprising: what was then known as 'underwater photography' or 'underwater film' was only on the rarest of occasions shot under water; most of it was taken in big aquaria or, worse still, was trick photography. We therefore had to work our much-mocked imagination even harder and decided to get a modern miniature camera and have a watertight case fitted around it.

Our first experiments in a Vienna swimming-pool were highly encouraging in spite of the far-from-clear water.

The following year, when I went to the area of Ugljan and Split, I found plenty of time to indulge my new hobby, underwater photography.

I was particularly pleased to find that our very first photographs confirmed our supposition that one should take pictures only in fine weather, that f5·6 was the best aperture and 1/100 second the best shutter speed for a film speed of 17 DIN, and that all other conditions could be worked out on this basis. With a little practice it is not at all difficult to judge the correct shutter speed. On particularly sunny days, against a light-coloured sea floor, I have even used aperture f8 and 1/100 second without under-exposing.

Close-ups, I noted at that time, need a particularly well-contrasted foreground as the background always remains a monotonous grey because of the transparency of the water. Objects more than thiry feet away appear pale even in clear water and at eighty feet disappear altogether. Make no mistake—the human eye can see considerably farther than the camera. And do not be deceived by brilliant colours—they never come out in the photographs. Perhaps one should make some experiments with infra-red photography, especially in view of recent developments in this field.

Sunny days are best, especially the hours between 11 a.m. and 2 p.m. when the sun is at its peak and its rays go straight through the surface. Before and after this period a considerable part of the rays is refracted, producing uneven lighting. I would also add that photographs at a depth of twelve feet are particularly striking because of the reflections of sunlight on the waves.

Altogether, waves are vital. They are to the underwater photographer what clouds are to the ordinary photographer. Whereas in calm weather the sun's rays penetrate the surface of the water uniformly, casting well-defined shadows, they are refracted and reflected in all directions when the sea is in motion. In a rough sea the lighting under water is totally uneven and, moreover, changes from one moment to the next.

Photographs of scenery and persons make no particular demand on the photographer's swimming skill; to photograph a fish, on the other hand, is difficult. Indeed I would say that it is usually more difficult than to spear it. Stalking has to be done just as cautiously and instinctively. The most difficult moment comes when instead of simply thrusting your spear you have to wait for the fish to be in a favourable position in front of the camera, with the right background and lighting too. As a rule it means spending far more time under water than for spear-fishing.

Diving itself is much more difficult too. For steady sighting one has to have both hands on the camera; all swimming and diving, therefore, has to be done with the legs. Rubber foot fins, which I first used that year, proved extremely useful. Unfortunately they also have irksome drawbacks—some fish perceive the movement of the fins at considerable distance and escape, presumably in the belief that a big fish is approaching. But in encounters with big fish, which show no fear, they have proved their value.

The whole question of the right footwear had been most important. We had experienced some bad trouble with barefoot diving: the soles of our feet, injured by jagged rocks and the spines of sea urchins, often took a long time to heal. We had tried wearing shoes, but we did not really enjoy it. We found them an impediment in swimming and diving. This, therefore, was another point in favour of rubber fins, which not only enabled the underwater hunter to swim faster but also served him as footwear.

About that time I also conducted an experiment of which I was particularly proud. What I did was fasten my camera to my left hand in such a way that I could work the shutter with my forefinger. In my right hand I held my harpoon and on my feet I wore fins. My feet did the swimming and diving, my right hand speared the fish, and with my left hand I photographed the whole proceedings. No one can do more at a time. I soon gave up these experiments, if only because the bulky case of the camera was difficult to fasten to one's hand. But a lighter camera case in later years frequently enabled me to combine hunting and photography in this manner. The pictures taken in these circumstances are particularly instructive in that they clearly show the behaviour of different fish when faced with a harpoon. Obviously, a cine-film would be more interesting still.

In the course of my reading about diving I also came across a suggestion made by William Beebe, the famous American deep-sea explorer. In one of his books he said: 'Ten years of diving on collecting expeditions for the New York Zoological Society have taught me everything that one needs to know. All one requires is a pair of swimming trunks, a pair of plimsolls, a copper helmet with a glass eye-piece in front, an ordinary rubber hose and a small hand-pump.'

William Beebe's helmet was basically nothing but a small diving bell, weighing about sixty pounds, which is tipped over one's head. Fresh air is fed into it by a hand-pump with a one-way valve and an ordinary thin hose; the surplus air escapes at the bottom edge of the helmet. Because the helmet is open at the base the air in it is approximately under the same water pressure as the thorax of the diver; this enables him to breathe normally. Since there is also compressed air in the hose there is no danger of it being collapsed by the water pressure and the air supply cut off.

Having carefully got together all this equipment we staged our first trials in Vienna, in the Old Danube. The water of this old arm of the river is particularly opaque. I went down first. To my great surprise everything worked perfectly. I dived down into the greenish depths without difficulties—except that I had to move slowly and steadily to get my ears used to the rising pressure. Any jerky up or down movement produces discomfort in one's ears and causes headaches.

'It is advisable to swallow while descending,' William Beebe wrote, 'in order to offset the increasing pressure. Anyone experiencing a severe headache a few feet below the surface should ascend at once and consult the nearest ear specialist—there must be something wrong with his ears that should be put right whether he intends to dive again or not.'

Encouraged by our first success we staged the craziest experiments. One of us would practise long jumps at a depth of sixteen feet, another would run up and down in a diver's helmet, and I myself crossed the Old Danube under water on the very first day, in spite of the tall algae and tangle of weeds. The consequences of this exuberance were not slow to take effect: atrocious headaches warned us against future excesses.

On the advice of our parents, who continued to view the helmet with some suspicion, we also made one sensible experiment. We wanted to find out if in an emergency one could cast off the helmet easily. We found this possible, and in fact so easy that I immediately attempted the opposite manoeuvre as well:

I dived down, put on the helmet cast off by my predecessor and stayed under water.

Our helmets now enabled us to take a new kind of walk under water. We encountered large pike, tench and catfish, and the sight of these great fish once more aroused our hunting fever and we were sorely tempted to try out our new harpoon against these fat freshwater fish. But we had been well brought up and avoided anything that might have brought us into conflict with the fishing regulations.

My deepest Descent

In the summer of 1938 I made what was my deepest descent until then off the Makarska Peninsula in Dalmatia. I just wanted to see how far down I could get. It was a particularly fine morning and we all strolled out to a promontory beyond the harbour. We found a suitable spot, I greased myself thoroughly and then began my descent. So that we could check my depth accurately we had fastened a string to my helmet; its other end was held by Karl Merz, who was swimming directly above me.

Slowly I descended, observing the small fish which approached me quite closely and gazed curiously at the rising air bubbles. From time to time I glanced upwards and waved to Karl who seemed to be hovering above like some dark bird. At a depth of thirty feet I could no longer see him. All I saw now was the hose which seemed to disappear into the bright sky. I was entirely alone, yet I did not feel uneasy in the least but, on the contrary, indescribably happy. The world was far away.

Presently the sea floor changed its appearance. Abruptly it dropped down, almost vertically, to an eery depth. Without reflecting for a moment I continued my climb down, and I must confess that I had a wonderful sense of security as never before in my life. Because of buoyancy my helmet now weighed only four or five pounds. I was able therefore to stand confidently on every minute ledge without fear of slipping and falling. Even if I had slipped I would not have come to any harm since I could have easily kept myself at the same level by swimming movements, or even risen to the surface. There was a regular soft hiss from the air entering the helmet and I was grateful for my friend's zeal above.

As I was clambering over a ridge of rock and looking down I saw two things which made my heart beat faster—a large dark fish with a yellow patch was moving past below me, and deeper down still I caught sight of an enormous

From the Red Sea across the Indian Ocean to the South Sea the coral reefs are built up by the same or related species of coral. These reefs rise from considerable depths; their outer slopes are steep while their flat tops are not infrequently dry at low tide. The most luxuriant coral growth is along the outer slopes, where they form overhangs and grottos.

Above: *The palmate branches of a stagshorn coral* (Acropora palmata) *in the Caribbean, where a different coral fauna has developed from that of the Indian and Pacific Oceans. Reef-building corals are made up of polyps which sprout out from one another like plants and produce a calcareous skeleton. With most species they are too small to be seen by the naked eye. By day they withdraw into their minute holes.*

Left: *Spherical porites coral on the Great Barrier Reef.*

Above: *The Stagshorn coral (acropora) of the Caribbean often forms thickets covering wide areas of the sea bottom. Sponges and algae settle on the dead branches.*

Right: *Brain coral in the Indian Ocean. The especially large polyps with their extended tentacles are arranged in a meandering pattern so that the colony has the appearance of a gigantic human brain.*

Above: *Compressed air apparatus
ensures safe diving down to 130
feet. At greater depths a dangerous
kind of intoxication is experienced.
After a prolonged stay in deeper
water, strict rates of ascent have to
be observed to avoid caisson
disease ('the bends').*

Left: *For notes and communication I used an aluminium plate
tied to my arm. Even under water
it is possible to write on aluminium with a pencil.*

Dr Georg Scheer was in charge of the classification of corals, while Dr Ludwig Franzisket (right) carried out physiological investigations. The coral polyps depend on symbiotic algae living in their tissues and suppling them with oxygen; that is why the formation of their calcareous skeletons depends on the solar irradiation required by the algae. This is also the reason why reef-building corals thrive only up to a depth of 130 feet.

The origin of ring-shaped atolls has been the subject of much speculation by scientists. According to Darwin's theory they are caused by islands sinking into the sea. In the Maldives, however (see page 227), there are atolls which in turn consist of smaller reef rings; the picture above shows one of only just over a mile in diameter. I was able to establish that the internal structure of these reefs is by no means solid: in my view, the reef plateau sags in the middle—the larger a reef is the more it sags. As the water can only slowly drain from the ring at low tide it exerts a continually recurrent pressure on the centre of the atoll. This may well contribute to the sagging of the loose substructure.

funnel-shaped sponge. I had to have that sponge! When I had got to the spot and broken it off I found it was half my own size.

My appetite had been whetted. I saw another sponge growing out of the rock face a little farther down. I wanted to have that one as well. Like a child picking flowers and getting deeper and deeper into the dark forest, I was climbing further down. Just as I was bending over to cut off the sponge I suddenly felt a tug on the hose—the world above was calling. I saw that the hose was taut and for a moment I lost that wonderful sense of security and was almost alarmed. A great pity. I should have liked to descend even farther.

Before setting out on my difficult return journey I once more stepped on an overhanging piece of rock and looked down into the mysterious depths. I understood the urge to descend deeper and deeper, and I understood that great scientist William Beebe who had constructed a steel sphere in order to dive down into the sea to a depth of nearly one kilometre—well over 3,000 feet—in order to gaze upon the unknown.

Reluctantly I returned and began my ascent. Only now did I realize how deep I had been and notice the coldness of the water. On my way up I found an old iron cross from a grave and took that up with me too. Thus laden I rejoined my friends who cheered my return. We were curious to see what depths I had reached. The string showed nearly sixty-five feet.

Fishermen's Jealousy and Police Wisdom

Near the island of Lopud, where we soon afterwards pitched our tents, there were not only particularly interesting groupers but also a lot of other fish, so that right from the start our catches were heavy. At first we ate the fish ourselves but soon found the diet too monotonous and sold them. The fishermen around the island of Lopud caught but a few fish, and not as a rule the most tasty kind, and our merchandise therefore was in considerable demand, much to the annoyance of the local fishermen.

A few days after our arrival we decided to have a rest day. I wanted to write a few letters and Karl went off to sunbathe. But very soon he was back again, and I could tell from his face that there had been trouble.

'Would you believe it?' he exploded. 'Do you know what they're saying?'
'Who?' I asked.
'The fishermen. They say we poison their fish or we fish with dynamite.'
'Idiots,' I said. 'But let them talk—they are just jealous.'
But things were not quite so harmless. The next morning we had a

summons to the police. There we were received with the curt statement: 'You have been reported by a fisherman for poisoning the fish.'

I had to smile. I asked the severe official, 'You really believe we slip poison into the fishes' mouths under water?'

But the official had no taste for argument or much interest in what we had to say. He merely informed us in a cold official manner that fishing with poison was prohibited and we must therefore stop doing it or else leave Lopud.

After an hour's debating I eventually suggested that I would lend him a pair of goggles and he could swim by my side to see what was really going on. This invitation to the hunt was declined because he could not swim. But fortunately a respected citizen of the locality was found who declared himself ready to inspect our activities.

The comedy started at twelve noon. Word had got about and a curious crowd had collected on the shore. Conscious of the greatness of the moment I personally fitted a pair of goggles to our visitor, got my harpoon ready with great panache and preceded my companion into the water. He followed with the dignity due to his mission. But no sooner had he cast his first glance under water than he squeaked with pleasure and was as excited as anybody else who looks under the water with goggles for the first time. The problem now was to spear a fish, and that was by no means easy. The reason was that no fewer than three boats were accompanying us, and my companion, moreover, was by no means a noiseless swimmer. Our quarries were scattering before us and, besides, I was so excited I missed all the time. But my judge was delighted with my efforts and entirely on my side. When, after a great many tries, I eventually speared a grey mullet I found myself the hero of the day. I was carted in a boat from one 'particularly good' spot to another, with more and more people asking to accompany me and to be allowed to look under water with goggles.

I had learnt one new lesson—to become famous is an exhausting and difficult business.

When I met my local diving companion that evening he said to me, 'Everything is settled with the police. You can fish as much as you like, only you must not sell the fish—that is forbidden. But of course—' he dropped his voice a little '—you can sell them to me!'

Adventures with Jörg

A really spendid time began with Jörg Böhler's arrival at Lopud. He was an ideal companion, enthusiastic about our sport and so skilful that he succeeded in spearing a fish on his very first day. We now went hunting in a team of three: Jörg and I speared the fish and Karl was our photographer.

Most of our hunting was done at Soon, a sandy bay on the south-east coast of Lopud. Among many other kinds of fish there were sting-rays, on which we were particularly keen. These flat fish have a long, whip-shaped tail with a sting which nature has equipped with a vicious barb, capable of inflicting quite frightful wounds. Wyatt Gill reports:

> The point of this terrible weapon almost invariably breaks off; if it remains lodged in the body there is no hope of getting away with one's life. If the point is lodged in the foot or the leg it is customary to make an incision from the opposite side since the serrated point can only be withdrawn in the direction of the thrust.

This point is said to be covered with a poisonous mucus which causes atrocious pain. The ray uses its weapon very skilfully and the greatest caution is therefore required in landing this dangerous fish. The best thing is to hack off its tail as soon as possible.

I usually encountered these fish towards the evening on a flat sandy bottom; during the day they presumably hid in the sand. They look very droll when swimming: they flutter like nocturnal spectres. They are not easy to harpoon because their eyes are directed upwards and any attacker is spotted a long way off. It is a little easier to creep up on them when they lie half hidden in the sand; they probably think they are invisible then.

I made one particularly interesting observation. I repeatedly saw smallish sting-rays escaping in panic before a few sheepsheads. I never quite understood what these fish wanted with the sting-rays but it appears that the sting-ray is not feared quite as much by other fish as it is by us humans.

Struggle with a Shark

Our beautiful holiday on the Dalmatian coast was drawing to an end. One fine late summer morning we drove up the coast to Dubrovnik. There, to our annoyance, we were told that the steamship we were to board was all of twelve hours late. What were we to do? Naturally we went for a swim and observed that the water was considerably warmer than along the parts of the coast we had been to. So we promptly unpacked our tackle again and went off hunting for a last time. And this was to prove our most successful day.

At the very outset we speared two particularly colourful wrasses. We next decided to swim out to the far reef for the last time, in the hope of encountering a tunny after all. Jörg, who accompanied me, had the camera and the fins while I had the harpoon.

As we rounded the reef we suddenly caught sight of a huge fish approaching rapidly. With great excitement we recognized the hideous grimace of a young shark. Fortunately we had often discussed just how we would act in the event of encountering a shark. Without exchanging a word we knew exactly what we had to do. Jörg tightened his camera strap and I gave him the harpoon.

The shark was approaching with elegant movements. The moment had come. Jörg dived towards the huge fish, whereupon it likewise dipped down and described a wide arc. The moment it was in position Jörg hurled the harpoon behind its gills with such force that my heart leapt with joy. While Jörg was making for the rocks with a racing swimmer's crawl, his rope uncoiling meanwhile, it was my task to prevent the infuriated shark from escaping. I therefore clutched the cord and allowed myself to be pulled along.

At last Jörg had gained a secure stance on the rock, his line was taking the strain, and things were now up to me. I had to kill the shark because otherwise there was a risk that the line might break, as had happened with the tunny. I pulled myself along by the line towards the shark. It was thrashing about furiously and several times evaded me. At last I succeeded in getting a grip on it and ran my knife into its belly several times. Desperately it tried to shake me off. It took all my strength to hold on.

I was running short of air and ascended to the surface, but the shark was already bleeding from several wounds and swimming along slightly arched to one side. I dived once more, carefully avoided its hideous mouth and thrust my knife into the region of its gills several times. Soon my giant opponent was overcome. With wild shouts of triumph we hauled it ashore and finished it off. Only later did I notice that my stomach had been badly grazed by the shark's rough skin.

My hopes of spending my next holiday in some tropical sea encountered considerable difficulties. The year was 1939. Austria was part of Germany and the political situation was tense. There was no ban on leaving the country but there were two obstacles—for one thing, no foreign currency was authorized for a journey of this kind and, for another, we needed an entry visa for the country we had chosen.

My party consisted of Jörg and, as a newcomer, Alfred von Wurzian, a strong swimmer I had known for many years. We had chosen Curaçao, the small Dutch island in the Caribbean. It was served by a German shipping line, which meant we could pay for our return ticket in our own currency. I had applied for a permit for a two months' stay for the three of us, but had received no reply. We had long since made our bookings for the passage and our equipment was all ready—but we still had no Dutch visa. As for the other hurdle, I cleared that by mere chance. One of the members of the sports club to which the three of us belonged was a Dutchman, a wealthy merchant. After a game of tennis the conversation got round to our proposed journey to a Dutch possession.

'I could arrange for money to be available in Curaçao when you get there.'

'But how could I repay you?' I asked.

The Dutchman thought for a moment. Then he laughed: 'You know what? We'll do business together. I'll give you 400 Gilders which I'll have transferred to a bank at Willemstad. You may rely on it—the money will be there. In return you give me ten per cent of all your earnings from this expedition—I mean from books, lectures or anything else. Agreed?'

'Agreed.'

Two years later—war had broken out in the meantime—things were not going well for the Dutchman. He was sick and had other difficulties as well, and certainly needed money. I offered to redeem his ten per cent for ten times the amount of our debt—i.e., for 4,000 Gilders. This suited him very well and it also suited me. I had found it rather a bore to account individually for every lecture or newspaper article, and I felt sure that his share should ultimately come to that amount.

The visa problem was rather more of a headache. Eventually an answer came from Holland—a refusal. It was regretted that permits to stay in Curaçao could not at the moment be issued. I was downcast for a day and a night—after that my decision was made. I told both Jörg and Alfred that everything was all right. I thought that once we actually were in Curaçao the authorities would be open to negotiation.

What I had overlooked was that the shipping line was also involved. I did not realize that, if we were not allowed to land at Curaçao, the law required the line to carry us elsewhere without payment. The moment we arrived in Hamburg to board our ship we were therefore asked: 'Where is your entry permit?'

I replied coolly, 'I am very sorry, but we only got it at the last moment, by telephone. We understand from the Dutch Foreign Ministry that it will be entered in our passports in Curaçao. The authorities there are being notified.' I gave the man an ingenuous grin. 'It's a special permit, you understand, since we intend to hunt sharks under water.'

My bait was accepted. The official wanted to hear more about our crazy intentions and a longish conversation followed.

'I'll turn a blind eye, then,' he said. 'But strictly speaking we must not carry you without a written permit. But as you've been promised it and have come all this way from Vienna we don't want to be too bureaucratic.'

I felt like falling round his neck but did not betray myself. As for Jörg and Alfred, I felt that their honest belief in the existence of our permit would help us in the difficult negotiations ahead. I was determined to act the outraged man of honour and to stick to my claim that our expedition had been approved. By the time inquiries were made in Holland our ship would have moved on.

I followed a similar course many years later. In 1957, when we were sailing to the Nicobar Islands in the Indian Ocean aboard the *Xarifa*, I did not even bother to apply to the Indian authorities for the required permit. According to my informants this was difficult to obtain, and even to get a decision would frequently take two years. Once it had been refused it would be difficult to talk one's way out of it. So we set off without permits, trusted to luck, and chose an island which seemed the least likely to have a police station. Only the captain was in my confidence. Things did not work out then as I had planned— as the reader will find out later.

In describing these tactics I do not wish to suggest that I approve of illegal action. But anyone following a new road invariably encounters official suspicion and difficulties. Officials as a rule are lacking in imagination and are, moreover, paid to be suspicious in carrying out the letter of the law.

Anyway, we had cleared our two hurdles and we were off.

AMONG CORALS AND SHARKS

Fishing in the Spanish Water

The Spanish Water is about six miles from Willemstad, the administrative centre of Curaçao; it is a large, widely-ramified inland sea. Its shores are hemmed with mangroves, and on its eastern side the slopes of the tall table mountain are densely grown with trees and shrubs. That was where the Boca was situated, a small lagoon linking the Spanish Water with the open sea, and where Mr Evers, a friendly official of the Chamber of Commerce and the owner of a boat, was now taking us.

We parked the car near a small plantation by the inland sea, changed, and covered the last part of the way on foot. Alfred and I carried the outboard motor while Mr Evers had his fishing rods and a rifle. He intended to fish in the Boca and to observe the *ala blanca*, a species of pigeon with white wing tips, among the mangroves at sunset.

While we were chugging across the peaceful Spanish Water Mr Evers explained to us the origin of the big inland seas of Curaçao. In the Quaternary period the island had been considerably lower and had been partially covered by the sea. At that time massive coral reefs had formed on top of the ancient volcanic mountain ranges and these had, in more recent periods, been raised up from the sea in a series of thrusts. The south-eastern part of Curaçao, which has low mountain ridges along its entire coast, is shaped like a trough and is in fact a raised ancient atoll. In a few places, however, where the ring is intersected by narrow valleys, the sea has been able to enter and form the inland seas which are shaped like multi-lobed leaves.

At last we reached the spot where the Boca ran into the sea. 'You won't see much in the channel,' Mr Evers said. 'It is ebb tide now and the sea is drawing out the opaque water from the Spanish Water. But over there, by the reef, the water is certain to be clear—you can tell by its colour. But for heaven's sake watch out for sharks.'

Our brass harpoon heads were already gleaming on the long shafts. We quickly put on our foot fins and with thumping hearts entered the water, full of excited anticipation.

We kept close together, keeping a careful look-out in all directions, and hastened to get to the far bank. Swimming in opaque water is an unpleasant sensation—you never know whether some invisible danger is not lurking close by.

The current was pushing us along and the reef moved closer. Abruptly the veil broke, the grey wall was left behind, and before us lay a picture of un-dreamed-of beauty.

William Beebe has likened the coral reefs to a moonscape, to a primeval forest from the early days of our world, and to a fairy-tale landscape peopled by scarcely visible dwarfs and gnomes. Now I understood what he meant.

· But I only stopped for a moment to absorb the new impression; then I breathed in and let myself glide down into the strange magic world. And it was a totally different world, far removed from all familiar landscapes of this earth, a world which only few had seen before.

I was swimming through a coral forest. Like tall trees, rust brown in colour and with thick gnarled trunks, these corals grew from the sea floor. Their branches were not slender but broad and spreading, reaching out into the water like those of fir-trees. Bizarre and massive, supporting the illusion of an enchanted forest, a grove of elkhorn coral lay before me.

But this forest was not dead. Everywhere were flashes of light—red and green, yellow and blue, and even in the dark shadows several pairs of eyes were winking at me like ghosts. I was swimming below the branches, almost brush-ing against the roots of the trees, along the edge of the forest, peering into the mysterious twilight. For a moment I was in danger of falling under the spell of this underworld as strange shapes suddenly emerged between the coral trees, huge fans waving to and fro like the fins of supernaturally huge fish lurking on the seabed. But these were only supple horny coral, *Gorgonia flabellum*, the 'Venus fans', waving rhythmically with the swell of the sea.

I passed between the gorgonians, turned my gaze upwards and now en-joyed a new picture. The tree-tops of this enchanted forest were alive with elves—small brightly coloured fish with minute lively eyes. They were all in motion, dancing and waltzing about the branches. I had the happy sensation of being no longer in a strange hostile world but among cheerful, happy creatures well disposed towards me.

But this was the end of my first invasion of these regions—I was out of air and had to surface. I avoided all movement, and felt myself lifted upwards by some invisible benign hands. With relief I expelled my air, happily I filled my lungs again and once more glided down, towards a grotto formed in the coral forest by trunks and branches. Through that grotto came sunlight. As I approached it slowly and noiselessly I saw, in the unsteady light below me, a shoal of red-patterned and brilliantly blue parrot fish. They were peacefully browsing, and I could hear the grating of their teeth against the coral. They were about twelve inches long and had not yet spotted me; I took care not to cast a shadow downwards. With my left hand I held on to a rough slippery branch and aimed my spear.

Just then I caught sight of a fish whose behaviour immediately fascinated me. It was a thin snake-like creature about the same length as the parrot fish but only about two inches across at its thickest point. Its head and mouth were elongated, looking like a trumpet. The eyes of this 'trumpet fish', as I mentally christened it—and in point of fact, that is its actual name—wore a rigid expression, and its whole posture was altogether rigid. It was hanging in the water, head downwards and its small tail pointing upwards, near a gorgonia bush and looked almost indistinguishable from a branch of this coral.

While I was watching it the trumpet fish suddenly abandoned its position and, moving in the shadows, approached the peaceful parrot fish. I could not make out its intention, since the parrot fish were about ten times as fat as itself. With a sudden jerk it made for the biggest of them and descended on to it. The parrot fish was clearly uneasy. It did not know what was happening and swam off in alarm. But the strange thin fish was not to be shaken off. Skilfully it followed every single movement of the parrot fish, always keeping close above the fat back. Quickly I let go of my coral and followed too, but they had disappeared in the depths of the forest.

I had to surface again. But no sooner had I filled my lungs than I caught sight of a huge fish hovering just under the surface, near the top of the coral trees. It was about five feet long and looked like a large pike. Once it angrily opened its mouth, as if to yawn, revealing its numerous sharp teeth. I instantly recognized the predator about which I had heard such a lot—it was a dangerous barracuda, feared even more than the shark by the natives of many coasts. But while I was watching it I witnessed an incredible incident. A minute light-brown fish, barely two inches long, came shooting out from the corals, straight at the large predator. It must be out of its mind, swimming towards its certain death!

But things happened differently. The little fish was now close to the barracuda and bit the giant in its tail. The barracuda was most annoyed and flicked its fins angrily, but the little fellow would not let go. Again and again it bit the large tail fin until the big fish abandoned its dignity and fled. Only then did the tiny hero swim back, satisfied, to its coral home which no one, not even a barracuda, was allowed to approach with impunity.

I tried to spear some fish, but soon realized that this was not so easy as I had imagined it would be in view of the great wealth of marine fauna. I first stalked a blue parrot fish, then I caught sight of a large grey fish with a round mouth which interested me. But as soon as I started to trail it a most interesting creature, glittering like gold, moved across my path—and so it continued. Things had been easier in Dalmatia. There a large fish was encountered only now and again, and one could devote oneself to it at leisure. But here, in this swirling maze of new and unfamiliar things it was almost impossible to concentrate on anything in particular.

Where was Alfred? I had completely forgotten him in my excitement. I could not see him anywhere and felt alarmed at the thought of sharks, but then I discovered him not far away, among the corals. I watched him chasing the barracuda with wild leg strokes; at last, realizing the hopelessness of his efforts, he angrily thrust the harpoon into its tail. Clearly it was not the barracuda's day!

'Such rotten luck,' Alfred panted as he saw me. 'Twice I was quite close to him! And a blue parrot fish only got away by a whisker! And my goggles keep misting up all the time!'

'Smear some saliva on the inside,' I advised him from long experience. I was delighted to see that the hunting bug had bitten him.

We now swam together into deeper water. Here the sea bed was covered by quite different corals. In between green hemispherical brain corals with their meandering patterns and stagshorn corals growing like tall thick hedges stood large gorgonians, the long arms of which reached upwards like bony spectral fingers. Under a broad Venus fan, about twenty-five feet down, I spotted a strangely shaped large fish calmly floating above a stagshorn coral. Here was a suitable object for showing Alfred how to spear a fish.

Soundlessly I sank under the surface. Then, with a movement of my left hand, I turned over so that I was looking down, and without splashing, with cautious slow fin movements, I swam downwards. I had worked out the necessary tactics. I intended to reach the bottom about twenty yards away from the fish and then creep up on it from the side, through the tall coral bushes.

At a depth of about twenty feet my ears reminded me that they needed accustoming again to the pressure at lower depths. There was also a slight pain in my sinuses, but I took no notice of it and descended the last few feet to touch down among several massive gorgonians.

I pushed the thick branches aside, cautiously crept between the bushes and soon spotted my quarry. It was about three feet long, grey with blue patches. It was also very flat, had a proboscis-shaped snout, and on its forehead a curved horn. The eye of this unicorn fish particularly fascinated me—it was like the eye of a recluse or a philosopher. The unicorn fish loves solitude to ponder its problems.

The creature was still unaware of danger; it was leaning slightly to one side, the delicate fins alongside its body moving gently. But I was unlucky. I was just about to strike when a small yellow fish which had spotted me shot out from the coral in alarm. This disquieted my unicorn fish which now began to move slowly and uncertainly. I struck quickly, but my aim was short and I merely jogged the fish's side with my harpoon head without wounding it. This threw it into indescribable panic. It was as if, abuptly snatched from its dreams, it was suddenly terrified by its whole environment.

It jerked forward, knocked its proboscis against a coral bush, got even more alarmed, flapped its fins and laid its horn flat against its back. For a moment I saw its eyes—they were most expressive, reflecting terror and helplessness.

I had to ascend for air. From above I could see the fish still straying about among the coral, like a child that has lost its way in a maze. Just then Alfred called out to me. He was pointing his arm towards the open sea.

Swimming straight towards us was a whole shoal of large silvery fish. There must have been over a hundred of them, swimming in serried ranks, alongside each other and on top of each other, their large unwavering eyes staring towards us. It looked like an attack. Muscles taut, harpoon ready in my hand, I dived towards the fish, But suddenly, hard in front of us, a flash of lightning streaked through the water. As if by a word of command, the fish had about-turned and were swimming away—still in the same perfect formation in which they had come. We had penetrated into an exceedingly strange world.

Jörg had been anxiously awaiting us. We told him our experiences in great detail. Yet it was he who produced the most important piece of news that evening. Timing himself with a watch he had been practising holding his breath as long as possible and now informed us that he had managed a full four minutes. 'It isn't really difficult,' he declared. 'All you have to do is breathe as fast and as deep as possible for about two minutes beforehand.'

I tried out Jörg's new technique and at my very first attempt reached three and a half minutes. The intensified breathing reduces the carbon dioxide content of the blood and in consequence enables one to manage longer without fresh air.

In point of fact such performances are only rarely necessary in skindiving. Few people realize how long sixty seconds is and all the things one can see and do in that time. That is the great thing about spear-fishing—each stalking barely takes a minute and you experience more in a single day than a normal hunter may in a whole month.

Four days after our arrival we were at last informed that our entry permit had been approved. Jörg's weapons, however, were not being released by Customs.

The diplomatic part of our task was completed. Now came the equally difficult preparations for our expedition proper. The most difficult problem was supplies. We were complete beginners and had no idea what we would need in our tent. We shopped quite wildly—tinned milk, vegetables and fruit; sardines and corned beef; coffee, tea, bread and soup cubes; rice and potatoes; fat, butter and jam in tins; oil, sugar, vinegar, salt; methylated spirit, petrol, eggs and coconuts. As there were no fresh water springs in Curaçao we also wanted to take metal drums of water with us. Later, especially on Bonaire, we learnt to manage more modestly. There we lived mainly on fish, buying only bananas, oil, flour and cornflour, sugar, tea, and finally, as a source of vitamins, the cheap *limunjes*, small green lemons growing in Curaçao.

First Encounter with the 'Tiger of the Sea'

Without any doubt the Boca—where we eventually received permission to camp—was one of the most charming spots in Curaçao. Between two steep slopes the narrow arm of the Spanish Water here ran into the open sea like a dark lazy river. Our bank was densely grown with mangroves and other tall trees. In the thickets up on the slopes we observed a herd of wild goats. The opposite shore was considerably steeper and more sparsely grown. Among the larger boulders, we often observed iguanas lazily basking in the sunshine outside their caves.

The spot assigned to us for camping was on the bank of a calm lagoon, only a few hundred paces from the open sea. In the shelter of tall, spreading trees we put up our tent on the very edge of the minute beach which had survived between the dense mangroves.

'We will put all our underwear, the medical supplies, your telescope, photographic things and anything else that's got to be kept dry into the case,' Jörg said to me. Our cooking utensils and pots were arranged by Alfred in a wooden case, and the sack with the food supplies was put under the fly-sheet to keep it out of the rain.

'I'll see to the rest,' Jörg suggested. 'You go and catch us some dinner.'

He did not have to ask us twice. This time we had better luck. At the very beginning, as I was peering into the confusion of the coral forest, a large green parrot fish emerged suddenly from among the branches and made straight for my harpoon. I thrust and struck it in the middle of the head. The fish was instantly dead. I stowed it away in my fish carrier, readied my harpoon again and continued the hunt. The large barracuda was here again and so were the little dancing elves in the tops of the coral trees—but we could see no sharks this time.

After a few less successful attempts I bagged a large horned fish. Then I had a strange adventure. I had been following a coral fish with blue and yellow stripes and was watching a couple of small graceful butterfly fish when about six feet below me, in the shadow of a broad coral branch, I caught sight of a strange object swinging regularly to and fro. It looked like a large delicately patterned lump of jelly. I dived down and to my surprise discovered that it consisted of countless small copper-coloured fish pressing quite close against one another. The little creatures had strikingly big breasts and we were to encounter them frequently in the future. They could be found in the same spot day after day, in their hundreds, never moving an inch and spending their lives in a close community.

While I was watching these big-breasted fish, scattering them a little with my hand, I noticed behind them in a dark hole two big shining eyes. I was instantly seized by the fever of the hunt—this was certain to be a very big fish!

I checked my harpoon line and head, descended, slowly crept up on the hole in the coral and took careful aim between the two brilliant eyes. This was a thing I had discovered before—whenever a fish faced me I had to aim straight at its head; as it saw the harpoon moving it would turn swiftly to the side and the harpoon head would strike home behind the gills.

I could feel I had hit it. The harpoon head had detached itself and was lodged in the fish's body, and the line which held it was disappearing in the recesses of the cavern. I tried to pull the fish out by the seven feet of line, but it had got entangled in the hole and would not move.

Although I was getting very short of air I swam up close to the cave and cautiously followed the line into the dark hole with my hand. It is a rather uncomfortable feeling to reach into the unknown—anything might lurk in there. But I found the spot where the line had fouled and freed it.

Now I really had to surface for air. I pulled the harpoon shaft and line behind me, the resistance ceased, and from the jerk I could tell that I had pulled my quarry from its hole.

After gasping for air I looked down expectantly and had a surprise. Dangling from my harpoon line was not, as I had imagined, some huge fish but a very small miserable creature. It had a large square head with enormous rigid eyes, and behind the head a tiny little tail. The body seem to be missing altogether.

Angrily I hauled up my ridiculous trophy, but just then I had another surprise. The fish began to gulp down water with eager movements of its lipped mouth. It gulped and gulped, its body grew larger and larger and fatter and fatter, it got more and more inflated, and eventually completely changed its appearance. It was now as round as a ball and the spines which had been lying against its tail were now erect in all directions. Now I recognized it. It was the porcupine fish, dried skins of which can be seen hanging around the lamps in harbour taverns.

Subsequently we have always spared the porcupine fish. I always felt sorry for them and regarded them as the personification of an inferiority complex in the fish world. Aware of their weakness and deformity, they hide in coral holes and look out from wide-open round eyes which betray boundless fear. Only occasionally—who knows why?—will they venture out and gaze in astonishment on the world around them. At the approach of supposed danger they fly into a panic and with a desperate thrashing of their little tails they retreat to their holes. Only when it is too late for escape do they resort to their ultimate weapon—they pump themselves full of water and turn into a spiky ball which no fish can injure.

Towards noon we were fishing near the reef. Jörg had just bagged a fine silk snapper when we caught sight of a large creature, at least twelve feet long, approaching us with regular flicks of its huge tail fins.

A shark!

And now something happened to me that I must try to explain. I am deliberately saying 'happened to me' because in recounting it I feel as though some alien will had taken possession of me. What I did, in fact, was swim straight at this dangerous creature, without hesitation or reflection, and photograph it.

I photographed it coming towards me, in its full majesty, assurance and perfect grandeur. Behind the giant fish was deep water, so the background was dark; its contours were gleaming with the light of the sun so that its shape stood out clearly and impressively against the background.

I was clicking my shutter, getting closer to the shark, meeting it at an angle. I got to within ten feet when it did something totally unexpected. With a sudden frightened jerk it raced away.

Back on the surface I asked myself: What had happened just then under the water? I was, to be perfectly honest, appalled by what I had done. I was gasping for air, and my heart was still thumping from excitement. The shark had run away from me!

Why? Surely I was only a small fish, nothing that it need fear, a miserable creature in the water, compared to it, a king in its own domain.

I believe I know why the shark fled from me. Imagine it swimming along, sure of itself, feared by all the creatures of the sea, and then suddenly something it has never seen before makes straight for it. This is outside its experience and therefore frightening.

Since that day we have learned how to treat sharks. Our first commandment was: never betray fear but swim straight at it, just as if you wanted to attack it. But keep a firm hold on your nerves because this is easier said than done.

Hunting for Rays

There was a spot nearby where we could climb ashore comfortably. There we lay down in the sun to absorb some warmth into our bodies. It seems to be a skindiver's fate that he should always be cold on his hunting expeditions. In Dalmatia, while sitting on the rocks under the hot midday sun and shivering with cold, we had dreamt of the scorching tropics. But here too, in the warm Caribbean Sea, we were feeling chilly. During the prolonged stays under water too much of one's body heat is drained away by the sea.

I loaded my spare film which I invariably carried on me in a small tin sealed with beeswax. We also ate our food. This was naturally watertight, consisting as it did of oranges which I had carried in my fish carrier.

We slept a little and felt refreshed and cheerful as the evening was beginning to close in.

Off, then, to hunt the rays! A fisherman who had visited us at our tent had told us that towards evening the giant sting-rays came up from the deep sea towards the sandy bed. If his dramatic accounts were to be believed, their whip-like tails alone were over six feet long. Maybe we would be lucky.

We once more glided through the waves and immediately had an unpleasant experience. I felt a stinging pain on my cheeks, along my legs, on my body—it was impossible to see anything but we knew that there must be minute jelly fish barring our way. We stopped and probed around us. Since the jelly fish could not be seen we had to feel them. If we sensed the stinging in our outstretched hands then there were jelly fish in that direction; if there was no stinging then that presumably was the edge of the swarm we had strayed into. A few brief but painful minutes later we had escaped from them. Now that the sun was no longer high in the sky all contours on the sea floor were blurred. Without the hard light with its black shadows everything looked flat and the three-dimensional effect was lost. The bottom, about twenty-five feet down, had become grey and unfriendly, and the gorgonians whose waving branches had looked so charming in the sunlight had turned into grey spectral arms which would seize us the moment we dived down.

Suddenly we turned in alarm. Close to us something was hissing through the water. But this was no ray, merely a turtle we had disturbed. It was swimming away with incredible speed and a few moments later had disappeared in the dark distance.

Jörg was swimming a little way off while I stayed with Alfred. We had split up because this would give us a better chance of spotting the rays. I stared down intently. Alfred and I were in luck. Down below, among the grey menacing coral trees a dark shadow had appeared in the distance—a ray.

It really looked like a ghost. It was not swimming like a fish but rather flying through the water. With slow regular undulating movements of its two sides, very much like flapping wings, it was approaching just above the sea bed.

It was all black, like some hideous evil spectre of the night.

Slowly it came closer. I realized at once that this massive creature was too large for us to attack; even if we succeeded in harpooning it we should never get it up to the surface.

But Alfred had already dived down, harpoon ready in his hand. For a moment I was appalled: I had no harpoon with which to come to his aid, and in the excitement I even forgot to take photographs. Now they were closing— Alfred and the sting-ray. Alfred was slightly in front of it and for a moment I caught sight of the ray's tail with its dangerous poisonous sting.

The ray had noticed Alfred and was making a sudden effort to turn away. Its movements were clumsy and reluctant—big fish always find it awkward to have to diverge from their path. Clearly the sting-ray wanted to escape; its tail was curving for the turn—and just then Alfred struck. To my delight I saw the harpoon entering the ray's head behind its eyes.

There was an enormous turmoil in the water. Thrashing its sides powerfully and lashing the water with its tail, the ray raced off into the corals. Alfred, gripping the harpoon shaft with both hands, was being carried along, and so the two together entered the ghostly underworld. Alfred and the fish, or rather the fish with Alfred.

I called to Jörg and followed the two as far as I could on the surface. I could see Alfred eventually succeeding in slowing down the monster and then in holding it. Admittedly he could not pull the ray to the surface but at least it was no longer able to drag him further down or make off with him.

It was now up to me. I dived down to Alfred and saw his chest twitching spasmodically—he was short of air. He had thrown his head back looking out

Calcareous algae play an important part in the building of coral reefs. They envelop the dead clumps and turn even loose debris into solid stone slabs.

Above: *An elkhorn coral (millepora); next to it a dead clump already covered by calcareous algae.*

Left: *The result—a massive stone slab.*

Right: *The delicate stagshorn corals (acropora), which grow to a height of several feet, are similarly transformed once they have died. It is this cementing activity of the calcareous algae which produces the reef plateau.*

Above: *A shoal of yellow-tailed surgeon fish* (Xesurus laticlavius) *in the cloudy waters off the Galapagos Islands.*

Left: *French angel fish* (Pomacanthus paru) *in a Caribbean reef. Only by studying their natural habitat can biologists gain an understanding of the evolution of the fishes living there, that is, of the development of their forms and behaviour patterns.*

Preceding page: *Two ten-foot-long grey sharks* (Carcharhinus menisorrah) *on a reef slope of the Maldive Islands.*

The easternmost point of the Indo–Pacific coral region is tiny Cocos Island north-east of the Galapagos Islands. As in all border regions, the number of species here is small, but the number of specimens is large. The coasts of Cocos Island are reminiscent of the rocky coasts of the Mediterranean, except that these are clumps of coral and not bare rock. In the foreground a puffer-fish (sphaeroides).

for me. There was still a good distance between us, and it suddenly occurred to me that it would not be at all easy to hold the fish because I was still carrying the camera and the fish carrier and in consequence was rather less mobile than Alfred.

I reached him, took the harpoon shaft from him, and Alfred, relieved, made for the surface. But in the excitement I had not allowed myself time properly to fill my lungs with air. Besides, holding the struggling fish was quite a job. It was flapping first one way and then another, and suddenly it started gyrating, with its tail getting alarmingly close to me on one occasion. I strained against its pull with all my strength but I knew that I could not hold out much longer.

Just then Jörg and Alfred arrived. Alfred took the harpoon shaft from my hand and while I ascended to breathe I could see Jörg, now holding the harpoon, lunging towards the ray and hitting it once more, this time in its back. I had reached the surface and was filling my lungs with air. My heart felt as if it were bursting and I was painfully cold. But I had to go down again.

My friends had by then ascended half way. I once more took over the shaft, and slowly the three of us pulled the fish to the surface—a very difficult job against the water resistance produced by its flat body.

The shore, fortunately, was not too far away. Exhausted but happy about our quarry we dragged the sting-ray towards the beach. We moved with great caution—one of us swam to the right of the creature with the harpoon line and the other to the left, so that it could not get near either of us. Although the ray was heavily wounded, as it was swimming just under the surface its tail was now wildly thrashing the air.

We dragged it up the beach and while the other two were holding it I found a stone and flung it on the beast's tail. Then I struck swiftly with my knife. The monster was defeated.

This sting-ray was our last major quarry at New Port. Our beautiful reef seemed to be getting depopulated from one day to the next. No doubt the large fish had been telling each other about our ravages.

Local fishermen advised us to move to the island of Bonaire where, so they said, fish were extremely plentiful. This island was about sixty miles from Curaçao. The idea appealed to us as we were wanting to leave Curaçao for other reasons as well. We had discovered that we were being continually watched by detectives who had even searched our tent during our absence. The Curaçao police evidently still did not trust us.

There were no oil refineries on Bonaire and therefore, presumably, no military fortifications. It seemed reasonable to assume that we would be left alone there—this assumption, however, was not borne out.

On my last dive before our departure I had one more memorable experience. The sea off Curaçao evidently wanted to give me a parting reminder of its danger. Evening was falling and the light under water was getting murky when I killed a rare brightly-coloured horned fish. I detached it from the harpoon, killed it, but had some trouble threading my carrier line through its gills. I let my harpoon float—its long wooden shaft made it slightly lighter than the water—forgot about my surroundings and concentrated fully on my problem.

At last I succeeded. I turned, tried to retrieve my harpoon—and was paralyzed with fright. I could feel my heart missing a beat. Barely six feet from me, quite motionless, was a large fat shark. It was facing me, watching me closely from small vicious eyes. The harpoon, my only weapon, had drifted far away.

For a moment we were facing each other, motionless. Then the shock made me jerk unwittingly and air was expelled from my mouth. Abruptly we had exchanged roles. I had scared the shark at least as much as it had scared me. With a hasty movement it turned about and raced away. The next moment it had vanished in the darkness.

Our Robinson Crusoe Island

Towards 9.30 a.m. we reached Kralendijk, the seat of the Dutch administration of Bonaire, and made fast at the pier alongside several large sailing schooners from Jamaica and Puerto Rico. Kralendijk, on the flat part of the island, consisted of small white stone houses scattered along the beach. Amidst them, above the pier, towered the Fort and the great house of Mijnheer Gezaghebber.

The inhabitants, crossbred Negroes, Venezuelans and ancient Indians—or rather those of the inhabitants who had not drifted to the more prosperous Curaçao in search of jobs in the docks and factories—were simple fishermen and skilled boat-builders. Bonaire had long been famous throughout the West Indies for the seaworthiness and elegance of its schooners. On the long beach, among tall scaffolding, we saw the hulls of ships in various stages of completion.

Right: *The Great Barrier Reef fringes the north-eastern edge of the Australian continent over a total length of 1,250 miles. The outer face is twelve to ninety miles offshore and drops steeply to a depth of 6,600 feet. The picture shows the particularly long tenth Ribbon Reef not far from Lizard Island (see page 165). North of this point Captain James Cook, on his famous voyage in 1770, succeeded in passing through the Barrier.*

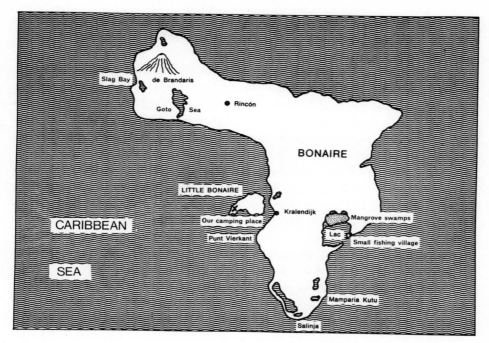

The Dutch island of Bonaire in the West Indies. We camped on the flat, uninhabited neighbouring island.

But again there was trouble with our papers. After a great deal of argument we were taken to Mijnheer Gezaghebber, the Supreme Commander of the island, who wanted to send us back to Curaçao there and then. But this time we knew we were in the right, so we turned obstinate and compelled the corpulent gentleman to wire for instructions from Curaçao.

Since the reply was not expected until the afternoon we left our luggage on board and set out to search for a Dr Diemond, a Dutch veterinary surgeon, who was said to be staying on Bonaire. Dr Diemond, we had been told in Willemstad, was studying fisheries and would surely be able to give us valuable information. At the Pension Hellmuth, where he was staying, they sent us to 'old Katchi' who was building a boat for him, but we did not find him there either and eventually located him at the schoolmaster's house, at the extreme end of the beach.

'You must be the Viennese students,' he greeted us. 'I have heard a lot about you and instantly recognized you by your splendid beards.'

Dr Diemond was interested in our fish observations. He made us give him

49

exact and detailed accounts and he was able to give us the scientific names of many of the fishes we had seen. When we mentioned hiring a sailing cutter he immediately promised us his help.

We decided to pitch our camp on the small, uninhabited island of 'Little Bonaire', just over a mile out in the Bay of Kralendijk. The fact that Mijnheer Gezaghebber was being difficult seemed to annoy Dr Diemond a good deal more than it did us. He was going to champion our case with him.

Accompanied by Dr Diemond we first went to the Venezuelan Consul to ask for permission to sail to Los Roches and Las Aves, two minute Venezuelan island groups about forty miles from Bonaire. The Consul was very charming but had no authority to give us the permit asked for. He advised us to get the German Embassy in Caracas to make an application to the proper authorities.

For lunch we were Dr Diemond's guests at the Pension Hellmuth. He showed us his own extensive researches on fisheries and provided a new experience for our palates. For hors d'oeuvre we had some small parchment-coloured objects which looked like squashed table-tennis balls and tasted delicious. They were turtle eggs.

When we called on Mijnheer Gezaghebber again we were informed, a little irritably, that we might stay on Bonaire after all. Still accompanied by Dr Diemond, we therefore went off to buy the necessary supplies. There was not much choice in the shops, but what struck me were the large stocks of chamber pots everywhere. I asked Dr Diemond why the demand for these articles was so great here.

'It isn't,' he replied with a smile, 'but we used to have a particularly efficient chamber pot representative in Kralendijk. And people here are so naïve. They don't know anything about business.'

Dr Diemond took charge of the entire organization. The schoolmaster was to take Jörg, Alfred and the luggage across to the island at once and come back for me later. Meanwhile Dr Diemond and I would try to find a rowing boat in Kralendijk and, if possible, a native boy.

It was pitch dark when we reached the island. After an impromptu meal we slept on our air beds among the thorny shrubs.

When I woke up towards 7 a.m. Bernardo, our new servant, was already crouching on a nearby stone, awaiting our commands. We at once assigned to him the duties we enjoyed least—dishwashing. Then, on our morning hunt, he accompanied us in the boat with a spare harpoon. This made our hunting a great deal easier. Whenever we had speared a fish we would pass the harpoon with our kill up to Bernardo and were at once handed another by him.

As soon as we had caught enough fish I got Bernardo to cook us an ample breakfast, especially as we were expecting a guest with a good appetite. Carrying a large water barrel in the bows, Dr Diemond came rowing over from Kralendijk in a tiny boat, and we were afraid that his little cockleshell might vanish under the waves at any moment.

'Unfortunately something's the matter with the schoolmaster's boat,' he explained. 'We will just have to try to carry your whole baggage in the two little *bootjes.*'

Our search for a favourable camping site took us half way round the island. At last, near the shore, we found a tall shady tree standing alone in a desolate spot.

Little Bonaire is entirely flat and overgrown with low thorny scrub and many kinds of cacti. The trees which used to grow here had fallen victim, over the centuries, to the charcoal burners and boat builders of Bonaire. Only at the centre of the island had a scruffy forest thicket survived. This harboured our only companions in this uninhabited corner of the earth—wild asses and goats which lived on the sparse foliage of the shrubs and quenched their thirst at a brackish waterhole. At night we were often startled from our sleep when one of these wild asses, either from exuberance or tormented by a nightmare, galloped past our tent, its hooves pounding, and in the morning we were invariably woken by the bleating of the wild goats feeding on the scrub.

We got our luggage from the boat and while I was erecting our tent under the shady tree Jörg and Alfred dragged along some large stone slabs to build a table and seats. These jobs finished, we hastened to explore our hunting ground. While my friends went straight into the sea from our camp site, I walked with Dr Diemond to a more distant spot to reconnoitre the area.

The water here was exceptionally clear and I took photographs of unending bushes of stagshead coral which covered the sea bed as far as the eye could see. Since few large fishes kept to this tangle of coral we swam on towards deeper water, as far as the edge of the coastal shelf.

This edge—a steep step where the sea floor abruptly drops down—extends all round Bonaire as it does around Curaçao. In a few places it is close inshore, elsewhere it is a few hundred yards out, but everywhere it occurs at a depth of about thirty-five feet and, moreover, so suddenly that only a short distance beyond quite considerable depths can be measured. The islands of Curaçao and Bonaire, which are of volcanic origin, rise up like towers from the depths of the sea.

At the point where we were reefs of large round clumps of coral had formed on the edge of the shelf, and in their crevices and holes there were large numbers of groupers. I made several dives to take photographs, and on one of these Dr Diemond drew my attention to a pair of angel fish. I was particularly keen on these black creatures with their golden-edged scales because I had never yet seen a fish whose appearance so well matched its general character—seen of course in human terms.

These black angel fish were a well-to-do couple, attaching importance to breeding and good manners. They were proud and disdainful. They were flat and of circular shape, and their movements had an old-world touch about them.

The couple invariably stuck together. They were jointly curious, they were jointly nervous, and whenever anything happened they arrived jointly, always remembering their dignity. They never ventured too close to anything 'new', they were easily frightened and hurriedly turned to flight, always keeping close together. As soon as their first fright was over they would rally again and, almost as if ashamed of their cowardice, shift about embarrassedly in the water. Then they would gracefully dance away, full of love for each other and of disdain for the world around them.

As soon as we had settled down a little we began experiments with our diving helmet and roughed out a scenario for our filming. Before going to bed I checked the camera case, packed the spare film in a watertight bag and got everything ready for the next morning.

After breakfast we were about to carry our diving helmet to the boat when Bernardo pointed to the sea. A large motor yacht was approaching. It cast anchor directly off our camp site. We watched a man in a white suit climbing into the dinghy and being rowed ashore by a native servant. A few minutes later he appeared in front of our tent. He was short and skinny, with serious, cunning features and a morose air. The Dutchman greeted us with striking courtesy and a smile that froze on his face: Mijnheer Gezaghebber was aboard the yacht, Mijnheer Gezaghebber would like to speak to us, would we please come out to Mijnheer Gezaghebber.

Even at a distance the thin man had looked to me like a plain-clothes policeman, and now that he was trying to lure us away from our tent my suspicions turned to certainty. This was a manoeuvre we knew from Curaçao. Evidently we were going to be spied upon even on this small uninhabited island. Very well, we had no objection—the man was welcome to look around our tent. We strolled down to the beach to pay our respects to Mijnheer Gezaghebber.

We knew quite well what suspicions the Curaçao police had about us. They believed quite seriously that we had secret communication with U-boats.

We were curious to find out the meaning of this visit. Mijnheer Gezaghebber welcomed us with great cordiality, told us that he happened to be passing this way with some friends on a fishing trip but had left his bait at home, and so it had occurred to him that we might perhaps do a quick dive with our harpoons to catch him a few fish for bait.

It was clear that Mijnheer Gezaghebber wanted to find out whether we were in fact able to catch fish. Very well—he would get his bait.

Back at our tent to collect our harpoons we caught the plain-clothes man searching the bushes nearby. But all he found was a few fish heads which we had thrown there.

Off we went to catch some bait for Mijnheer Gezaghebber. The first major fish I spotted was a beautiful creature with yellow and blue longitudinal stripes which the natives called *rode bekki*—meaning 'red mouth'—because of its brilliant red palate. I had no intention whatever of delivering this delightful creature to Mijnheer Gezaghebber. Looking out for my two companions, I saw Jörg hunting offshore in the deep water while Alfred was engaged in his favourite occupation of lurking by the huge shapeless corals in shallow water. These corals were a labyrinth of passages and Alfred would spend hours lying in wait at the entrance to these caves. He was after a particularly large fish which was at home in this maze and was making a fool of him. While he was sitting in front of one hole the fish would emerge at the far side, and the moment Alfred moved to the other side the fish would calmly return to its former place.

As always when I needed a fish urgently I was unsuccessful. Half an hour had passed when I heard a shout from the rocks. Jörg had climbed ashore a few hundred yards from our tent and was now leaping over the rocks waving excitedly and shouting. I got out of the water as quickly as I could. Jörg, speaking hastily and excitedly, told me he had spotted a sleeping shark.

There was instant chaos. I raced back to the tent to get the camera and remembered that I had to load a new film. Jörg, running alongside me, panted that he would instruct Bernardo to get our boat ready. We would fasten the harpoon point to a long rope and tie the other end to the boat. In this way, provided we succeeded in harpooning the shark, we should be able to tire it out from the boat and land it.

Bernardo leapt into our boat, Jörg followed him, and at last I had my camera ready for action. But we were not the only ones who were excited. The corpulent Mijnheer Gezaghebber, failing to understand what possessed us, was standing in his boat, shouting. He wanted to know what this was all about, but we had no time to answer him. As soon as we got near the spot indicated by Jörg we handled our oars as gently and as silently as possible so as not to awaken the sleeping shark.

This then was the spot, with the sea over thirty feet deep.

Jörg got into the water first, looked searchingly down, and swam in front of the boat. We followed him. Then he suddenly turned his head and from his excited signalling I could see that he had found the sleeping shark again. Now I too slipped into the water with the camera. The end of the harpoon line was already fastened to the boat. Jörg's face was white with excitement: this was the opportunity we had been waiting for. We had never before succeeded in killing a shark with the harpoon, and I wanted to be in the water with the camera at the same time.

Jörg went down first and signalled to me to follow him. The camera was round my neck, ready for action.

And there was the shark. It was lying between tall green coral rocks on a light patch of sand, its contours clearly outlined against the bright background. It was a fine creature, certainly over seven feet long—the species to which this shark belonged hardly ever grows bigger. It was perfectly motionless except for its gills slowly opening and closing.

I forced myself to remain calm and, moving close behind Jörg, crept up to within twelve or fifteen feet of the shark, in such a way as to keep both Jörg and the shark in the viewfinder. Jörg had now reached the creature but still was not striking at it. He was advancing with incredible patience—indeed, it seemed to me, with excessive patience.

My eyes were riveted on the shark. It was not moving, it had not noticed anything, it was sleeping. With barely perceptible movements Jörg was swimming along its side. I knew exactly what he had in mind—he wanted to strike it with the harpoon at its most vulnerable spot, behind the last gill cleft. If it was hit there, the harpoon would go straight into its heart. I was holding the camera pressed to my face, clicking the shutter and waiting for the great moment. It was an incredible picture I had in my viewfinder—the dangerous beast dark against the light sand, and Jörg's gleaming brown figure cautiously moving in for the kill, his eyes probing the large fish, all muscles taut. At last he had reached the spot. Now he thrust his spear, with lightning speed and with all his strength.

Within a fraction of a second the water, until then clear, was opaque. In its agony the shark raced off with all its enormous strength, furiously thrashing the water. Jörg, holding on to the harpoon and the rope, was swept along. Then the shark twisted round a clump of coral, which immediately crumbled, and zigzagging wildly, still dragging Jörg behind it, it raced on among the corals. Jörg, clutching the rope, was flung first against one piece of coral then against another, and finally, realizing that it was hopeless to try to drag the shark to the surface, let go and, utterly exhausted, drifted up.

Meanwhile I too had surfaced. We breathed deeply and immediately looked towards the boat. It was a comical sight: suddenly, as if gripped by some invisible force, it slewed round and raced off. Bernardo yelled—it was not quite clear whether from delight or fear. At any rate he was standing up in the boat which was rocking alarmingly as it was being towed along by the shark.

We followed as fast as we could and a moment later Mijnheer Gezaghebber's motor yacht came chugging along too. Mijnheer Gezaghebber was quite pale. Clearly he could not understand the strange and highly suspicious happenings at all. Perhaps he thought that a U-boat was somehow involved—but we had no time to worry about his shouting. Action was now imperative; otherwise the shark would tear the harpoon line against the sharp coral. Suddenly the boat made a sharp turn—Bernardo almost fell overboard—and came racing straight towards us. For a moment it slowed down and I reached in to get my long sharp hunting knife. A glance below water had shown me that the shark had entangled itself with the harpoon line among the coral at a quite considerable depth, almost certainly over forty-five feet. As I was filling my lungs with air I suddenly saw Mijnheer Gezaghebber's pale face close above me. His corpulent body was leaning over the rail and his large eyes were staring down at me.

With a ferocious cry I waved the flashing knife over my head, then, in order to swim faster, I put it between my teeth and dived down. It was an incredibly long distance, that forty-five feet. The water pressure painfully forced my mask against my eyes, I felt I could not stand the pressure in my ears and nose any longer, but I saw the shark below me and that gave me the necessary strength. It was lying close to a clump of coral around which the rope had twisted, and its tail was thrashing furiously in all directions. At last I had reached the bottom but unfortunately my vision was blurred because the water at this depth was forcing my mask inwards so that my eyes were filling with tears. I first tried to strike the beast in its back, but that did not work because its skin there was too thick. Instinctively I held on to the coral with my left hand, slipped my right hand under the shark, pressed my body against its rough back and several times from the side thrust my knife into the area of its heart.

As the shark's blood began to stain the water I let go and gripped the rope. Though scarcely able to act any longer from shortage of air, I succeeded in getting the rope clear of the coral and then made for the surface with vigorous kicks of my finned feet. With a bad headache from the water pressure I floated on the surface, exhausted. When I opened my eyes I saw Jörg and Bernardo hauling the shark into the boat. Mijnheer Gezaghebber was still at the rail of his motor boat, speechless. With a casual air, as if nothing out of the ordinary had happened, I called over to him: 'Your bait, Mijnheer Gezaghebber!'

Battle with a Moray Eel

The next day, after prolonged and unsuccessful filming attempts and a considerably delayed lunch, I felt like going hunting at nightfall. Jörg and Alfred did not want to come along, so I set out on my own. In addition to my nose-clip, fins and harpoon I also took the camera. I made for a spot on the north coast of the little island which Bernardo had recommended.

I got there after half an hour and found that getting into the water would be exceedingly difficult. There was a large coral reef about twenty or thirty yards offshore, and between it and the shore where I was standing the water was only a little over a foot deep and the bottom covered with countless sea urchins. Only after a long search did I find a spot where a narrow twisting strip of sand ran between these colonies of sea urchins out to the reef. There I tried my luck.

I carried the camera in one hand and the harpoon in the other, and I had on my fins. Admittedly they were an obstacle to walking in the shallow water, but it was better than having to tiptoe barefoot among the sea urchins. Having reached the reef I had to clamber over a few rounded clumps of coral, covered with slippery coral animals. But at last deeper water lay ahead.

The sea bottom dropped gradually until about seventy-five yards from the shore I came to the steep slope where I wanted to spear some perch. The underwater landscape was by now familiar to me—tall coral mountains, deep gorges and luxuriant 'vegetation'. The first fish I spotted was a small grouper of about four pounds.

I dived, but the camera hanging round my neck and dangling before my nose was a great hindrance. To dive properly with a long harpoon one needs one free arm—so I had no choice but to carry harpoon and camera in the same hand while descending.

The grouper belonged to the species which changes its colour quite strikingly. Sometimes these creatures were such a light grey that from above they look almost brilliant white, then again they could turn almost black; their normal colouring was brownish with white spots and a narrow dark stripe. My grouper changed colour as soon as it observed me, but the place it had found for itself seemed so attractive to it that it was reluctant to leave it. That was to prove its doom.

A sharp thrust and a moment later I was pulling the wriggling fish to the surface. There I killed it, detached it from the harpoon head and placed it in the net which I carried on my belt.

Shortly afterwards I had killed a second grouper of the same size and was just wondering whether these two fish would be enough for supper when I caught sight of a quite enormous snapper below me. It came swimming up among the coral, its eyes rigid, and although I was not quite sure whether to tackle this powerful creature I dived towards it. I was on my own, there was no one to help me, and underwater the fish was undoubtedly stronger than me. Besides, the camera round my neck and the two fish in the net round my waist made swimming difficult. Undecided, I was approaching the reef from seaward when suddenly the large snapper chased off in a fright and I found myself facing the head of a hideous eery creature.

Without much reflection I arched my body and thrust the harpoon straight through the thick neck of the snake-like monster.

At the same moment the harpoon shaft was snatched from my hand and I could see it bouncing away and disappearing among the coral.

Back on the surface I realized the kind of opponent I had got involved with. Judging by the thickness of its body the moray eel must have been at least as long as myself. Besides, the creature's bite was said to be poisonous. But what I had started I wanted to finish. I peered down to spot my harpoon. It was wedged between clumps of coral at a depth of over thirty feet and the line disappeared in a dark hole.

I dived down, gripped the shaft and tugged as hard as I could. But the moray eel stuck to its hole. I sped to the surface again to fill my lungs with air, hurried down again and tried once more. I dived three, four, eight, twelve, perhaps twenty times, tugging the rope in all directions, wedging myself against the coral, thrusting with the harpoon into the dark where the beast was hiding—I tried everything that was humanly possible but I did not succeed in budging the moray eel by as much as an inch.

I was exhausted and needed a short rest. The sun meanwhile had sunk lower and the blue of the sea seemed darker than before. While I was resting and reflecting I noticed that a small crowd had collected below me—no fewer than five large and seventeen lesser groupers. They had been lured from their holes by the commotion and they had collected to witness our battle. There were also some grey snappers and small barracudas. If my harpoon had not been lodged in the moray eel I could have speared as many fish as I liked.

I was diving again, determined to force a decision. I wedged both my feet against a clump of coral and gave a mighty tug. I reeled back, losing my balance for a moment—the line had broken.

But I was not giving up—I had to kill the monster no matter how long it took. Fortunately I had a spare harpoon head with me; I fastened it to a double length of harpoon cord, to prevent it breaking too easily. I descended once more, swam around the coral and peered into its many caves. In one of them I believed I could see the greenish body of the moray eel. I thrust at once. A sharp jerk proved my suspicion to be correct. But everything else was just as before. My harpoon was once more lying by the clump of coral and the line once more disappeared into a hole, though a different one this time.

To make matters worse, I had run into new trouble. While ascending I had brushed off my nose-clip by a clumsy movement. It had dropped down and was now lying on a round coral, at least thirty-five feet down. Without stopping to think I dived down to get it back, but instantly felt a pain in my sinus which at a depth of about fifteen feet got so bad that I could hardly bear it. I gritted my teeth and forced myself to continue. It simply had to be done.

The pain unfortunately made my eyes water, and when I reached the bottom the nose-clip had become very blurred. Dazed, I clumsily groped for it, trying to pick it up—and pushed it off the coral. It dropped another three feet into a narrow crack. By then I had ceased to care. Although I felt that something was going to give way in my head at any moment I descended the additional three feet and, forcing myself to move with patience, tried to extricate the nose-clip from the crevice. But time and again it slipped back. Then my air gave out and I had to surface.

I was exhausted and had to float on my back, resting. Should I not give up this unequal struggle with a moray eel and my bad luck? But something in me rebelled. It was possibly just pigheadedness—but I refused to admit defeat.

I swam into shallower water and removed the camera and the two fish which had been greatly in my way during diving. I realized with some annoyance that in my excitement I had not taken a single photograph and had merely carried the camera with me as needless ballast.

I filled my lungs with an extra large amount of air and dived back to my nose-clip. This time I was pinching my nose with my left hand and therefore felt no pain. But at the bottom I just could not manage to pull the little thing out of the damned crack. It was so narrow that I could hardly get my fingers in. As the seconds sped away—seeming like eternity—I tried and tried again until, at long last, I had it out far enough for me to reach it with my other hand. But that other hand was pinching my nose and I had to overcome considerable hesitation before I let go of it.

I was holding the clip now but at that instant I felt such a frightful stab of pain that I raced up to the surface like a man demented. The pressure had acted on me too abruptly. My nose was bleeding heavily and I had to wait a while before being able to fit my nose-clip.

I must have been out hunting for a good two hours. I was shivering all over with cold and the sun had sunk so low that only a little time was left to me. My hunting fever together with my stubbornness undoubtedly lent me far greater strength than I normally possessed—otherwise I could not have stood the strain.

I decided to have one last try. The eel, I reflected, would have calmed down in the meantime and it might be possible now to get it out of its hole by an unexpected jerk. I descended as calmly as possible, gripped the harpoon shaft with both my hands, levered my feet against a clump of coral and gave the cord a violent jerk.

The result was staggering. Just as if I had touched off an explosive charge the whole clump of coral, about five feet high and as much across, shattered into countless fragments. At the same moment the moray eel came shooting out of the opaque water. Only then did I realize its huge size. The ugly snake-shaped beast was racing to and fro alongside me and below me, its mouth opened menacingly, trying to reach me. Fortunately the harpoon line—as a result of my having doubled it—was now much shorter and if I held the shaft at its lower end the eel's head could not quite reach me.

With rapid fin movements I made for the surface. I was gripping the shaft with both hands in order to check the furious beast. I knew that if it managed to bite me I would hardly reach the shore alive. This was one thing the natives had told us time and again—once a moray eel had sunk its venomous teeth into something it would not let go again but would bite deeper and deeper into the flesh.

At the surface I quickly gulped for air and continued the struggle. One moment the moray eel was pulling to one side, then it would gyrate furiously, and it took an all-out effort with my finned feet to hold my own. Then again it would shoot up towards me in unexpected snake-like undulations. It would not keep still for a moment.

Only slowly did I manage to drag it towards the shore—but there I faced a new problem. My camera and the two speared fish were lying in the shallow water. How was I to pick them up? If I dived my moray eel might hide among the coral once more. While diving, therefore, I had to hold the harpoon shaft vertically upwards in one hand, so that the eel would chase about above me, and with the other quickly picked up the camera, hang it round my neck, and pick up my creel and fastened it to my belt.

Having accomplished this acrobatic feat I found myself faced with an even greater difficulty. There simply was no clear path through the countless sea urchins in the shallow water. The water, in fact, was quite black with these spiky creatures. But I had no time for reflection: the sun had nearly reached the horizon and I could not risk going ashore with the moray eel in the dark.

I tried therefore to pick my way through the expanse of sea urchins. There were occasional spots where the black creatures were lying less close, and sometimes I could push them aside a little with my fins. I was cautiously advancing while the moray eel still struggled with undiminished energy in the shallow water. Then something happened that might easily have ended tragically for me.

I stepped on a small rounded coral, slipped on the slimy surface, lost my balance and crashed down right among the sea urchins. Instinctively, to protect my face and body, and also to prevent my expensive camera from striking the ground, I put my hands in front of my chest. There was a sharp stab of pain—my hands were pricked by countless spines. But at least I had checked my fall to the extent that only my legs and my left arm touched the sea urchins. But at that moment another horrible danger stared me in the face.

As I instinctively opened my eyes in the water I saw the eel's hideous teeth-studded open mouth close to my face.

By bringing my hands to my chest while falling I had involuntarily brought the harpoon shaft closer to me and very nearly given the enraged moray eel its chance of attacking me.

During my hunting on Curaçao I had been through a good many adventures and had often displayed a reasonable presence of mind—but I shall never forget this moment. I can still see the small vicious eyes and the greedily opened mouth hard in front of my face and I still wonder how I managed to stretch out my arm with the harpoon quickly enough for the beast to be snatched back at the last moment.

The eel, angrily gyrating, succeeded in getting a hold of the steel shaft on top of the harpoon, and so furiously dug its teeth against it that, as I discovered later, it broke every one of them on the metal.

Once ashore, I tried to kill the creature. I threw a large stone on the back of its neck and repeatedly thrust my knife through its head. Even so the green slimy body continued to lash the ground with undiminished strength for quite a while.

These fish are at least as tough as big snakes and I have repeatedly admired their physical strength. I once speared a somewhat smaller moray eel with a trident spearhead of the best American steel. The trident spun through the water, the eel tore itself free, and when I hauled in my weapon I found that the beast had bent the outer spikes almost through a right angle. It was this huge physical strength that had enabled the eel, in its rage at the sudden pain, to burst the coral clump apart.

With my large trophy on my back I staggered to our tent. I was filled with an indescribable sense of triumph and power. True, my hands and legs were stinging with the pricks of the sea urchins, my head was aching, and my nose was still bleeding—but I was happy enough to embrace the whole world. Thus, victor of a three-hour battle, I struggled across the desert island, my camera and the two groupers in my hand, the huge serpent on my back, while in front of me the sun was plunging into the sea with a glow that flooded the whole sky.

'There's going to be a War!'

One evening after supper we were sitting on the deck of the sailing cutter we had hired when a dark shadow appeared out of the night and a moment later a large boat had made fast alongside. Two strangers leapt aboard our boat. One of them, carrying a torch, climbed down to our cabin, while the other, short, wiry and with piercing eyes, made straight for us. I felt sure I had seen him before.

'Where were you all day?' he snapped at us. No sooner had we replied than he barked: 'And what were you doing there?'

We did not know what the man wanted with us, especially as he presently turned to Leonardo, our captain, and talked to him excitedly in Papiamento. I was outraged at the behaviour of the other man, who, without a single word, was turning our cabin over. But just as quickly as they had arrived they vanished again with the curt instruction that we were to present ourselves to Mijnheer Gezaghebber at twelve noon the next day.

Only after they had left did I remember where I had seen those piercing eyes before. Our short visitor was Mr van de Kroef, the head of the Aliens Department of Curaçao, with whom we had fought such a bitter duel on our arrival there. Leonardo told us that the official had questioned him about all our activities. While we were still guessing at the purpose of our nocturnal visitation there suddenly came a shout from shore: Dr Diemond, our trusted friend. Bernardo hurried across in the dinghy to bring him over.

'I have very important news for you,' Dr Diemond began, all pale. 'The German army has marched into Poland!'

That certainly was unexpected news. So that was why Mr van de Kroef had come to Bonaire.

'And, of course, Britain and France have guaranteed Poland,' Dr Diemond continued. 'If war breaks out now, what will become of you? Will you get back home?'

We did not sleep much that night. Hunting, filming and photography, the wonders of the sea and our adventures, everything that normally filled us with enthusiasm, now seemed unimportant and trivial. Only one thing mattered— how were we to get back home?

For the moment there was no answer to that question. Nor were we greatly encouraged the following day when we presented ourselves to Messrs van de Kroef and Gezaghebber.

'Have you heard the latest news?' the head of the Aliens Department asked us. When we nodded he continued: 'From now on you will report to Mijnheer Gezaghebber at twelve noon every day!'

In the afternoon, while we were watching him work on his boat, Dr Diemond told us that the Curaçao policeman had been so furious the day before because he had not been able to find us anywhere during the day. We were still thought to be spies—that explained everything.

The afternoon passed, then the next morning, and we were still waiting. We did not feel like doing anything, we were thinking of home, of our future, and of the war. During the night we had listened to the radio at the Pension Hellmuth, hearing news bulletins from different stations, but at that time there were still no new developments. Mijnheer Gezaghebber, to whom we again reported at twelve noon, likewise knew no more than we did. Not until the afternoon did Dr Diemond bring us the disturbing news.

'Herr Hass,' he shouted. 'There's going to be war! I've just heard it. Britain and France have declared war on Germany. What's going to happen to you now?'

What indeed?

We had no choice but to wait and to reflect once more on our situation. Naturally we had to give up the *Etna*, our sailing cutter. After paying our debts we should be left with about 200 Gilders. With these we would have to manage as economically as possible. We decided to pitch our tent at Punt Vierkant where we could live cheaply by catching our own fish.

'Today is our fiftieth hunting day,' Alfred said one morning. He little suspected that this anniversary was to be unlucky for him.

Because the water was especially clear we decided, after our call on Mijnheer Gezaghebber, to film near the lighthouse of Punt Vierkant. Alfred, wearing the open helmet, descended into an exceedingly romantic coral landscape. He was to film Jörg looking for a coral fish among the spherical brain corals and clumps of gorgonians. I was sitting in the boat working the air pump.

At first all went well, but suddenly the pump failed. Jörg had just gone down and in the excitement of the moment I did not know what to do. I pumped furiously, but there was no pressure at all. The leather around the piston had dried out from the heat and we had forgotten to take spare oil and grease with us. What was I to do? I dipped the pump in the water, in a fleeting hope that this might make it airtight again, but of course, this did not work. I had to wait inactively for Jörg to surface.

When I first started diving (1937-40) masks had not yet been invented. We used watertight goggles, like the ones made for pearl fishers. My first watertight camera case was made for me by a Viennese master craftsman.

Our first encounters with tropical sharks were in the Caribbean in 1939. The creatures were not nearly as aggressive as was generally believed. We were able to chase them away by swimming straight at them. However, when we speared sizeable fish the sharks would race up to us at great speed (left). By chance we discovered that we could scare them off by yelling at them under water. This 'weapon' subsequently proved effective in other seas too and saved the lives of, among others, three German sailors drifting off the West African coast in 1943.

Above: *At first I used a tripod for filming but subsequently I learned to hold the camera steady even while swimming.*

Right: *The six-foot moray eel with which I battled for two hours. In those days underwater fishing was still a fair struggle: armed only with a hand spear it is difficult to outwit a fish. Against the modern catapults, on the other hand, the fish hardly stand a chance.*

Off the Maldives we discovered fish which were rooted to the spot like plants and which, as we approached them, withdrew into the sand. We placed a television camera near their holes and were able, on a near-by island, to watch on the screen the behaviour of these previously unknown 'tube eels' (Xarifania hassi).

Preceding pages: A shoal of barracudas. Like the sharks, they are not as dangerous or aggressive as is generally assumed.

'Jörg,' I yelled to him; 'the pump's broken down. Get down fast and signal Alfred to come up at once!'

Jörg took a deep breath and was gone. Another painful minute passed. Why wasn't Alfred coming up? Surely he must hear that there was no more air flowing into his helmet. And what was keeping Jörg?

At last Jörg reappeared. He was utterly exhausted.

'The fool doesn't want to come,' he groaned. 'I tried everything. He has got some idiotic fish there which he intends to film and he's just sitting there quite calmly!'

A moment later Jörg shouted, 'That fool is moving back now—he evidently wants to get to the line. He's running now—he's jumping—he's short of air. Ah—he's got rid of the helmet!'

A moment later Alfred appeared on the surface in an utterly exhausted condition. He immediately disappeared under the water again but we had grabbed him and were pulling him into the boat. What had happened? He was as white as a sheet, his features were distorted and he was groaning pitifully. It was not really a groan but a kind of whistle, as if the air was being squeezed out of his body. He tried to say something but could not utter a word, he pressed his arm against his chest and painfully tossed his head about.

Jörg had climbed into the boat and was seeing to Alfred. I leapt into the water because the diving helmet and the camera had to be brought up. Halfway down I realized that I had left my nose-clip behind, but I was past caring about my pain.

With trembling hands I unscrewed the big weights from the diving helmet and took them up to the surface one by one, and finally the heavy helmet itself. I hardly took time to breathe at the surface between dives. Finally I picked up the film camera which Alfred had likewise left on the sea floor, detached the anchor and dropped into the boat, exhausted.

Alfred's pains had not yet abated but at least he was able to speak a little.

'My arms—I've lost all feeling in them,' he breathed. 'I can't move them—they are like rubber!' And between these words came the same uncanny whistle of air being forced out of his mouth.

I glanced at Jörg. He was a medical student and must know what the trouble was with Alfred. He was pale and rowing towards the shore with hasty movements. I did not have to ask any questions.

While Jörg was making the boat fast I dragged Alfred ashore. I supported him under the arms because he was almost unable to walk. His movements were clumsy and his arms dangled helplessly from his shoulders.

I put him down on a patch of sand and wanted to help him but did not know how. Alfred evidently saw my anxiety and, to reassure me, tried to smile

63

in spite of his pain. But it was a mere grimace.

'Just listen,' he whispered to me and pulled my head down to his chest. And there, in the area of his heart, I could hear an eery gurgling sound. Suddenly he got up by himself and began to hobble up and down, bent double, with gritted teeth.

Jörg came to my assistance and together we dragged Alfred the long way to the tent. There we laid him on a mattress and Jörg at last was able to apply his medical knowledge.

'Let's try this,' he muttered to himself and boldly sat down on our patient's chest.

'Ah!' Alfred groaned. 'Stay there, that's much better.'

. Jörg sent me to get a sheet and we wound it round Alfred's chest as tightly as possible. This treatment seemed to relieve his pain considerably and he asked for a drink. We got him some tea and then Jörg quietly sent me off fishing.

He was quite right—there was nothing I could do for Alfred. So I went off, plagued by anxiety, to catch our supper. I pursued a few large fish but nothing went right. My thoughts were with our patient and I was so jittery that I missed every time. I was about to give up when I came across a fat angel fish in the shallow water. Angrily I speared it. I had what I wanted. Jörg was waiting for me by the tent. He said in a whisper, 'He's sleeping now, and he is a little better. He's told me what happened. He says he didn't feel anything at all while ascending; only when he got to the surface did he suddenly feel that he was being torn apart from inside.'

In the evening Dr Diemond brought us some letters from home. He was greatly concerned about Alfred's accident and returned early next morning with the Bonaire doctor. Alfred was still feeling very sick. He had not slept all night, he had again lost all feeling in one arm, and he was complaining about pains in his neck. There was still, from time to time, that same gurgling sound near his heart. The doctor examined him very thoroughly, then took Dr Diemond and Jörg a little way aside, and I could guess from their serious expressions that Alfred's condition was causing them concern.

'He must be kept absolutely still,' I heard the doctor say. 'If possible he should not move at all—then we may hope that he'll pull through.'

As soon as we were alone again Jörg explained to me that Alfred was suffering from what was known as caisson disease, 'the bends', a condition caused by subjecting the body to rapid changes of pressure. The nitrogen normally dissolved in the blood forms little gas bubbles and causes an aerial embolism which can cause paralysis and even death. To prevent this, divers ascending from considerable depths must undergo slow 'decompression' and caisson workers must be brought back to normal pressure conditions slowly and gradually.

Since our diving helmet was open at the bottom Alfred, while below water, had been breathing air which was under the same water pressure as his body. During his rapid ascent he had preserved this great internal pressure inside his lungs and blood vessels while the external counter pressure was rapidly diminishing. This sudden change had caused an air embolism with partial paralysis and also explained the escape of compressed air from his mouth.

Alfred's condition improved during the next few days but when we were ordered to return to Curaçao the doctor still maintained that the voyage was too dangerous for him. There was still no prospect of our returning home, and since the intention was merely to accommodate us on board some German ships lying in the harbour of Curaçao, Jörg and I went ahead on our own and left Alfred in the care of the small Catholic hospital.

In Willemstad our appearance caused a general sensation. Our hair, bleached by sun and salt water, our tan, our beards and our shorts—we certainly looked like daredevil adventurers or, in fact, like spies. At the Aliens Department and the Hapag office we were told that an Italian steamship might sail for Europe towards the end of the next month. Meanwhile we were to live on board the *Vancouver*.

The *Vancouver*, a Hapag liner of about 5,000 tons, had been linked up into a kind of island with eight other German ships. The connection between this 'island' and Willemstad was provided by a ferry operated by the cheerful old Mairo.

Our arrival on board likewise caused a stir. Jokes were cracked about our appearance, with the result that Jörg shaved his beard off again. I, on the other hand, stuck it out, in spite of such nicknames as 'Robinson Crusoe', 'Holy Ghost' and 'Herr Professor'.

Two weeks later we returned to Bonaire aboard the *Mississippi* to collect Alfred and the rest of our baggage. It was early morning when we tied up at Kralendijk. Alfred was awaiting us at the pier. He had grown incredibly fat and looked reassuring.

'Do you know that I should have been dead long ago?' he greeted us. We were told that a thorough medical examination had revealed the presence of air in his heart and a haemorrhage in the spinal cord. In hospital he had been the first white patient in many years; he had been pampered in every respect and the fat black nurses had secretly slipped him love letters.

'Besides, I had to break bounds to meet you here,' he added. 'Mijnheer Gezaghebber has strictly forbidden me to leave the hospital.'

In the afternoon I went with Jörg over to Punt Vierkant, where we had kept several shark skins and ray skins as trophies. Then we said goodbye to the island, to old Katchi and even to Mijnheer Gezaghebber. Dr Diemond saw us off to our ship and repeatedly reminded the captain that 'these gentlemen like a lot of strong coffee'.

Soon Bonaire disappeared behind us like a beautiful dream. I shall never forget it.

Saved by a Cry

Shortly before Christmas the *Vancouver*, together with two other ships, moved to Caracas Bay. This was a welcome change because it meant we could hunt by the reefs near our first camp site on the Boca. For the ships' crews on the other hand, the monotony of life in Caracas Bay became well-nigh unbearable. True, during the day the men knocked the rust off the decks and the captains then had them freshly painted, and when one side was finished the men started on the other—but even so the sailors suffered from boredom. Of course, there were exceptions. The officers, for instance, went sailing in the lifeboats, the engineers and technicians used to study or else work on the engines, a steward from the first class collected cacti, and our barber practised the piano and gave small recitals. But most of them, especially the real sailors, did not know what to do with their time in the scorching heat.

Swimming, which at least would have been refreshing, was impossible because of sharks, and going ashore was strictly forbidden because of the anxiously guarded fuel tanks and oil pipelines.

Christmas on board was most impressive. Our captain had conjured up a Christmas tree and on it flickered the flames of small coloured candles. For a short while at least, while the old carols were sung, the men forgot the strain, the heat and the boredom and talked of home.

After the New Year the weather at last allowed us to go hunting off the northern coast. Our first dive was near Boca Tabla at the north-western tip of Curaçao, where the surf had cut a large grotto into the cliffs. The waves that day were less high than usual, the water was exceptionally clear, and we swam out to the deep water in high spirits.

We soon saw a large grouper hovering near a cave. To prevent the fish when struck from getting entangled in the coral we tied the harpoon head to a longer cord and dived down, all three of us together. At the moment when Alfred thrust the harpoon into the fish's body Jörg and I vigorously snatched at the line, and in this way we succeeded in getting the wriggling fish clear of the coral.

Unsuspecting, we were ascending with our catch when suddenly Jörg froze rigid. He had every justification—three sharks were making for us from different directions at hair-raising speed.

We have often since been similarly attacked by sharks after spearing some fish and have estimated the speed of the attacking sharks at forty, fifty and perhaps sixty miles per hour. But words cannot even begin to describe what it feels like to be attacked by a shark at such an uncanny speed. That is something which must be experienced. The shark appears in your field of vision at one moment, and the next it is on top of you. The flicks of its thrashing tail are so rapid and powerful that one cannot see them but can clearly hear them under water.

At this moment of supreme danger I instantly realized how utter pointless it was to carry a knife as a weapon against sharks. Even if it were possible to whip the knife out of its sheath in time, what could one hope to achieve with such a ludicrous weapon against such a huge monster? No, a knife was utterly useless, and on future occasions we usually left it behind. When a shark attacks it comes like a flash of lightning, performs its bloody business while racing past, and the next moment has disappeared with its victim, no matter what one does with one's knife.

These sharks, then, were racing up towards us. For a moment we were incapable of movement, then one of us screamed with fright. None of us subsequently recalled clearly which of us it was—but one of us, fortunately, uttered a shrill note into the water, and this had a startling effect. As if whipped back by some superior power, the three sharks slewed round at the last moment and chased off as fast as they had come.

One of them, a beast with a light longitudinal stripe, a moment later seemed ashamed of its panic, because barely thirty yards away from us it about-turned again and mounted another, even more furious, attack. But now the three of us yelled in chorus. And this time it was really knocked sideways. It raced off and was gone.

Breathless and totally exhausted we reached the surface, realizing that we owed our sound limbs to pure chance. A benign providence had led us, at the moment of supreme danger, to find the only effective weapon against an attacking shark under water—one must yell at it.

This method has proved highly successful on many occasions since. Our experience also led us to devote a great deal of interest to two problems. One, why do sharks race up suddenly when one has harpooned a fish? And why are they alarmed by a human shout? A number of experiments have led us to believe that the two questions probably have a common answer.

I have mentioned before that movement in water produces noise, in other words, sound waves. Strong movement, as for instance the roar of the surf or the hum of a ship's propeller, or even the rapid fin flip of a large fish, are audible even to the human ear little though this is adapted to functioning below water. Fishes possess a much more highly developed sense of hearing for such noises than does man. We have ourselves frequently observed the acuteness with which fish sense vibrations in the water. Any rapid or unharmonious swimming motion will alarm a fish even when it cannot see its attacker. This convinced us that fish not only sense movement in the water but are also able to interpret it, that is, to draw conclusions from the kind of vibrations in the water.

Why then does a shark turn up as soon as a fish has been harpooned? In popular belief the shark is attracted by the blood of the wounded fish. But in our experience the shark invariably turns up within seconds, and from such a great distance, that it is quite impossible that the minute amount of blood which the fish might have lost by then, or the smell of such a minute quantity, should have been perceptible over considerable distances within a fraction of a second.

Clearly the shark is attracted not by the blood but by the peculiar way in which a harpooned fish beats its fins. This is proved also by the fact that sharks will show up when a large fish dangles from a rod without losing any blood at all.

The question that interested me was: were the sharks attracted by the beating of the fins as such, or were they able to interpret vibrations at con-siderable distances and understand them? Did a shark come racing up because it knew that a certain fish was in trouble and would be an easy prey, or was it attracted by the mere noise?

To discover the answer to this question I dived at many locations which we knew to be full of sharks, and made as powerful and rapid movements with my rubber fins as I could. My fin beats certainly were no less vigorous than those of a small wounded fish, but nevertheless I have never been able to attract sharks in this way. And yet they showed up the moment a fish was harpooned. This led us to believe that the sharks were able to distinguish between my fin beats, which were strange and meaningless to them, and those of a wounded fish.

We also made similar observations with jacks and various species of mackerel, but one need not go to such lengths to find support for this hypo-thesis. An angler will take a small fish and use it as a live bait on his hook. Does he really expect a pike or some other predator to just happen past, or is there not perhaps a better reason for the use of a live bait?

I am convinced that my hypothesis applies also in this case, since pike do not as a rule swim about for the pleasure of it but instead lie in wait, motionless, on the bottom. It is again the fin beats of the unfortunate bait which attract the predator. The little fish, in fear of death, beats its fins in a quite unusual way which the pike interprets correctly even at a distance.

These observations and reflections, and also my instinct, have increasingly led me to believe that fish are neither deaf nor dumb. They, too, communicate —by the vibration of their fins.

One may often observe pairs of fish close to each other, hovering at one spot or dancing about each other without touching, moving their fins with infinitely delicate and rapid movements. This no doubt represents their murmured lovers' talk.

The quite exceptional sensitivity of the sharks, which enables them to sense and interpret fin beats over a distance of more than seventy-five yards, also explains their alarm when shouted at by humans. By comparison with the noise produced by a distant fin beat a human shriek at close quarters must produce sound waves striking their sensitive organs like a clap of thunder.

Jörg's Accident

The moment of our departure was drawing near and my box of unexposed 16 mm. cine-film was still in the cold store of the *Vancouver*. Since Alfred's accident near the lighthouse of Punt Vierkant we had not shot any film because to do so without boat or helpers seemed impossible to us. But I did not want to bring my films back home unused, and so I reflected on how I might do some filming on the sea bottom without a diving helmet.

My first attempt at setting up a tripod-mounted camera on the sea floor among the beautiful coral and letting the film run the moment a fish happened past proved exceedingly laborious. So I thought of another idea which was to prove spectacularly successful. Why, I asked myself, should it not be possible to operate a hand-held camera while swimming under water?

The main difficulty was that first I had to learn how to hold the camera steady in spite of the waves to avoid the picture wobbling on the screen. I tackled this new task with great zeal and I actually managed during our last few weeks to make some very satisfactory shots of most of the coastal fishes off Curaçao.

I shall always remember our last Sunday in the Bay of Plow because it ended badly for Jörg. The day started with a pleasant surprise: unexpectedly our good Dr Diemond turned up from Bonaire in his new boat, the *Dolfin*.

'In Bonaire,' he told us, 'everything is much the same. The people are still talking about you. Mijnheer Gezaghebber has been transferred and everybody is pleased about it. Old Katchi sends you his regards; he is as lazy as ever. The money I paid him for my *Dolfin* he immediately invested in booze.'

In the morning we dived in the bay, using several helmets. Even Alfred, who had long since forgotten his accident, cheerfully went down to the bottom and I photographed and filmed him sawing off a particularly fine piece of coral which we subsequently sold to an American for fifteen dollars together with an underwater photograph and our autograph.

At noon we rested comfortably in the shade of some tall trees while Dr Diemond prepared *awa di playa*, a fish soup which had been a favourite of ours back at Little Bonaire.

In the afternoon we intended to film and spear a shoal of jacks which we knew to be 'stationed' at a point not far from the bay, on the edge of the coastal shelf. That was when Jörg had his accident. Having split up into two groups we were swimming along the coast; I was keeping close inshore with Dr Diemond because I wanted to show him a small thread-tailed spotted drum, the only specimen of its kind I had seen around the whole island. The others —Jörg, Alfred and a few friends of Dr Diemond's—were swimming in deeper water along the coastal shelf.

First, still in shallow water, we encountered a rare hogfish with a large pig's snout, then some pretty butterfly fish and silvery barbels which I both photographed and filmed. To be ready for all eventualities I had both my photographic and my film cameras hanging around my neck—and this led me to make an interesting observation. When we first got to Curaçao, I clearly remembered, the underwater camera had been so heavy that even when I had breathed in deeply I only had a very slight buoyancy in the water. But now, with lungs filled, I was able to carry both photographic and film cameras and still remain lighter than water. It seemed unlikely that the specific weight of my body should have diminished. I concluded therefore that the volume of my lungs must have increased over the past few months—and this would not be altogether surprising, considering the vigorous manner in which we filled our lungs before every dive.

'A *tapa-tapa*!' Dr Diemond exclaimed, pointing to a small, blue-patterned flatfish which came gliding along close to the bottom. Like all flatfish this one was swimming along with one of its sides facing the sea floor, and for this reason its other eye had gradually travelled from the lower side across the forehead to the top. These two eyes, close to each other and facing the same way, enable flatfish, unlike most other fishes, to have three-dimensional vision. We have often found that they have observed our approach even if conducted motionlessly.

In other ways, too, the *tapa-tapa* displays little symmetry. While its underside is colourless and white, its upper side, which can rapidly change colour, usually displays a fine blue patterning. When alarmed, the *tapa-tapa* buries itself in the sand with such speed and such skill, that once the water has cleared again, one cannot even discover its outline.

'The Bonaire fishermen', Dr Diemond told me as we were swimming on, 'call this fish *sobra de dios*—meaning "what God left over". Because it is coloured on one side only and thus looks like half a fish, they say that God ate half of it and flung the other half away because it contained too many bones. This half then continued to live and became the *tapa-tapa*.'

Dr Diemond had hardly finished speaking when something unexpected happened. A large dark shadow, certainly thirteen feet long, detached itself from the distant background. A huge creature came swimming towards us from the side. The head of this monster had a strange shape—it resembled a broad flat hammer head, with small evil eyes on its outer edge. A tall dorsal fin pointed steeply upwards and a powerful crescent-shaped tail fin was thrashing the water. It did not take me long to realize what kind of giant was approaching us here in the shallow water. It was a hammerhead shark, even more feared by the natives than the tiger shark.

I grabbed Dr Diemond's arm—he was still looking in the opposite direction. For a moment I could not decide whether to photograph or film the hammerhead shark. After a second's hesitation I descended vertically, put the still camera on the ground and filmed the shark as, without considering us worth a glance, it sailed past us with majestic movements at a range of barely ten yards. The water at this point was scarcely ten feet deep. The tall dorsal fin of the creature and its fat body were so impressive that it seemed to fill the whole space between sea floor and surface.

The film camera was running in slow motion until the film ran out. Then, without going up for air, I went down to the bottom, exchanged the two cameras, and tried to take some stills of the hammerhead shark as well. Unfortunately I was too late; the beast was a long way off. I therefore turned towards the open sea, straight towards the point where our friends were.

Dr Diemond still seemed to be petrified by the sight of the shark—not from fear but with fascination at the strength of the powerful creature. 'What a splendid creature,' he was muttering as I reached the surface. I hardly had time to reply because I had to warn my friends of the hammerhead.

As loud as I could I yelled across the water. Just then there was wild, excited shouting from them. I could not make out the words but the tone of their voices and my instinct convinced me that some accident had happened. Greatly worried, I swam towards the shelf edge as fast as I could, trying to count my friends' heads among the waves. Swimming in front of them with a hasty crawl was Jörg: the others were following him, shouting excitedly.

At last Jörg came into my vision and a load dropped off my mind—he still had all his limbs. But he was pale and breathless, and clearly in a hurry to reach the shore. As we passed each other he called out to me, in a voice that tried to sound casual, 'My ear-drum's just burst!'

I had now reached Alfred and discovered that they had not even seen the hammerhead shark.

'Jörg went completely crazy,' Alfred panted as we were following Jörg towards the shore. 'We were swimming near the shelf edge when suddenly this rare species of pompano, with the long threads on its dorsal fin, appeared far below. Jörg at once dived down at a furious speed. He thrashed his legs so hard that one could no longer see his fins. Of course the fish noticed him and escaped down the scarp—but Jörg followed. We nearly lost sight of him. At last he came up again and I immediately noticed the odd way he was swimming. Obliquely, one moment to the right and then to the left, then he would look up, swim straight for a little way, but presently lose his bearing again. Finally he got to the top and told us that his left ear-drum had burst with a loud snap. After that he completely lost his sense of orientation.'

We later measured the depth at this spot. Jörg had dived down fifty-eight feet. To appreciate this achievement one must remember that the pressure at that depth is the same as in a fully blown up car tyre. Once ashore, Jörg got into the car of Mr Jonghoudt who took him to a doctor in Willemstad. Poor Jörg, I thought, this is the end of your underwater career. But I was wrong. True, Jörg was no longer able to dive with us on Curaçao, but a few months later, when we were exploring the submarine gardens of California, his ear-drum had fully healed and he was once more diving with his old enthusiasm, if with a little more caution.

At last came the hour of departure, the moment when we had to say good-bye to friends whose kindness and helpfulness we would always remember, and to the bare rocky island which had become a second home to us. Our farewell was somewhat impaired by the fact that the American shipping company, the Grace Line, whose *St Paula* was to take us to New York, was creating great difficulties at the last moment. By a strange irony of fate Mr van de Kroef, the chief of the Aliens Department, was now our staunchest ally. The man whom we had caused so many headaches was now anxious to get us far away from his fuel tanks, and I well remember the amused satisfaction with which we watched him conducting endless telephone conversations with the representatives of the Grace Line, eventually taking full responsibility for us.

But before leaving Curaçao with its coral reefs and sharks behind me I would like to tell of an experience on its north coast, an incident which occurred shortly before Jörg's accident and which represented the highlight of our adventures with sharks.

I was anxious to take some slow-motion shots of sharks in the expectation that this would probably earn us a good deal of money in America. Sharks had never before been photographed or filmed in their own habitat. For this purpose Ascencion, a sandy bay on the north coast, seemed to us the right spot.

For once it was a calm day, the sea was clear and less choppy than usual, and all prerequisites of success seemed to be present. We were the more disappointed when we found no trace of any large fish whatever at the shelf edge. But we knew by then how to attract the sharks. Jörg harpooned a small mackerel and almost instantly three sharks appeared in our field of vision. One of them was still keeping a little way off, but the other two came rushing up at an incredible speed and in an elegant arc circled round Jörg and his bait. One of them was impertinent enough to snap at the wriggling mackerel, but Jörg snatched it away and yelled so shrilly at the two sharks that they wheeled away with an alarmed thrashing of their fins. The whole thing had happened so quickly that I had not had time to dive and get my camera ready.

The third shark, too, had disappeared and I was beginning to be annoyed with Jörg for shouting, when suddenly I saw a very large grey shovelnose shark approaching slowly across the sea floor. It was certainly over thirteen feet long, but there was no need to be afraid since this species invariably kept close to the bottom and had never yet attacked us. However, there was something about it that led me to forgo all caution and made me snatch my camera up to my eyes. Close to its dorsal fin, where the pilot fish is normally found, there was a pompano weighing about nine pounds. This is a grey fish with a hooked nose; when young it has dark transversal stripes and exceedingly long black tips to its fins which it later loses. This pompano, for reasons incomprehensible to me, was swimming close above the shark and time and again butted the giant's back with its head. The shark seemed to take no notice.

This inexplicable procedure fascinated me so much that I forgot how dangerous a spot this was and that on the north coast of this island one should really be on the look-out from time to time. With no other thought but of filming this crazy pompano I dived down. But at the very moment when I raised the camera to my eyes I heard a shrill shout and simultaneously felt a strong blow against thigh and hip, and I was flung aside. For a brief moment I saw two hazy striped shadows, one following the other and disappearing at lightning speed.

It all happened so quickly that I had no time to be frightened. I surfaced again, intending to crack a joke with Jörg and Alfred about the familiarity displayed by these sharks—but my words stuck in my throat when I saw their faces. White as I had never seen them before they were staring at me, and I could tell that for the moment their minds were not on conversation but on getting out of the water as quickly as possible.

Not until we were ashore did I discover the danger I had been in. While I had been busying myself with my camera Jörg and Alfred had, by a mere chance, noticed the two tiger sharks racing towards me at an incredible speed, and with great presence of mind they had yelled into the water. Jörg and Alfred firmly insisted that the first and larger of the two had already turned over sideways and opened its mouth wide, straight at my left leg. Only their joint yell had deflected it at the last moment so that it had merely struck me with its tail while passing. Since that day my left leg has belonged not only to me but, in equal shares, to Jörg and Alfred who had saved it.

We returned to Vienna by way of the United States, Hawaii, Japan and right across Russia by the Trans-Siberian Railway. Vienna was not yet greatly aware of the war and the three of us, for the time being, had our call-up deferred so we might pursue our studies.

My original intention was to read law but I soon took the fateful decision to switch to biology. I felt convinced that what I had begun as a sport and an adventure could open new avenues to undersea research. In the past marine creatures had only been observed in aquaria and little was known about their behaviour and mode of living. In a diving bell or an open helmet one was much too clumsy for observation. The skindiver, on the other hand, could make direct contact with marine creatures. He could come to know them as they really were. What I lacked was a breathing device which would allow me to stay below water for longer periods. I made inquiries and discovered that something suitable already existed—the escape apparatus used in U-boats. These were strapped across the chest and were small and handy. A person surfacing from a submarine breathed pure oxygen, and the exhaled carbon dioxide was absorbed in a potassium cartridge. The oxygen was inhaled from a breathing bag lying around the neck like a safety belt, and the exhaled and purified oxygen was recirculated into that bag. The positioning of the oxygen bottle at the belt seemed to me convenient, but the shape of the breathing bag did not. In order to give the skindiver a correct weight distribution the breathing bag had to be on his back. I travelled to Lübeck, where these devices were being

74

manufactured for the German Navy, and discussed the matter with the design staff. By 1942 I had an opportunity of testing the new equipment in Greece. The use of pure oxygen seemed to me to have the advantage of no fixed rate of ascent having to be observed. On the other hand, my experiments showed that at depths of over sixty feet oxygen became toxic to the system.

Cousteau, who marketed his diving apparatus after the war, continued the tradition of his compatriot Le Prieur who before the war had walked about under water with a compressed-air bottle on his back, shooting fish with a harpoon from a real rifle. His 'aqualung' soon conquered the world, whereas we decided not to commercialize our oxygen apparatus. We continued to use it for a long time because it had many an advantage—notably the absence of noise caused by escaping air bubbles. We were interested chiefly in coral reefs, and there a diving depth of sixty feet was quite enough. I myself—and many others—even descended a good deal lower, but that involves a serious risk. During one descent to a depth of over sixty feet I suddenly fainted and I was lucky to have been carried up to the surface and pulled out of the water.

At any rate, we were probably the first to use independent diving apparatus—'scubas'—for skindiving. With this equipment we penetrated into submarine grottos and there encountered an until then totally unknown sponge and coral fauna. This provided me with the subject for my doctoral thesis on which I worked at the Zoological Station in Naples. In certain grottos I had found coral-like structures which resembled a newly-opened rose, with leaves resembling the finest muslin. They were bryozoa—more particularly reteporidae—and we also found very similar ones at a depth of over ninety feet in a ravine with a strong current. Here the rose petals were much smaller, and the tissue of which they were built up considerably more robust. The question arose: Did the fine-mesh reteporae in the grottos belong to the same species or not? Was their totally different appearance due to entirely different environmental conditions or not?

Only the prismatic microscope reveals how this fine-mesh structure is created by countless small polyps. They build their little shells, into which they can withdraw, in rows of two, three or four, separating from each other and then reuniting. In this way the mesh is formed. It was in fact the current which influenced the different growth under different conditions. In two years of work I succeeded in reducing the behaviour of these creatures in the building of their colonies to basic mathematical formulas. For my thesis, 'Contribution to the knowledge of reteporidae with special consideration of the laws governing the formation of their zoaries and report on the new method used for investigations on the sea bottom', the Friedrich-Wilhem University in Berlin awarded me a *summa cum laude* degree. These were awarded rather sparingly, and no zoologist had gained one for seven years. To me this research was of particular importance as it gave me an understanding of systematic zoology, an understanding of the problem of 'species' which was to engage my attention to a much greater degree in the future.

These activities, like so much else, were then interrupted by the war. I had just about managed, by giving lectures, to collect enough money to acquire a ship with which I intended to pursue my diving activities more scientifically after the end of the war. This was Count Felix von Luckner's *Seeteufel*. Luckner, who became a good friend, told me so much about the Galapagos islands that I decided to make them my first objective. But things worked out differently. By the end of the war the ship had been lost, and so had all the equipment I had collected. Several years were to pass before I could think again of new operations.

All my efforts were now concentrated on acquiring a new ship and turning it into a floating research station. It was to provide accommodation and laboratory facilities for a team of zoologists—a small floating institute to be anchored directly above the coral reefs. Each one of the participating scientists was to be trained as a diver to enable him to pursue his own researches on the sea floor himself. The realization of this project required a great deal of money which had to be earned. The Red Sea was not too far away. No one had so far dived there. Its coasts had a reputation of being heavily 'infested with sharks'—just like the Caribbean. This time I set out on my own. It was an expedition on which I had to look after no one except myself and be responsible only for myself. It was an unforgettable expedition.

DEVIL RAYS IN THE RED SEA

An exciting Departure

The destination of my voyage to the Red Sea was to be the area north and south of Port Sudan. Ten years earlier, shortly before the outbreak of the war, I had applied—then in vain—for an entry permit to the British Protectorate. Now the situation was more favourable. I called on one of the gentlemen of the British Council in Vienna.

As a visiting card I put my book about our expedition to the Caribbean on his desk.

'That's most interesting,' he said, having looked at some of the pictures. 'How on earth did you cope with the sharks?'

'You mustn't show any fear,' I replied. 'That's something those creatures sense very acutely.'

'And that's all?'

'Yes. If you encounter a shark under water you must swim straight at it as if you wanted to attack it. The sharks aren't used to that. No other creature swims straight at them. That's why they believe one is stronger—and make off.'

'And suppose one of them isn't afraid? Couldn't that happen?'

'Oh yes. In that case you must yell at it hard.'

'Yell? Under water?'

'Yes. You expel air into the water with a shrill note. You can try it in your bath. Sharks are very sensitive to pressure waves in the water—that's why they about-turn and make off.'

The man shook his head and took me to his superior. He promised me his support. I was to address my application for a tourist visa to the Sudan direct to Khartoum, and he would support it. I also asked the Vienna Natural History Museum and the Ministry of Education for letters of support. Then I posted my application.

My prospects looked less favourable with the shipping lines. Most of the ships passing through the Red Sea were bound for South Africa, India or Australia, and were sufficiently well booked for the lines not to be greatly interested in carrying a passenger only as far as Port Sudan. I was told that all passages were fully booked for six months ahead. I therefore called on the representative of the Swedish airline who, I had discovered, was an enthusiastic fisherman. He promised to recommend his directors in Stockholm to grant me a reduced fare. Within ten days I had his reply. They were prepared to meet me half way, but as for my baggage, they could only allow me a certain free limit.

I gleaned some valuable hints on the Red Sea from the publications of the Austrian naturalist Klunzinger who had worked as a quarantine doctor at Quseir on the Red Sea from 1862 to 1875. I wanted to study a little Arabic but time was too short. I called on a few people who knew the country, and they tried to dissuade me. The sharks, they were sure, would devour me on my very first day. There was only one shark-catching station in the whole world which invariably ran at a profit, and that was at Massawa on the Red Sea. A passenger who had fallen overboard at Port Sudan had been torn into pieces by sharks in front of the other passengers before help could reach him. A professor who had himself travelled down the coast of the Red Sea told me how two sharks had savaged each other in the shallow water before his eyes.

I was also warned against the heat which everyone said was unbearable for a European. The Red Sea coast was the hottest region of the world. As soon as news came from Khartoum—my visa had only been approved for a fortnight but I could assume that once I was there it would be extended—I fixed the day of my departure for 14th October.

It was pouring with rain. I was riding around Vienna in a taxi, settling a few last-minute jobs, had a quick lunch at home, and punctually at 2 p.m. turned up at the airline. With some misgivings I watched my voluminous baggage being weighed in and the tariff for excess weight being worked out.

Lotte was with me; she wanted to see me off to my plane. We hung about until half past four when eventually they loaded us into a bus.

'It seems unbelievable that I shall sleep in Rome tonight and in Cairo tomorrow,' I said as Vienna's grey suburbs dropped behind us.

After a few miles there was a screech of brakes and the bus halted. A police car had overtaken us and made us stop. Our driver got out and talked to the policeman. Then he turned the bus and drove us back to the airline office.

Heavy rain had prevented our aircraft from taking off from Prague. We were to be back at the airline office at seven the next morning.

Punctually at seven I arrived. Lotte was again with me. It was still raining and the aircraft was still in Prague.

We waited until noon, then we were allowed out for an hour for lunch. It was positively embarrassing to walk through the streets—I kept meeting

78

The research vessel Xarifa in the Indian Ocean. A three-master, she had a length of 164 feet, carried 5,900 square feet of canvas, and her masts were 100 feet tall. With our auxiliary motor we could make 6 knots, carrying fuel for 4,000 nautical miles. Under sail we reached over ten knots. The ship needed a crew of twelve and had accommodation and working quarters for twelve scientists and technicians.

The cleaner wrasse (Labroides dimidiatus) rids other fish of their skin parasites. If a fish wants to be cleaned—as the sweetlips (plecto-rhynchus) in the picture do—it goes to the cleaners' 'place of residence'. In response to a nudge at the corner of the mouth it will open it to admit the cleaners. When it wants to close its mouth again it indicates this by a brief movement. Here a kind of innate code language has developed among the fish.

By intensifying their colouring or by producing new skin patterns male fish get the females into a receptive state for mating. This 'wedding suit' is particularly marked in the unicorn fish (Naso tapeinosoma), *which lives in shoals. Normally unpatterned, the sexes cannot be outwardly distinguished. The wooing male, however, displays a brilliant white colour signal which disappears within seconds as its excitement subsides.*

Above: *The growth pattern of certain coral species varies considerably according to environmental conditions. In calm, oxygen-poor water the elkhorn coral forms long thin branches instead of the reticular structures normally typical of it.*

Right: *At nightfall the feather-stars (crinoidea) come out of their hiding places, open their feathered tentacles and catch the plankton which at night rises up from lower levels of the sea. 'Primeval' relations of starfish, sea urchins and sea cucumbers, the feather-stars have hardly changed over millions of years.*

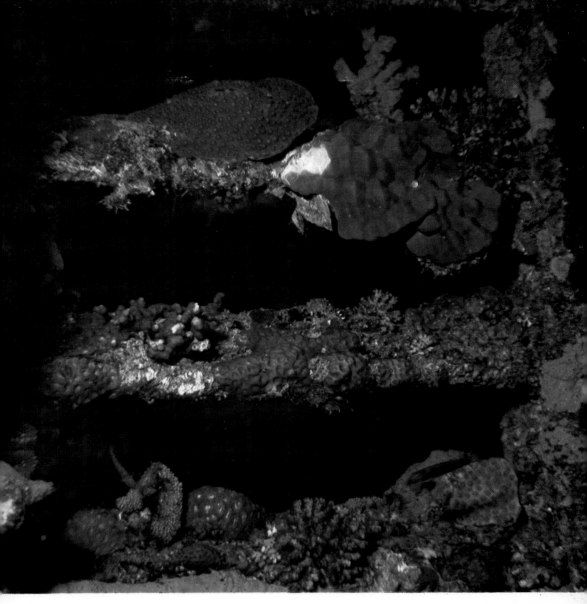

Above: *The encrustation on a steel ladder of a ship sunk only twenty years ago. The interiors of wrecks, like grottos, are often inhabited by light-shunning organisms normally only found at much greater depths.*

Left: *The remains of sunken ships are most instructive: if the date of sinking is known it is possible to establish the growth rate of different kinds of coral that have settled on the wreck.*

Over: *To the cardinal fish (Siphamia versicolor) a sea urchin moving about on the sandy bottom offers protection and safety. Normally it could not seek its prey there; it would be at the mercy of predators. Between the sea urchin's spines, however, it is safe and can venture on sorties into the neighbourhood. As a collateral it cleans the sea urchin, which holds its spines so that the fish can move among them in its search for parasites.*

acquaintances who all believed me to be in Cairo. A journalist in one paper had made things easy for himself and had most touchingly described my departure without leaving his desk. He could have hardly foreseen that my plane would not take off.

At 2 p.m. we once more boarded the bus and this time got as far as the airport. Our luggage was checked in, passports were stamped, foreign currency was examined and entered in the passport. Then we all sat down in the restaurant and waited.

At 6 p.m. the radio interviewer said he could wait no longer. He had brought his recording van and wanted to cover my departure for the 'Evening Newsreel'.

'The programme's got to go out at seven,' he explained. 'We'll just step outside the hangar and you say a few words into the microphone. We'll add the propeller noise from our archives.'

'And suppose we don't take off?' I laughed.

But there was no longer any need for anxiety. The aircraft had arrived and its captain was only awaiting a weather report before taking off. All the passengers were therefore asked to go out on to the apron, and against a background of general goodbyes I explained the purpose of my trip.

The radio van drove off. Half an hour later we were informed that we would not, after all, take off until the next morning. At dinner in a restaurant in Vienna I listened to my own farewell message. The propeller noise was most impressive.

The following morning there were no further formalities at the airport. We boarded our plane and a few minutes later were climbing through a grey cloud blanket into a blue sunny sky.

In Cairo, the second stop after Rome, I found some unexpected support for my project. When I had my visa entered in my passport by the British representative for the Sudan, he also gave me a personal letter of introduction to Bill Clark, the Commissioner of Port Sudan.

We took off on our next lap at midnight. I soon sank into a deep but shivery sleep. When I awoke the sky was already lit up by the dawn. We were flying over the Red Sea. Far below I saw a blue-black area crossed by irregular lines, melting along its edge into an uncertain haze. Gradually this haze turned red under the rising sun.

I kept speculating about the white patterning in the sea. As it was motionless it occurred to me that it might be due to jelly fish drifting in vast numbers under the surface. Such accumulations are known to occur in many parts of the world at certain times of the year. Not until it became light did I realize how high we were flying. What I had seen below were undoubtedly the white crests of big waves. Viewed from over 6,000 feet they naturally did not seem to move.

Soon the first coral reefs appeared. They were the first real reefs I had seen in my life, for those in the Caribbean and at Hawaii had only been growths of coral on steep coastal slopes. But here were massive walls rising straight from the sea far from any coast. Some of them had the shape of long barriers or of looped chains; others, quite small ones, were like small reddish mushrooms against the blue-black deep. Like slender turrets they rose straight from the sea. The prolonged reefs sloped obliquely on one side; I was able to see the light-coloured sandy bottom with large individual clumps of coral which, at greater depths, melted into a blue haze. On the other side the reefs dropped so abruptly that immediately alongside the clearly defined edge there was blue-black bottomless deep water.

More and more clearly the Arabian coast came into view. A flat band of desert along the sea, and behind, at a considerable distance, the silhouettes of several mountain ranges, as if drawn on the sky with a sharp pencil. The coast was likewise hemmed with reefs which on the seaward side dropped vertically. A few fishing vessels anchored at the edge emphasized the majestic grandeur of these structures created by minute creatures. The ships seemed no larger than flies on the edge of a wall.

We circled above the port of Jiddah, where a number of fairly large ships were riding at anchor, and then over the city itself which gleamed like white marble against the brown desert. As the cabin door was opened, hot air flowed in as from an oven—so solid that I was tempted to push it away with my hands. A heavy oppressive something settling on chest, lungs and every limb—an unpleasant fur coat impeding all movement.

'And in this climate I've got to do duty now,' sighed a young Englishman who was flying to Eritrea to do his military service somewhere on the Abyssinian frontier.

'How long's your turn of duty?'

'Nine months,' he replied without enthusiasm.

In the shade of a primitive building we were served two large jugs of iced grapefruit juice. Then we rose up again into the refreshing sky. After barely two hours we had re-crossed the Red Sea and the Sudanese coast hove into view. It looked just like the Arabian coast. Here too a broad desert belt was hemmed with distant mountain chains, but these were considerably higher. There were also some striking deep lagoons reaching into the desert from the sea like long thin tongues and widening out at their tips into the shape of a quatrefoil. The origin of these natural harbours, called *mersa* by the Arabs, is still an unsolved problem. On one particularly large quatrefoil I noticed the chequerboard pattern of a modern city.

I stared down intently at the position of the off-shore reefs. That was where success or failure of my enterprise would be decided. We had reached our destination. We were at Port Sudan.

The first Day

We skimmed over a flat strip of desert with a few shrubs growing—Bill Clark's golf links, as I was to discover—and touched down. Passport and customs control was in a minute timber building. A tall ebony-black negro in uniform examined my papers.

'And a certificate of your yellow fever immunization?' he asked in excellent English.

'Unfortunately it is impossible to be immunized against yellow fever in Vienna at present.'

'Impossible? Why?'

'Because there's no serum available. Immunization is possible only in Switzerland and I was in no position to travel to Switzerland specially for that purpose.'

The man nodded and contented himself with certificates of immunization against smallpox, typhoid, paratyphoid and cholera. There was no yellow fever in the coastal area anyway, he said. Only if I wished to travel into the interior would I have to get immunized.

Down the dusty streets of the city, through crowds of shouting children, caravans of camels, lorries, and donkey carts we made our way, sounding our horn all the time. Ugly vultures were looking down on us from a tall steel scaffolding. Gradually the streets grew wider and the rusty corrugated tin huts gave way to groups of stone buildings with shady arcades in front. They housed the shops and stalls of the merchants. Then we drove past a park and a number of very European-looking villas and stopped in front of a large stone building with a few scattered tables on the terraces to both sides of a flight of steps.

This was the Red Sea Hotel.

A servant carried my suitcase into the hall, which was permeated by that dignified quiet typical of all British-managed hotels in the tropics. Under the framed picture of a fish, no doubt some record catch, an Englishman sat in a wicker armchair in white shorts and briefly glanced at me from behind his paper. At the back of the hall was the entrance to the bar. Next to the reception desk was a display case containing silver articles, carved ivories and other souvenirs for sale. Next to it, framed, was the latest set of Sudanese postage stamps with and without special postmark.

The black receptionist opened his large book with weary lassitude. Yes, there was a room available. No. 25 on the first floor. He reached for a bell which, after a while, summoned another servant. He picked up my case and, striding in front of me with great dignity, led me up to my room.

I washed quickly and put on a clean shirt. Armed with my book and my letter of introduction I got into the car again and told the driver to take me to the Commissioner.

Three blocks further down we stopped outside a large, solidly built villa standing in a very well-cared-for garden. Under the stone arch of its drive stood a large American car. Hesitantly I entered the garden and passed through the open gate. Surely this could not be Government House. But of course, it was Sunday. And the time was 9 a.m. This must be Bill Clark's private residence.

In the hall there was no trace either of a servant or of the master of the house. To both sides of the stairs in the background hung cavalry standards. On my left, in a clothes closet, I saw fishing rods and a bag of golf clubs. Next to it a door led into a spacious living room.

'Hello,' a voice said behind me.

In the door opposite stood a man of sporting appearance, whose tanned face contrasted strangely with his grey wavy hair. He had on him nothing but a pair of shorts and an unbuttoned polo shirt which he was wearing like a jacket over his shoulders.

'Hello,' I stammered in reply. 'I am looking for the Commissioner.'

'That's me,' he replied. 'Come in, I am just having breakfast.'

We stepped into a large dining room where the Commissioner was having his solitary breakfast at a long polished table.

We sat down. Suddenly the Commissioner turned his head and in a stentorian voice roared, 'Ahmed!'

Soundlessly a servant entered. He was a study in black and white. Starting at the bottom with his bare black feet, there next came a long white nightshirt from which his black hands peeped out at the sides, and his black head at the top; on his head was a huge brilliantly white turban. There was also a brilliant white patch in the middle of his head—his teeth which he flashed cheerfully to greet me.

The Commissioner gave him a few instructions in Arabic—clearly he was to lay a second place. There was coffee, a fish swimming in oil, toast, butter and grilled bacon. As soon as the Commissioner saw the first pictures in my book—he had only cursorily glanced at my letters of introduction—he pushed back his chair and began to question me about many details. He was particularly interested in anything to do with sharks. He absolutely refused to believe that one could swim towards a shark with a camera.

'Those must have been very friendly sharks you have encountered,' he said. 'I am certain your method won't work here. I've been in this part of the world for twenty years but no one has ever thought of getting into the water by the reef. I'm afraid you're in for some nasty surprises. But of course I'll be delighted to help you.'

To start with he invited me to stay with him. He was a bachelor and I could sense that he would be glad of company.

'We can go out this very afternoon if you feel like it,' he said. 'I've ordered the Government motor boat for three o'clock because I want to do some fishing. Why don't you come along and try your luck?'

When I mentioned my customs difficulties he put on a pair of slippers and we drove out to the customs shed in his car.

By the jetty I saw my first brightly coloured coral fish. There were also a few corals in the shallow water, but they were rather stunted since coral thrive only in clean and moving water. As soon as the formalities were finished we drove back and Ahmed showed me to my room. It was on the first floor and opened on to a large flower-grown stone balcony. Adjoining it was a private bathroom. I was delighted to find that it could easily be blacked out: I would be able to develop my films here.

Lunch was just as informal as breakfast. There was soup, baked fish, then mutton with potatoes and beans, followed by chocolate cream and finally coffee. As I discovered later, this menu hardly ever changed much.

'My food isn't anything to write home about,' the Commissioned explained. 'But having been to England this won't greatly surprise you.'

'By the way,' he added, 'I find it a bore to keep addressing you as "Doctor". I suggest I simply call you Hans and you call me Bill. This is customary with us.'

He wanted to lie down a little until three o'clock. I went to my room to unpack my things and get ready for our expedition. One problem was the harpoon shaft. In order to save weight I had taken with me only the steel shaft to which the detachable head was fitted. Where was I to find a suitable shaft here, and moreover on a Sunday? I called for Ahmed and explained to him what I needed. He disappeared and presently returned with a broom and a half-round strip of wood which must once have been part of a huge picture frame. As I did not wish to rob the house of its equipment I settled for the moulded strip. But the wood was so hard that it took me half an hour's whittling before it fitted into the collar of the steel shaft.

'Hello!' Bill was ready, waiting for me in the hall.

Carrying spear and fins I ran down to the car.

The police barge was waiting for us in the harbour. It was a rather worm-holed crate with an elderly engine operated by two military-looking negroes. With their white shorts they wore sailor's caps. After some reluctant spitting and snorting our craft got under way.

There were no fewer than four large freighters at anchor in the port. Cotton, groundnuts, ivory, and other animal and vegetable produce from the interior of the country were brought to Port Sudan by rail and here loaded on ships. The deck of one of them was crowded with cattle mooing pitifully and being hoisted one at a time to the jetty by a large crane. At the end of the jetty, immediately behind the last ship, I saw a strange hut surrounded by a few bushes with several veiled women moving about.

'That is the tomb of Sheikh Barghut,' Bill explained. 'Some time in the early eighteenth century the shrouded corpse of a man was washed up here and cremated by the sailors on the beach. Rumour went round that a saint had been cremated here, and ever since the sailing ships have poured a little fresh water into the sea at this spot whenever they have come past. *Barghut* in the local idiom means "flea" or "louse". The man is said to have been as small as a flea but when they tried to lift him he was too heavy for them. When the harbour was built here we wanted to move the tomb, but the people objected and so we left it where it was. Now it is a popular place of pilgrimage for Sudanese ladies praying for fertility.'

'And out there,' Bill continued after a little while, pointing to the strip of water along the jetty, 'out there are the submarine gardens of which you may have heard. We have a big ship here with a glass bottom for the tourists to gaze down on the corals for a few piastres. At the moment she is in dock for repairs. But of course the coral here, at the harbour mouth, cannot even compare with those further offshore.'

The sky had meanwhile clouded over. The moment we left the shelter of the harbour entrance we found ourselves in rough water. The police barge was not suited to this kind of weather: it smacked down hard on every wave crest so that we got soaked to the skin.

Bill had cast out his drag line. I was astonished at the direction we were taking. The coastal reefs, where I had expected to dive, were behind us and we were making straight for the open sea. Bill was standing up in the boat, hair flying, gripping his fishing rod. The sea was surprisingly warm. When a wave unexpectedly washed over my hand it was just like bath water.

The coast behind us was a grey line, with the dock-side cranes and the masts of the ships rising above the low red roofs of the warehouses. The mountains in the distance were taking on more substantial shape as the sun sank lower. It was a panorama of several hundred jagged peaks, the nearest ranges darker and the more distant ones, reaching right up to the sky, shimmering in the most delicate hues of blue. We had been on a straight course for a good half-hour without a single fish showing the slightest interest in Bill's rod and line when before us the foaming spray of a reef appeared. Bill ordered the helmsman to slow down.

'If you really feel like getting into the water you can do so now,' he said to me. 'Certainly I should be very sorry to see anything happen to you—but you know your own mind.'

'Can't we get nearer to the reef?' We were a good hundred yards away.

'Impossible. The waves are too high.'

This meant that I had to go overboard in the deep water and swim over to the reef. No doubt my photographs had inspired the Commissioner with great confidence in my ability. But this certainly was not what I wanted. I had intended to start in shallow water and gradually familiarize myself with my new environment. After all, this was the Red Sea and seven years had passed since I had lasted dived in any sea.

'I am really curious and I am also seriously worried about you,' Bill said, regarding me expectantly. 'But you must know what you are doing.'

Unless I was to lose face I had to make the best of a bad job. I was already wearing my swimming trunks; I quickly slipped on my foot fins, put on my mask, dispelled my misgivings and leaped overboard. The boat with Bill moved on while I stayed behind. I quickly glanced below water. All round me, as far as I could see, was a dark yawning void. I was floating over an abyss which might be three hundred feet deep or three thousand.

I rapidly finned towards the reef, which was easily identifiable by the flying foam. My heart was thumping. Never before had I surrendered myself in so foolhardy a manner to the unknown. I had certainly not thought that I would set out on my first submarine adventure in the Red Sea armed with a length of picture frame.

At last the first outlines of the sea floor became visible below me. And what I saw coming up towards me took my breath away. Rising up from blue nothingness towards the steep reef barrier the sea floor was totally different from the coral floor I remembered from the Caribbean. Large slab-shaped structures covered the bottom like tables, surrounded by large dark fish, like diners at a banquet.

A moment later I was floating, relieved, over a bottom I could see clearly.

My sense of assurance returned. Deep water is frightening not because one can drown in it more easily than where the bottom is visible at sixty feet, but because in the empty water one has no point of reference for judging one's visual range or the distance at which an approaching creature becomes visible. As soon as one finds a point of reference, no matter whether it is a rock or even a small fish, the spell is instantly broken. One has around one a clearly bounded field, almost a kind of rampart, a distance which an enemy has to cover and which thus gives one time to arm oneself. Floating on the surface like a bird, I looked down on the landscape below me. Although it was getting dark I could still see everything clearly. There were so many brightly coloured shapes that it took me a while to distinguish details. In contrast to the West Indian reefs, which are predominantly green, yellow or brown, the principal colour here was red. There were no elkhorn or stagshorn corals, but instead jagged madrepora like flowerbeds in bloom. It was these corals which formed the table-shaped slabs; their tangled growths covered the large crude clumps of other coral species.

I descended to thirty feet and discovered that my ears had to get accustomed again to an amphibian way of life. What struck me was the marked buoyancy. The Red Sea is not only the warmest but also the saltiest sea in the world.

I stopped at the foot of an overhanging creviced reef wall and looked upwards. Hundreds of minute, brilliantly red fish, each one like a ruby, were bobbing up and down along the rock face, and between them, like arrows, flitted the silvery rays of the oblique sunlight. Blue, yellow and multi-coloured parrot fish were playing around the coral. Further away, in the deeper water, swam a shoal of green unicorn fish with clearly visible single horns on their foreheads. Looking into a hole by my side I could see the vibrating pectoral fins of a green-brown flecked grouper of considerable size. As in every other ocean, it was hovering in front of its hole, plump and square, goggling at me with its round eyes.

In particular I noticed a strangely arched formation peeping out between the coral in a brilliant blue. I swam closer—and the formation contracted like a slit and the brilliant blue double edge disappeared. They were the opened halves of large shells which were embedded among the coral and closed at my approach. I stopped motionless—and they began to open once more. From their size it was obvious that they were tridacna, close relations of those giant clams one reads of in books about the South Seas, where it is claimed that pearl fishers can be trapped between their jaws. On the Australian coast they reach a size of more than three feet across and a weight of some six hundred-weight; the ones here were considerably smaller. They were remarkably sensitive to vibrations in the water. A slight movement ten yards away was enough for the shells to close, just as if they had eyes to see me.

I was ascending and descending—I had completely forgotten the world above. Some of the coral fish looked as if the Creator had tried out his entire palette on them. In the shallow water, in particular, they looked like a collection of jewels. At the same time, these swimming butterflies were moving so fast that frequently I did not know their heads from their tails. They would suddenly emerge from a crevice and almost at once vanish into another.

The whole reef was pervaded by a labyrinth of caves which extended far into the shallow water. In the mysterious darkness of the grottos the walls were alive with strange shapes. Some of these were firmly attached to the coral rock —these were the sponges or bryozoa, forming their own curious ornaments. Others abruptly sailed away; these were bristly batrachids or ugly broad-headed scorpion fish which, pressed hard against the rock, were lying in wait for their prey.

I had been in the water a good three-quarters of an hour. I had completely forgotten about Bill. When I looked up for him I saw that the boat was looking for me. I hid by the reef and then made a long dive, surfacing immediately alongside the pinnace.

'There you are at last!' Bill sounded relieved. 'We looked for you everywhere. I am getting terribly cold and want to go home.'

I apologized and, to cheer him up, described the wonderful things I had seen under the sea.

'And what about sharks?' he interrupted.

'None appeared. Next time I'll bring a second mask and then you can come and have a look at the reef for yourself.'

'I'll be damned if I do,' he grunted. 'If you are determined to end up in a shark's belly that's your business. I certainly don't want to be eaten by one.'

Back home we had a bath to get the salt off our skins, and then drove across to the English Club where most of the British living in Port Sudan were playing billiards or cards, drinking whisky or beer, swimming in a fine modern pool or spending the evening dancing under Chinese lanterns.

I was dead tired and glad to leave. I had not slept much on the plane and the change of climate and my first dive had exhausted me. But at home Bill informed me that the Governor was on a visit to Port Sudan and had invited us to dine with him at the Red Sea Hotel.

'Me too?' I asked.

'Of course. He specially instructed me to bring you along. He is a nice old boy and knows quite a lot about fishing.'

Ahmed had laid out my dinner jacket on my bed, complete with silk shirt, tie, socks and shoes. We had a whisky in Bill's sitting room and drove over to the Red Sea Hotel where the rest of the guests were already assembled on the first floor terrace.

The food was a little better than at Bill's. After dinner a visit to the cinema had been envisaged, but it had begun to rain and the ladies in their long dresses did not want to venture outside. My recollections of the final part of the evening are a little hazy because it took all my willpower to stop myself from falling asleep in my chair. At long last the Governor rose and declared it was time to go to bed. At home I just about managed to get out of my dinner jacket before dropping into a deep death-like sleep.

The Wreck

I was awakened by the sound of Ahmed placing a small pot of tea and a plate with three sweet biscuits on my bedside table. In the garden below, wearing a dressing gown, Bill was inspecting his flowers. His driver, whose name was also Ahmed, was polishing the car.

'Breakfast at eight!' Bill called out to me when he saw me. 'The Governor and his wife are coming for breakfast. Did you sleep well?'

'Very well. But not long enough.'

Half an hour later Bill was wearing a white gala uniform with gold braid. He confessed to me that he put on this finery only on special occasions. The Governor was due to come round again in the afternoon, to tea, and would leave Port Sudan that evening.

Breakfast was a formal affair. But I was greatly interested in what the Governor told me about an island further north, where he had himself been two years ago. At one side of the island a steep cliff dropped vertically into the sea, and from the top he had once observed over a hundred sharks basking in the shallow water.

'Over a hundred?' I asked respectfully.

The Governor cleared his throat. 'Certainly over a hundred. The water was full of them. Besides, I had seen something similar once before—it must be a good fifteen years ago now, near Tallatalla Island, over towards Eritrea. The water there was so full of sharks that you could put an oar into the water and it would remain standing upright. What they were doing there, or whether this was their mating season, I don't know. But certainly the sea was full of them.'

'And by this island here—were they large sharks?'

'Oh yes, there were some fine specimens among them. Certainly six to ten feet long. I am convinced you would see all you want to see if you went there.'

'Those are the best fishing grounds along the whole coast here,' Bill added. The island, he explained, was about a hundred miles to the north, near Muhammad Qol. Whereas Tallatalla Island could be reached only by a big ship, it was possible to drive to Muhammad Qol by car through the desert and to reach the shark island by boat from there.

The police chief, to whom Bill had sent me, gave instructions for a suitable boat to be found for me. As for the price, he would negotiate with the owner on my behalf to make sure I was not cheated. The boat, a felucca, would be ready for me at one o'clock.

At one o'clock I went down to the small jetty with my equipment and a packed lunch. A little while later a good-sized boat came sailing in. It was of elegant shape, about sixteen feet long and rather narrow. The mast was sloping forward in the Arab manner and the pointed sail was relatively small. As she made fast I noticed that the floor was covered with attractive mats.

The crew consisted of two tattooed natives, one of them looking exceedingly grim and the other very cunning. The cunning one evidently was the spokesman. He jumped ashore, saluted me by placing his hand on chest and forehead, and conveyed that his name was Mahmud and that he was entirely at my service. The second man tied up the boat and similarly saluted me. His unsure grin suggested limited mental faculties. Mahmud informed me that his colleague was called O-Sheik.

My gear was stowed away in the boat and I settled down on the mat. Mahmud, at the tiller, was in command; O-Sheik crouched in the bows, pulling the sail tight.

As we approached the tip of the jetty, where the submarine gardens were, Mahmud gestured that this was a good place for diving. I replied, likewise by gestures, that I wished to dive not here but outside the harbour, along the lateral fringing reef. This decision seemed to alarm them both. Eyes rolling, Mahmud bit the air and violently shook his head, to convey to me the fate awaiting anyone entering the water there. Delighted as no doubt he was to have found a well-paying stranger, he was anxious now not to lose him immediately.

'*Girsh! Girsh kabir!*' he kept repeating. His gestures suggested that the sharks there were particularly aggressive.

'*Kois, kalas,*' I replied. They were the only two words I had learned. They meant 'O.K. All right.'

The fringing reef started immediately outside the jetty and ran parallel to the coast in a nearly straight line. To judge by the clear difference in the water colour, the reef dropped vertically along a shelf between twenty-five and thirty feet deep. We were sailing exactly above this line where the sea abruptly turned deep blue.

I ordered the anchor to be dropped at a little bay which intersected the straight line of the reef. My crew were not too enthusiastic—they evidently feared that the anchor would not hold and the wind might drive the boat against the submerged rocks. But I assured them that I personally would secure the anchor to the bottom.

A moment later I was overboard. Now, in the bright midday light, the coral looked even more brilliant and colourful than the night before. Directly below me was a peach-coloured bush; from Klunzinger's writings I immediately recognized it as a cup star coral. There were violet-hued bunches of pistil coral, and between them I spotted a vermilion coenopsammia. There were luxuriant growths of dozens of species of star coral in the shape of brightly coloured balloons and blisters; snow-white thistle coral filled the hollows and stagshorn coral extended their delicate rose-coloured tips. And brilliant coral fish were flitting about these fairy-tale gardens like butterflies.

The spot where we had cast anchor was a bare ten yards from the edge of the underwater shelf. The seaward side of the reef really dropped down vertically to such a depth that, in spite of the clear water, I could not make out its bottom. I was quite prepared to believe Mahmud's assurance that there were sharks here. I decided to postpone a closer investigation of the reef face for when I had my diving equipment, and to confine myself to the shallow coral zone.

I wedged our anchor between two large clumps of coral, where it could not possibly break loose, and clambered back into the boat. In order to test the camera case before using it under water I removed the camera, closed the empty case, and let it down on a rope. On opening it after a little while I found that it was watertight. I now picked up a pad, a pencil and noted down all the photographs I intended to take. This first day was to serve mainly for an examination of lighting conditions and the effect of different special filters.

Mahmud and O-Sheik watched me closely during these operations. The watertight camera case, in particular, seemed to exercise their imagination. When I let it down into the water on the rope O-Sheik's mouth widened and, in spite of his respectful demeanour, he burst into loud laughter over the stranger's naïve belief that he could catch a fish with such a bait.

When I had fitted the camera into the case again I slipped overboard. But since I had to open the case every time I wanted to change a filter a whole hour passed before my programme was completed. Lighting conditions were by no means straightforward. Although the water in the lower layers was beautifully clear, millions of microscopically small organisms were floating just under the surface and these turned the water into a kind of soup which only partially let the sunlight through, according to the density of the clouds of organisms. I also discovered that there were plenty of those invisibly small jelly fish about against whose painful stings one was helpless. While photographing I kept looking behind me and all round me. I should have preferred the first shark to have shown itself. Until I had encountered one I would not know whether the sharks here really behaved differently from the ones I had met.

I had a bite of food in the boat, loaded a new film and descended once more. I was lucky at once. Opalescent in wonderful blue hues, a large tropical medusa was floating close by. Its large bell or umbrella was rhythmically pulsating and it was trailing a large number of long barbed threads. Like umbels of yellow flowers its marginal tentacles stood out around its side. As I swam closer I saw several minute fish playing hide-and-seek under the large umbrella among the dangerous tentacles. These fish are spared, and indeed offered shelter, by the otherwise rapacious medusa. As I was taking my photographs two or three of these fish came swimming out from the forest of long filaments, boldly inspected the glittering camera lens and, as soon as I moved, scuttled back to cover.

The strong current drove the medusa against the shallow reefs and I followed it until it ran aground and was torn to shreds by the sharp points of the dead coral. The small fish now did not know where to go. They scuttled around the rock and hid in what fragments were left of the medusa. A tragedy in miniature of a kind that is repeated in the ocean a thousand-fold each second.

Suddenly I heard a shout from Mahmud and O-Sheik. The two had settled down comfortably in the boat but now I saw them dive overboard in their white nightshirts. The one was holding on to the boat while the other disappeared, kicking under water and presently surfaced again, still kicking and puffing. The anchor rope had broken, after chafing against the coral. I hurried over to help them. Within a few seconds the boat had drifted quite a distance nearer to the shallow reef. With a stiff wind blowing towards it we had quite a job to prevent us from foundering.

Back in the boat the three of us laughed about our recent panic and I committed the *faux pas* of offering Mahmud a ham roll. Being a good Muslim he firmly but cheerfully declined it and instead started to chew tobacco.

I was quite pleased with my first day's photography and now decided to spear a fish. Ahmed had got me a new stick that morning so that I was no longer dependent on a piece of picture frame. I left the camera in the boat and cautiously descended under water.

91

But I did not find it at all easy to outwit a fish. I would have to get used again to moving soundlessly. The slightest splash was enough to cause alarm, and this was worse in an area teaming with fish where one alerted fish would warn all the rest.

I missed several times but then saw a large red fish hovering motionless under a rock. This one, I decided, was for Bill Clark's supper. I drew breath and descended to the ground at a point where a well intersected the reef edge like a vertical gun barrel. I let myself glide down through this opening and cautiously approached the large clump of coral behind which I had seen the fish hovering in its hole.

Half way down I encountered two small parrot fish, one of which placed itself directly in front of my harpoon. I had to hold on to the coral and stay motionless, otherwise I might alarm these fish and that would be the end of my hunting prospects. It seemed as if the two parrot fish understood my dilemma and were laughing at me; they cavorted around me for quite a while before moving on. At last I was able to slip around the rock. Fortunately the red fish was still in the same place. A short distance behind it was a small crab, its pincers digging in a hole full of sand.

Cautiously I pushed through between two corals. Then I brought my harpoon forward with all my strength. I not only struck the fish, piercing it in the middle, but also struck my elbow against the coral hard enough to see spots in front of my eyes.

But I had no time to think about that because just then, immediately above me, a long slim body had appeared, with a pointed nose that was now looking down at me. A shark! Though, admittedly, it was the smallest I had ever seen. It was not even three feet in length and looked more like a fat impertinent pike. It turned and was gone. As my fish on the line had got entangled in the coral I ascended quickly for air. In doing so I had another glimpse of the shark. It was now gliding along the coral slopes, approaching the spot where my fish was lying. Could it be that it was trying to snatch it from me?

An instant later I had descended again and was freeing the line. Mahmud was beside himself with pleasure when I climbed back aboard with my colourful trophy. An hour later I was having tea with Bill and the Governor, and the fish was passed around among those present. It was a holocentrus weighing about eight pounds. Mahmud assured me that it was one of the tastiest fishes hereabouts.

On board the Umbrea

'You say the shark was going to snatch the fish from you?' the Governor's wife asked excitedly.

I replied that this shark could hardly be described as a shark yet.

'You really should dive out by the *Umbrea*!' she exclaimed. 'I'm convinced you'd have incredible adventures there!'

Bill explained that this *Umbrea* was a big Italian ship which was lying on the bottom about a mile off Port Sudan. The tips of her two masts were still showing above water. But it was strictly forbidden to go near the wreck.

'Because there's a lot of gold aboard?' I asked.

'Not gold but dynamite. No less than 18,000 tons of ammunition and explosives.'

The Governor cleared his throat. 'The *Umbrea* was carrying a cargo to Eritrea,' he explained. 'She happened to be lying at anchor here on the day Italy entered the war against us. We boarded her and were about to take the Italians off when suddenly there was a great commotion and the news that the *Umbrea* was sinking. In spite of our sentries the Italians had succeeded in opening the seacocks. It would have been easy enough to save her but the Italians claimed to have fitted time bombs, and so we had no choice but to let her sink.'

'She is in about sixty to a hundred and twenty feet of water,' Bill said. 'One can clearly see her hull from the surface. Moreover, there are about half a million Maria Theresa dollars in her. Only last year an Italian salvage firm applied for permission to raise her. But we turned them down.'

'Why?'

'Because in the opinion of the Admiralty the ship could still suddenly blow up.'

'Blow up? Under water?'

'Yes. Certain detonators will gradually rust through and then there is a danger of spontaneous ignition. About now, after ten to fifteen years, is the critical time—at least, that's what the experts say. We have considered blowing her up ourselves, because she is blocking the whole of the outer Wingate anchorage, but it can't be done. At Government House we have a seventeen-page expert opinion from two officers who came out here specially for the purpose. If the *Umbrea* blew up the entire eastern part of Port Sudan would be flooded. After all, 18,000 tons isn't peanuts.'

I could not get the wreck out of my mind. I raised the topic again at dinner and asked Bill if he could not get a diving permit for me. He would try gladly, he said, but told me not to be too hopeful. The harbour master was adamant on this point. No doubt he was afraid that I might blow up the ship together with Port Sudan.

'I wouldn't touch anything, of course,' I said. 'But I'd like to take a few photographs which might be of considerable scientific interest. Because as it is known how long the ship has been on the bottom of the sea one would be able to see how fast the various corals which have settled on her have grown. And it would also be interesting to see what fishes inhabited her. There could be a lot of useful lessons in that.'

Bill promised to do his best.

The following morning I got my two faithful attendants to take me to the reef where I had dived on my first evening. From there I could make out clearly the two mastheads of the *Umbrea* sticking out of the water at an angle of about forty-five degrees. The ship therefore must be lying on the bottom with a considerable list. I reflected whether I should wait for a permit or not—and then I took my decision.

'That's where we'll go now,' I commanded. I pointed to the masts of the sunken ship.

It really was too silly. Port Sudan was only a thin reddish line in the distance. How could anyone tell where our cockleshell was drifting just now?

The wind was favourable and barely ten minutes later we had reached the spot. At close quarters the tips of the masts were considerably higher than I had thought. Their upper side was encrusted white with the droppings of the many birds which perched there permanently. As we approached and made our boat fast to one of the steel guys the birds took wing and circled us with much screeching.

I leaned over the side. In spite of the waves I could clearly see the outlines of the massive hull. I felt like a knight of old facing a bewitched castle and about to enter it.

With trembling fingers I assembled my underwater camera and strapped on my breathing equipment. On second thoughts I decided to dive with my spear only and leave the camera behind. Mahmud and O-Sheik watched me wide-eyed. They both tried to explain something to me, something to do with the ship. As far as I could make out from their gestures, it was inhabited by some kind of mermaids who were very alluring but also very dangerous. Well, so much the better.

Mahmud gave me a hand with the straps, then I sucked my airbag empty, let it fill with oxygen from the bottle at my waist, put on my nose-clip, spat into my mask, rinsed it out and slipped it on. I was already wearing my fins and O-Sheik handed me the harpoon.

This was my first descent with breathing apparatus for seven years. If

Dr Irenaeus Eibl–Eibesfeldt succeeded in taking this particularly interesting picture inside a grotto of the Miladummadulu Atoll in the Maldives. The black-tipped soldier fish (Myripristis murdjan) swimming in the upper part of the grotto turn their bellies upwards. They orientate themselves towards the nearest rock. For them there is no 'up' and 'down' in our sense: their lateral line system enables fish to perceive remote impressions even in dark or opaque water. The position of the body, normally governed by the balancing organ in conjunction with the eyes, is here controlled by the lateral line system.

The rightly feared stone fish (Synanceja verrucosa) *is difficult to spot even for an experienced diver. At the centre of the picture its right eye is discernible, to the right of it the closed mouth, and obliquely below to the left of it the curved rays of its pectoral fin. The sting of its dorsal fin spines can have a lethal effect. Even if approached, the fish does not stir. If, therefore, one wants to sit down on a coral— for filming, for instance—it is advisable to strike it with one's shark spear first. I have known parts of putative 'corals' to come to life and swim off.*

The hammerhead shark (Sphyrna levini), *which reaches a length of up to twenty feet, is one of the few species of shark which occasionally attack humans. Its head is broadened on both sides, and at the ends of this 'hammer' are the eyes and the nostrils. Since this abnormality evidently results in no disadvantage to the creature, it has succeeded in holding its place in evolution—like many another non-advantageous mutation.*

Left: *Cheviot Bay, where the Australian Prime Minister Harold Holt, an enthusiastic skindiver, lost his life. The accident happened by the channels (just below the centre of the picture) which converge at an acute angle. When the reefs are flooded at high tide, the water flows back to sea through these channels, reaching a speed of up to eight knots.*

I investigated these highly unpredictable currents with my son Hans (above). On the fatal day Holt was walking on the beach with some friends. Although the surf was over thirty feet high he wanted to take a cooling dip in the shallow water. He got out a little too far, was caught by the currents, and perished in the surf.

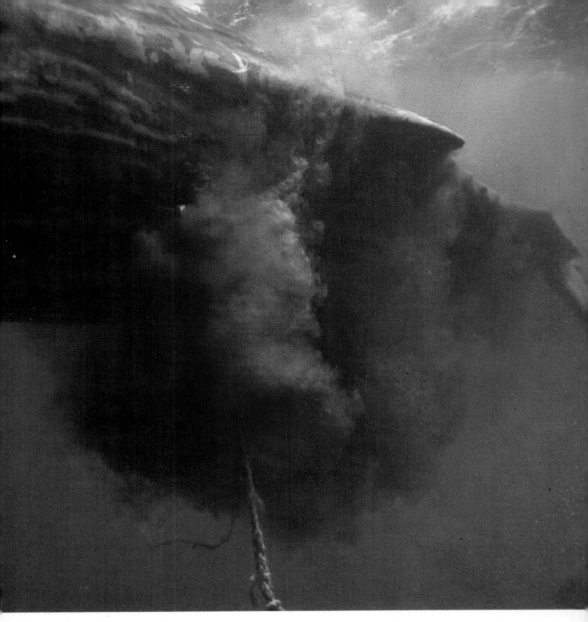

Left: *The largest predator of the seas is the sperm whale. It grows to a length of up to seventy-five feet and dives several hundred feet deep to hunt for squid. Being a warm-blooded mammal, it comes up after about thirty minutes and takes some sixty to eighty breaths. Off the Azores the sperm whale is still hunted from rowing boats with hand harpoons. We accompanied such whale hunters and succeeded in filming sperm whales under water—including the final struggle and death-throes of some harpooned specimens. The enormous quantities of blood pouring into the sea attracted several sharks. On that occasion, too, we heard the shriek of the sperm whale (above): it is reminiscent of the creak of an old barn door.*

Bodianus elancheris, *a wrasse, in the dark waters of the Galapagos archipelago. In the light of the photo-flash the fish shows up like a bright flame in the surrounding darkness. While there are hardly any places left on land where man can still penetrate into the unknown or see sights not seen by anyone else, the depths of the oceans will continue to offer this possibility for a long time yet.*

someone had told me in Vienna that it would take me to a sunken ship I would not have believed him. The pleasure of being once more able to float underwater and breathe freely at the same time was indescribable. With this equipment one moves about the ocean depths no longer as an awkward diver but transformed, as it were, into a fish gliding weightlessly through this three-dimensional world. The technical side of it is not much trouble. If there is too little air in the bag a pressure on the valve at one's belt is enough to feed more oxygen into it. This is also what one must do when descending lower. The lower one descends, the more the water pressure compresses the gas; buoyancy becomes less and, growing steadily heavier, one tends to sink down. As one ascends again the gas expands, and one has to blow it out constantly through the corners of one's mouth to prevent the over-inflated bag from bursting. Amidst a trail of bubbles, which in turn expand and grow bigger, one reaches the surface like a balloon.

I was floating above a blue-black abyss. Below me to my right was the steeply sloping deck of the steamer, one side rising relatively high while the other was lost in the opaque depths. Also towering obliquely was the massive round smokestack, surrounded by all kinds of superstructures and many strangely curved steampipes and ventilation tubes. Corals had settled and developed luxuriantly on all the iron parts and even on the stretched steel wires. Among them swam countless brightly coloured fish which clearly felt as much at home here as among a coral reef.

I hurried to get away from the open water. In a steep glide I sailed down towards the middle of the deck. At a depth of sixty-five feet I settled weightlessly as a bird on a steampipe and sat there for a few minutes in order to take in the view. It certainly was a fine ship that was lying here in the womb of the sea, overgrown with corals just as the Sleeping Beauty's castle was with briars. I tried to picture the view in fifty or a hundred years. By then the corals would have covered the whole body of the ship and blocked most of the open doors and hatches. And in two hundred years the ship would be merely a strangely shaped coral reef with, admittedly, enough dynamite hidden in it to blow up a whole town and with enough silver to rebuild most of it again.

From my steampipe I could see up to the two masts which ended abruptly at the artificial sky formed by the waves as they emerged above the water. Between me and the silhouette of the boat which hung near one of the masts hovered a large barracuda. As for other fish, I saw mainly blue surgeon fish, butterfly fish, parrot fish and black-and-yellow angel fish. Next to me some minute red fish were forming a circle around one of the steam pipes. Having observed everything, I let myself glide down between the rungs of a companionway to the next lower deck.

95

Here it was rather dark. Tilting my head so that the passage in front of me looked level I tried to picture sailors walking up and down. On the right was a door to some dark interior cabin. I waited for my eyes to accommodate to the darkness and then entered. A small amount of light was coming in through the door and two portholes. A lot of clutter had piled up on the low side of the tilting deck and was now covered with mud. A table at the centre was screwed to the floor and had therefore remained in position. I floated over to it, when above me I caught sight of something round and glittering. It was an electric bulb. I tried to unscrew it but it was slimy and had rusted into its socket.

Suddenly the door was darkened. A fat grouper was looking in. For some reason its appearance brought home to me the oppressive silence which hung over this corpse of a ship. Perhaps it was because I had encountered another grouper at the teeming coral reef the day before. Here all was as silent as the grave. Until then the wealth of my impressions had not given me time to feel fear, but now a cold shiver ran down my spine. The water, too, was noticeably cooler than outside the ship. The grouper came through the door, uncertainly, then it took fright and with a sudden flick of its tail streaked out. A clearly audible shockwave remained suspended in the oppressive silence.

I shook off my uneasiness. Through a side door I reached another cabin and from there, through a further door, a small, almost totally dark bathroom. The bath was beautiful white enamel and still fairly bright. The situation struck me as so grotesque that I laughed aloud into my air bag and sat down in the bath. On the sloping ceiling above me hung two thin plates. I carefully explored them with my fingers. Unlike the blind mirror on the wall these plate-shaped things were not part of the ship's inventory. They were shells. In fact, genuine pearl-oysters. I had a knife with me and cut them open. With my fingers I probed the bleeding flesh in case there was a pearl in them. That really would have been a story to strain anyone's credulity—to have sat in a bath in a sunken ship and found a pearl in a shell hanging from the ceiling. Unfortunately there was no pearl. On the other hand, several small fish appeared and in the darkness began to fight over the flesh of the shell. It was amazing: even in a place like this, with no living things in sight, a little blood was enough to attract greedy mouths from all kinds of hiding places. For all I knew a moray eel might be sitting immediately below my bath and already creeping up towards me. Hurriedly I stuffed the shells into my breast pocket and left. Pursued by the spectres of my own imagination I hurriedly crossed a large room with shattered planks dangling from the ceiling and forced my way out through a tight porthole.

I heaved a sigh of relief. That was the drawback of breathing apparatus— that one was not protected by a solid diving suit and helmet but was more naked and vulnerable than any fish or other marine creature. Without noticing it I had touched some jagged pieces of metal and little trails of blood were issuing from several long cuts on my arms and legs. The price for one's exceptional mobility as a skindiver is a heightened physical risk of which one is especially conscious in an unusual situation. Added to this was the fact that I was in no communication with the world above. If anything happened to me there would be no one to come to my help.

My dive had taken twenty minutes so far and it was time for me to ascend and get the camera. Mahmud and O-Sheik were clearly relieved to see me. I handed them my spear and took the camera. No, I had not seen any mermaids so far. And down I went again into the bluish twilight, down to the ship which already seemed to me almost my personal property.

If I were a sailor I might be able to describe the route which led me from the ship's bows to her stern. The dimensions of this steamship were enormous. I swam over the upper and lower decks, peered into her interior through hatches and doors, and reached an open loading hatch through which I saw huge piles of ammunition boxes deep down in the ship's belly. I smiled at the thought that at this very moment, Bill might be talking to the harbour master about my request. No, I certainly was not going to touch the dynamite. But I would not mind the Maria Theresa dollars if they were not locked up in some inaccessible strong-room. It was wonderful to be able to choose and consider each shot at leisure. If I wanted to stand on a ledge fifteen feet above me I just gave a little shove and up I went. If I wanted to descend thirty feet I bent forward and glided down like a bird. Never had I been so aware of what life in three dimensions meant as swimming in this wreck, where every companionway and every door invited comparison with a normal ship. No bird, however skilfully it dipped through the rigging, could surpass me. For me there was no gravity whatever. I was able to float how and where I pleased, and I could equally well hang motionless in space.

I was just suspended upside down in order to photograph a fat browsing parrot fish through the maze of stanchions when the camera suddenly jammed. I shook it but it was no use. Through the lens window I peered into the case. My worst suspicions were confirmed: water had penetrated into the case. And quite a lot of it, too. As fast as I could I finned my way back to the surface.

I climbed into the boat and opened the case. Over a pint of salt water ran out. The camera had been partially immersed in this water and the film was certain to be affected. I whipped it out, and as best I could, cleaned the inside with a handkerchief. Then I held the camera open in the bright sunlight and for five minutes worked the shutter. Perhaps the drops inside would dry in this way without damaging the mechanism by rust or corrosion. What it meant to have to take the camera to pieces I knew only too well from our West Indian expedition. But it looked as if I was lucky this time. It was again functioning perfectly. I loaded a new film and, having replaced my oxygen bottle and absorbent lime, I glided down to my ship once more.

Encounter with the Devil

One morning at breakfast Bill suddenly said to me: 'By the way, would you like to come to Khartoum with me?'

'To Khartoum? When?'

'In just over two weeks' time. To mark the King's birthday the Governor-General is giving a big reception and all the chiefs and dignitaries of the Sudan will be present. I've got to go, and I could easily get you an invitation.'

'How does one get there?'

'We'd go by sleeping-car—that'll take two days and one night, and we'll fly back. I'm sure you'd find it worth while. Besides, there will be a ball.'

'Oh!'

'Anyway, you think it over,' Bill continued. 'You'll meet a few of my colleagues today. We are invited first for a drink with the port manager and then we'll all dine on board the destroyer which put in today. The captain tells me all his officers are enthusiastic skindivers. I believe they dived off Malta and in the Gulf of Aqaba, where they've been during the past few weeks.'

That sounded interesting. I had been racking my brains for days about how I could find someone to dive with me. For my photographs I needed another human to provide a scale of comparison with the coral. So long as I only photographed corals and fishes it would be impossible to tell from the pictures how big they were.

'How long is the ship staying?'

'Four or five days, I believe.'

The destroyer was dressed all over with festive pennants. The cocktails were even stronger than the usual whisky we drank at Bill's. The officers were in animated conversation with some ladies in long evening dresses. When I was introduced to them they showed me their diving masks together with the schnorkels which were so popular in the Mediterranean. They had speared a few fish off Malta but had not dived in the Gulf of Aqaba. The sharks had put them off.

I turned to one of them who seemed particularly tall and strong and asked him if he would like to sail out to the reefs with me one day. I told him how beautiful and safe it was to dive there and how much I needed a human being for my photographs as a yardstick to judge the size of the coral.

'A yardstick?' A man with bushy eyebrows had joined us. He was the Captain. 'No, for that purpose we can't possibly allow one of His Majesty's officers to be eaten by sharks!'

'But there are hardly any there!'

'Hardly any isn't good enough!'

Bill was an enthusiastic and accomplished dancer. Between dances he told me that Mr Row, the Port Sudan diver, was sitting at a table on the other side. I must meet him.

'I told him about you the other day and he doesn't believe a word of it. It'll amuse you to talk to him. He's an odd fellow.'

We walked across together and Bill introduced me. Mr Row was a short, squat man with a large almost empty tankard in front of him.

'Oh, you're the famous diver,' he said with disarming frankness. 'I've told Mr Clark that I don't believe a word of your tales.'

Bill left us alone and we soon got into conversation. Mr Row had been working at Port Sudan for a number of years and knew every stone in the harbour.

'What don't you believe?' I asked him.

'That you swim about among the reefs in your bathing trunks. Don't forget, I know those sharks—you can't tell me any tall stories.'

I had intended to dive among the submarine gardens in the harbour entrance anyway, so we arranged that I would call on him the following day and he could watch me.

When I showed him my mask, fins and breathing apparatus the next day he viewed these objects much as an engine driver might view a child's model railway. He himself dived in a diving suit, complete with proper helmet and heavy lead boots.

We drove past the Customs and stopped at the last ship lying by the jetty. She was taking on large bales of cotton. Immediately behind the ship's stern, near the tomb of the saint, from where several veiled ladies were watching me, I strapped on my breathing apparatus. While Mr Row was walking up and down the jetty, giving me some last-minute advice, I climbed down a ladder and slid underwater.

Apart from a film of oil on the surface the water was fairly clear. The harbour wall went down about thirty feet and was encrusted with countless mussels and colourful vegetation. But what interested me far more was the clearly visible ship's hull with its large propeller and a shoal of fine silk snappers which were hovering immediately behind the keel in a motionless cloud.

I had taken my harpoon with me. I cautiously retreated a little towards the harbour wall, then dived under the ship and advanced along the keel towards the propeller. Down here, from the ship's shadow, the water outside was like a pale green curtain. The swarm of fish was still motionless. Only when I got quite close did it slowly begin to move away. Close to the huge propeller I thrust my harpoon. Scales were flying in all directions and my harpoon was almost snatched from my hand. A moment later the point was loose in the water and a fish with a large hole in its side was making off.

Almost simultaneously the large head of a grouper appeared from the deep muddy water below. It rose a little way and remained hovering beneath the open water. It stood out clearly against the pale green background. I quickly surfaced, handed my spear to Mr Row, with a scrap of skin still on its point, and took the camera. Needless to say, the grouper had gone.

The submarine gardens were a little way farther out to sea. I followed the line of the coastal slope at about thirty-five feet. Through the oil-smoothed surface I could see a distorted picture of Mr Row and two of the veiled women. There were also a few dockers staring down at me. On the bottom among the coral were all kinds of rubbish—odd bits of iron, baskets, a tyre and a number of pots and pans. There was an astonishing wealth of fish and other creatures. In a crevice I discovered two crabs with enormously long white antennae and long spidery legs. The shelf edge did not exactly inspire confidence. Since sharks in tropical waters almost invariably follow ships it was quite possible that one would suddenly emerge from the muddy water. I therefore kept close to the coral and regularly looked behind me and to the side. I had been swimming for some twenty minutes when I caught sight of a big shadow above me.

It was a boat—a very strange boat because in the middle of its bottom there was a large square window and through this window several faces were peering down at the sea bed. The boat with the glass bottom! I had not seen it while getting into the water. Evidently it had been repaired and was in use again. It meant that I had reached the renowned submarine gardens.

They looked no different from other coral-grown sea beds in the harbour and they certainly could not compare with the off-shore reefs. I had meanwhile been spotted by the people in the boat. I could see the faces moving excitedly one way and then the other, and so I ascended and photographed the staring faces from below through the plate glass.

There was great excitement when I surfaced. A young lady asked me to dive down again and bring her up a shell. When I had done so she invited me to visit her on board her ship, but as her ship was due to leave very shortly I thought I had better decline. Mr Row meanwhile had disappeared. No doubt he had got bored waiting. That evening when I told Bill about the young lady's advances, he called me a big fool. 'Do you know who she was?'

'Well?'

'That girl's father owns one of the biggest diamond mines in Johannesburg. If you'd been a little bit attentive to her no doubt daddy would have financed an expedition for you and she'd have come along too.'

'I'd rather dive from a rowing boat than have a woman on an expedition,' I replied. But on this point I was to change my opinion. A mere three months later, when I returned to the Red Sea with several companions, one of the most courageous of these divers was to be Lotte.

The following day brought a terrific thunderstorm and the rain pelted down.

'If this continues,' Bill said, 'we shall be without mail for a fortnight. Our airfield can't stand much rain.'

When I stepped out on my balcony the following morning I could hardly believe my eyes. The entire garden was under water. There were a few small islands on the lawn, but from the front steps to the garden gate was one vast lake.

The rain continued throughout the day, throughout that night and throughout the next day. One alarming report followed another. On the southern edge of the town the road to Suakin was cut off; the water there was over three feet deep and the current so strong that a taxi had been washed away. The airfield was turned into a swamp. Several houses had collapsed from the rain and had been washed away. Three people had been drowned in the streets, among them the chef of the Red Sea Hotel. His body had been washed down to the sea and by the time it had been found a shark had bitten off the head. Bill was most unhappy about the golf course.

The following day I walked down to the port and out on to the jetty. The sea was a sight of terrifying beauty. Gigantic waves were crashing over the tall stone sea wall, and the water by the reefs was pitch black.

I tried to picture what was happening in the sea. It would be a grand banquet with no creature knowing whether it would survive or end up inside another. Every second thousands of creatures were being killed in the breakers and tens of thousands were fighting over these tasty morsels, exposing themselves to the same fate. In these conditions natural selection operated more ruthlessly than ever. Anything that was not totally healthy and resistant was bound to go under in this struggle. And then, in a few days' time, the sea would calm down again and everything would look bright and cheerful as before. Only the fat bellies of the survivors would testify to what had happened.

In the harbour large masses of seaweed were floating on the surface, and between them small transparent medusas. Alongside the ships vast numbers of anchovies were crowded together so tightly that from above they looked like a compact mass. In spite of the disturbed water I dived among the fish. While I kept quiet they enclosed me totally and I could feel the movement of the many small bodies on my skin. The moment I moved this living wall retreated from me as if by magic. This was no longer action by individuals; the whole shoal was a huge super-individual entity whose particles seemed to be acting in accordance with a higher will. Not one of them was out of step when the community performed a turn. With their sensitive lateral organs the small creatures were in communication with each other like tuned electrical instruments, and each impulse directed the movement of them all. But if I kept still the individual once more emerged and a hundred inquisitive eyes moved up close to me.

Four days after the heavy rain the sea had calmed down sufficiently for us to think of going outside the harbour. While inside the harbour wall the water was still yellow; outside, beyond a clearly defined line, it had again assumed a greenish-blue colour. I dropped a few stones into the water from the boat to judge as they sank the extent to which the sea was clear again. We sailed out to the *Umbrea* and again tied up to the same mast. Meanwhile I had received permission to dive there.

Here the water was still very clouded. But when I descended to twenty-five or thirty feet it became clearer and the milky haze hung like a cloud over me. But even below this cloud cover I could see no farther than thirty or thirty-five feet. The gale had caused all kinds of damage. The search-light turret on the after-deck had snapped. The Harbour Master had made me promise not to touch any part of the ship in case it exploded. But even if I had had a thousand arms I could not have shaken her as vigorously as the gale had.

I did not feel happy on the sunken ship in cloudy water. I ordered our sail to be set again and we went out to the end of the Wingate reef where I had dived on my first afternoon and where by now I knew every nook and corner. Close to the corals the water here was relatively clear, but a mere thirty feet out to sea I found myself in a milky veil. The local clarity could well be due to the corals themselves; it was possible that the small polyps were cleaning the water with their minute tentacles.

I had brought the cine-camera this time and shot close-up sequences of butterfly fish and corals in the shallow water. Suddenly I heard excited shouting from the boat. Mahmud and O-Sheik were standing up, pointing out to sea behind me. As this was towards the sun I could not see anything myself except the blinding glitter of the water.

'*Girsh! Girsh!*' they cried excitedly. That meant 'Sharks! Sharks!'

The great moment had come. I was not too pleased that it should have come with the water so muddy. Involuntarily my knees began to shake and I retreated towards shallow water. But then I got a grip on myself and swam slowly and relaxedly to the boat and, with a good deal of relief, clambered in.

Since I had been declaring ceaselessly that I wanted to see sharks my situation now was a little equivocal. If these really were sharks then I could not very well refuse to get into the water and swim out towards them—otherwise I would lose face with my two boatmen. But to take such a risk in cloudy water was sheer lunacy. For the second time on this journey I found myself manoeuvred into a decision against my will.

The two were pointing to a certain spot, about a hundred yards from where I had been swimming. They were quite right: two dorsal fins were smoothly slicing the water. They seemed strangely soft and flexible and kept the same distance from each other. Clearly two sharks were playing just below the surface.

The longer I looked the stranger the business seemed to me. One moment one of the fins would appear, and then the other, and then both simultaneously, but they would invariably keep the same distance of about fifteen feet.

'*Girsh kabir?*' I asked.

'*Kabir! Kabir!*' the two replied in unison. To judge by their gestures these sharks must be enormous. Mahmud, moreover, tried to explain something about a long sting and devil's horns, but that presumably was a figment of his colourful imagination. The two creatures were presumably performing some kind of mating rites. The only odd thing was the soft flabbiness of their dorsal fins.

'Raise the anchor!' I commanded. We could at least row a little closer and then I could decide whether to get into the water or not. I tried to control my excitement. But I could not help feeling that until then I had been skating on thin ice very luckily and that this ice was now beginning to crack.

The anchor was wedged among the corals and in spite of much tugging the two were unable to free it. I vaulted over the side and dived. But I caught myself looking out towards the deep water more than once. I had to keep my nerve now. I quickly freed the anchor and ascended to the boat.

I ordered the two to row very cautiously without splashing. The two fins had moved away a short distance but they were still clearly visible. With feverish haste I loaded a new film. Suddenly the two fins had gone.

I am not sure whether I was disappointed or relieved. On the one hand I had been tremendously curious to discover what kind of sharks these were, yet on the other I felt that, given the circumstances, this might be the better solution.

Just then the fins reappeared.

Mahmud and O-Sheik regarded me expectantly. It had to be done. I was already wearing my fins and carrying my knife. I quickly put on the camera carrier, slipped my mask over my eyes and slid underwater.

Everything all round was greenish and opaque. The dark outline of our boat gave me some idea of how far I could see in this water—some twenty to twenty-five feet at best. At the same time, provided I got close enough, I might take some very impressive pictures in this haze. Assuming, of course, that I still had all my limbs.

Swimming in the direction where I had seen the flabby fin tips, I strained my eyes until they hurt. Then, suddenly, the fins disappeared again. My instinct told me that I must be in the immediate vicinity of the creatures but I could not see them anywhere. Floating solitarily in the greenish-yellow mist I glanced up to the boat. Mahmud and O-Sheik were standing up in it staring at the water. They did not see anything either. To avoid being taken by surprise I kept turning and looking all round. In between I came up briefly for air. It was a torture. My eyes were watering from the strain. Suddenly I felt a great movement approaching from the left.

It was a bodily perception even before I saw anything. Then an outline appeared in the mist, more like a gigantic blanket than a creature. Everything in me was staring towards the monster that was slowly approaching. In the middle of a huge body was a gigantic rectangular open mouth. At last I understood. The two fins which we had seen, which had kept a distance between them of fifteen feet, belonged not to two sharks but to one single monstrous creature which, in this opaque water, did not seem to have an end at all.

Just then, at the worst moment, I had to go up for air. A moment later I was down again staring ahead of me. I could hardly believe my own eyes. The monster had come closer still, it had turned a little, I saw one eye, and above it—two projecting devil's horns!

I only saw it for a fraction of a second. Then the water in front of me was one enormous foaming commotion. A wide flapping wing pushed me aside; I was caught in a vortex and spun around in a flurry of bubbles. A thin black thing glided past me—and the apparition was gone.

Only the trail of slowly rising air bubbles testified that this had not been a mere figment of my imagination. Back in the boat it took me a long while to recover from my excitement. A week was to pass before I discovered what it was that I had seen.

The first Sharks

A few days later, on a fine Sunday, Bill decided to take me out to a more distant reef where he assured me I would find a lot of sharks. On the way we saw on the horizon the distant silhouette of what looked like a miniature Eiffel Tower. Bill explained that this was the lighthouse of Sanganab, an atoll on the extreme edge of the coral reefs. A boat with supplies for the Egyptian-operated lighthouse went out every Thursday and would, if I wished, take me along.

'But if you really want to come back here with a larger expedition you could camp out there altogether. There's enough room in the lighthouse and the atoll is exceedingly interesting. There are plenty of hammerhead sharks there.'

For the moment I was more anxious to find out whether any sharks were to be expected at the reef we were making for.

'No doubt at all,' Bill replied. 'Last time I was out there, when I caught a bayard, there were no fewer than six of them round our boat. I know because I counted them.'

'How big?'

'Between six and ten feet. One of them probably even bigger.'

'Grey sharks?'

'I didn't look that carefully. But I think so. One of them, at any rate, had a terrifying mouth and was so impertinent that we had to keep it away from the boat with an oar.'

The wind had freshened and we were moving faster. On a command from Mahmud, O-Sheik fixed a plank to the ship's bottom, projecting at least five feet over the gunwale. He then crawled out on it to provide a counter-weight to the sail.

'Over there! Look!'

Bill had leapt to his feet and I could just about see a large tail disappearing in the sea. A moment later the fish leapt a second time. It was a sailfish. Including the sword projecting from its head, it was certainly over six feet long. Its vibrating serrated dorsal tail glittered magnificently in the sun. For a second it hung in the air, as if cast in metal, barely twenty yards from the boat. Then it fell back into the water, sword first, and all that was left was a ring of froth.

Hastily Bill fixed the biggest hook he had and cast his line. Soon the reel screeched and after a short, violent struggle we landed a splendid crevallé. I was amazed at the assurance with which Mahmud was piloting us through the increasingly numerous reefs. Some of them were visible by their crest of foam but there were also some which did not show at all above the glittering surface.

The sun was fairly high in the sky when, after two and a half hours of sailing, we at last reached our destination. We dropped anchor in deep water, a short distance away from a long reef barrier. On Bill's instruction O-Sheik had cut out a piece of flesh from the crevallé and Bill now hooked it on to a hand line which he lowered overboard.

'If we really want to see sharks,' Bill explained, 'what we need is one of those big perch which are around here. . . . Ow! Quick! Hold it! Hold it!'

With a mighty jerk the line had suddenly taken off. Bill tried to hold it but the pull was so strong that a piece of his skin went with it. Mahmud and O-Sheik then seized the line almost simultaneously. At the same moment both of them followed it overboard, head first. Mahmud succeeded in hanging on to the gunwale with one hand while not letting go of the line with the other. Either the fish would pull our boat down into the depths or Mahmud's desperate effort must halt it.

The boat was rocking as if in a storm. But the fish was held. Once its first impetus was broken it only defended itself half as fiercely. While Bill and I were belaying the line, Mahmud and O-Sheik hurriedly clambered back into the boat. Then Mahmud noticed that he had lost his turban and jumped overboard once more. There was still no sign of any sharks. We had got over our shock and were laughing at our recent discomfiture—though Bill's laughter was mingled with groans over his skinned palm.

Slowly we hauled the fish on board. It was a magnificent sea perch with red and blue dots, weighing probably some forty-five to sixty-five pounds. Mahmud had checked it just in time. If it had reached its hole in the rock we should not have been able to get it out.

We brought the boat closer to the edge of the reef and I went down to explore the submarine world. Bill was watching me with a wry smile. He was clearly envying me my swim.

'Why don't you come in?' I called up to him. 'You'll be perfectly safe. Take my spare mask and come on in!'

'I'm not completely crazy!' Bill retorted. But then he seemed to think it over. I saw him try on the mask, but a moment later he was pushing it up to his forehead.

'It's suffocating. How do I breathe?'

'Through your mouth. But first you must spit on the glass, wipe it off and rinse it out. Otherwise it'll steam up.'

Bill shook his head, did as I told him and presently swung himself overboard. His very first glance under the surface made him forget all sharks and other monsters. He got Mahmud to give him my spare pair of fins and he was soon diving among the shallow reefs.

The whole side of one rock was covered by a giant anemone. Among its many hundreds of tentacles, which spelled certain death to any fish, minute pomacentrids were scurrying about with complete assurance. What puzzled me about this friendship was how the sea anemone managed to identify these minute fish while devouring all others. This friendship goes so far that when in danger these small fish even take refuge in the sea anemone's stomach—the very place where all other fishes are digested.

'They clean the sea anemone,' I explained to Bill. 'They eat all kinds of parasites and as a kind of reward they are allowed to hide in it.'

Bill by now could no longer be persuaded to get out of the water. He had discovered a sea urchin with red club-shaped spines between two rocks and was trying to pull it out. With much puffing and spitting he was diving up and down.

As my camera had once again broken down, I decided to do some spear fishing with breathing equipment. The neighbourhood looked promising. There were considerably more fish than at the Wingate reef and in the blue depth below I could see the outline of coral formations such as I had never witnessed before.

I dived down. The scene was like an oriental temple city which had sunk to the bottom of the sea and whose ruins were overgrown with creepers in a hundred different colours. There were coral fortresses thirty feet high and more, with magnificently decorated façades and countless little turrets. Between them, vertical gorges crossed the rocks like streets. What gave the scene its astonishing colour was the exceedingly luxuriant growth of the leathery corals which spread over everything like a primeval forest of flowering plants. Unlike the petrified corals these do not excrete a calcareous skeleton and their polyps have not six but eight tentacles which, moreover, are feathered. They were like thousands of little star-shaped flowers, opening, rhythmically pulsating, and withdrawing again as soon as I approached.

Among the numerous fish which were scurrying about the ruins of this sunken city two large dark-hued groupers seemed particularly interested in my arrival. They were inquisitively pursing their thick, fleshy lips and regarding me sadly with their protruding eyes. But in spite of this demonstration of friendship they kept at a safe distance from my harpoon, unlike the brilliantly yellow angel fish which approached quite close and inspected me at leisure.

The streets of this coral city led obliquely downhill, ending in a precipice which was almost vertical. As I was emerging there between the clumps of coral, some twenty or thirty bluish-black fish appeared from the deep water.

Their shape and twin caudal keel suggested a close relationship with the green unicorn fish although they lacked the latter's single horn. I christened them 'idiot fish' because they really seemed exceedingly stupid. With undisguised curiosity they made straight for my bright harpoon head, gazed on it with cheeky eyes, flicked their bodies to and fro and pursed their little lips as if trying to play the flute with my harpoon head.

Without much hesitation I speared the first of them. The harpoon head separated, there was a powerful jerk, and I was being dragged through the corals behind my harpoon shaft. The fish developed a quite astonishing strength. After a few high-speed figures of eight the wire which held the harpoon head to the short rope on the shaft broke and the fish vanished down a side street.

The remaining members of the shoal were circling me in great excitement. If I had had a spare harpoon head I could have speared any one of them. As it was, I had to surface to get another.

Bill was greatly surprised to see me reappear so quickly.

'Something wrong?' he called out.

'Not at all. Everything's fine!' I replied, out of breath. I waved the broken wire and told him what had happened. When I descended again the blue fish were still there. But their behaviour had become noticeably more timid. This might have been due to those 'alarm substances' which are thought to enter the water when a fish is wounded and which, upon spreading, warn the other members of the species that there is danger at hand.

I decided to swim a short way along the precipice. The growth of coral was equally fantastic here. Several fish watched me as I passed their holes, as if I were some marine predator. And that was just how I felt, swimming along with my harpoon at the ready. I stopped under a tall over-hanging rock. From here I had a good view of the corals right and left and of the precipice. I did not suspect that this rock would very nearly become my gravestone.

I did not have to wait long for my idiot fish. A whole shoal of them had spotted me and were now approaching with dancing movements. I aimed at the fattest of them and harpooned it. Again the fish struggled mightily, but this time wire and line held, and I braced myself against the corals with my legs.

A cascade of fish poured over us while I tried to haul in my trophy. At last I had got it by its tail and killed it with my knife. A cloud of blood was spreading around me. Just then a black shadow moved in from the side.

I was so busy freeing my harpoon head which had caught in the fish that I did not notice the shadow until it had got to within six feet. Looking up I found myself facing a row of menacing eyes. No fewer than forty barracudas, each about five feet long, were making for me in silent formation.

I knew these greatly feared fish from the West Indies. There we had come across even larger specimens, but they had invariably been solitary and had not attacked us. I had never before faced a whole shoal of them. Perhaps Bill, Mahmud and all the others had not been entirely wrong when they had warned me of barracudas as insistently as of sharks. True, unlike sharks, barracudas cannot snap off entire limbs, but they pounce on their victim from all sides and tear his flesh from his body in chunks, while getting increasingly inflamed by the taste of blood. A lady of my acquaintance had once been within thirty feet of a man who was attacked by barracudas in water that was only waist deep. That was in Bali and although several people had immediately come to his aid and dragged him ashore, his wounds had been so severe that he had had to have a leg amputated and soon afterwards died. The barracuda's teeth are arranged like countless small daggers. All these thoughts flashed through my mind as the creatures were approaching with rigid expressionless eyes.

Holding my harpoon shaft in front of me—the head was still in the body of the idiot fish among the coral at my feet—I retreated into the niche formed by the rock. I was cornered.

Indefatigably the barracudas were patrolling in front of me, to and fro, coming a little closer each time. It was a regular siege, except that the signal for attack had not yet been given. Just as I had among the shoals of fish in the harbour, I again felt that I was facing not individual creatures but a vast super-individual entity whose communal resolution was steadily growing stronger. Unable to see a way out I lost my nerve. I thrust about furiously with the blunt steel shaft and here and there hit a fish.

I wounded some of them, but this merely intensified the eerie tension. At lightning speed the barracudas turned a circle and the next moment were back in their former position, just as if some electric field were keeping each individual fish in its accurately defined place.

In this situation help came from an unexpected quarter. Through the barracudas I caught sight of a large grey shape, followed immediately by another. Sharks! They were about nine feet long, well proportioned, with white tips to their dorsal and caudal fins. The sight of them made the barracudas seem like pigmies. For a moment I lost my fear—and that was enough. With a sudden movement I hurled myself forward among the barracudas, yelling and expelling air into the water at the same time. The swarm scattered and before it could rally again their common will, that invisible link between them, was broken.

Sharks! Here they were at last. A third one was just then approaching from the left, like an aircraft appearing between two towers. It floated along above one of those coral streets, barely six feet above me. In passing it turned a little, to look down on me with its laterally positioned eyes. This was the first time that I had seen a shark from directly below. Its belly, with two pectoral fins sticking out from it like pointed wings, was snow white, and in front behind its pointed nose was a clear-cut crescent—its mouth.

A wonderful sense of security engulfed me. These sharks, I sensed instantly, were no different from those I knew. Almost, one might say, good friends with whose movements and behaviour I was well acquainted. At long last the great uncertainty that had plagued me was gone; fabled monsters of limitless power had once more become flesh-and-blood creatures familiar to me from a hundred encounters. For the first time I no longer felt like a secret intruder among these reefs, but like a master. Like a solid protective armour this sense of strength and assurance enclosed me.

The first three sharks had disappeared, but a smaller dark one had come up from below. I swam down to meet it and it calmly turned away. The battle was over. The barracudas were hovering like a motionless cloud some hundred feet away in the deep water. I stepped right up to the edge of the precipice and gazed down into the uncertain blackness in which I again saw the outlines of a few sharks. Then the waves of assurance ebbed away again and I decided to call it a day. I picked up the idiot fish I had killed, which weighed some twenty or twenty-five pounds, and with a sense of relief ascended along the coral slope.

I was laughing into my breathing tube—I just could not help myself. Perhaps it was a reaction after the excitement. On my way, unexpectedly, I found the anchor of our boat with a length of chafed rope. I dragged it up to the edge of the reef and looked out for our craft. It had drifted a good distance. In response to my shouts Mahmud rowed her over and we knotted the rope together. Bill stared at me in some horror when, chuckling all the while, I told him about the sharks and the barracudas.

'You aren't seriously saying that there were sharks about while I was in the water?'

'But of course!' I laughed. 'And a shoal of barracudas!' As I was telling the story I gradually regained my composure. Mahmud, for whom Bill interpreted my account, rolled his eyes and shook his head. He in turn translated my story for O-Sheik who only understood Fuzzy-wuzzy and who, no doubt, was having my sharks passed on to him at twice their real size. When I had finished Mahmud solemnly stepped up to me, placed his hand on my shoulder and pronounced me 'Big Shark'—a name which stuck to me among the natives.

It took me a long time to go to sleep that night. I kept thinking about the sharks I had seen and compared them with those I had met in the past. I tried to recall every detail of their behaviour and their movements, and worked out

The oxygen apparatus which we used after 1941 was convenient and produced no noise from escaping bubbles; on the other hand, it limited the depth of our descents.

Above: Commander Jimmy Hodges (third from left), an outstanding diver, lost his life when he dived too deep.

Left: Captain Johannes Diebitsch, the first master of the Xarifa. After our expedition to the Galapagos Islands he was appointed to command the training schooner Pamir. Near the Azores, at a point where the Xarifa had been caught in a heavy storm, the Pamir went down in a hurricane.

Right: The Xarifa at the jetty of Sanganeb atoll in the Red Sea, at the spot where I had encountered a white shark ten years previously.

Above: *A shoal of small striped catfish (Plotosus lineatus) passing over the sandy sea floor like a caterpillar track. The fish at the back swim over the swarm to the front: in this way the sea bottom is very efficiently searched for food.*

Left: *The shy, easily alarmed angel fish (Pygoplites diacanthus).*

'*Any good aquarium picture is of greater scientific and instructional value than similar shots taken in nature, even if at the risk of one's life,*' *a well-known German woman zoologist wrote in a review of my first fish photographs. Views have changed: only shots taken in a natural habitat provide a true picture of living communities.*

Above: *Coral growth on an overhang in the Indian Ocean at a depth of one hundred feet.*

Right: *A bullseye (priacanthus) among the unfolded polyps of a leathery coral (alcyonaria) in the Red Sea. The particularly large eyes are indicative of life in dark grottos.*

A brilliantly coloured sponge, twenty-four inches tall, of the demospongidae family. Just like the corals, which are also rooted to the spot in the way plants are, the sponges are classified as animals because of their mode of feeding. They suck water into their bodies by way of a system of tubes and digest the plankton contained in it.

a plan of campaign for photographing them. I would sit down on a suitable coral and fit a harpoon head to a longish rope, tied not to the harpoon shaft but to the corals by my side. Then I would spear an idiot fish and keep it dangling from the rope tied to the coral. Its wriggling would therefore not worry me, and I hoped it would attract sharks and barracudas while I would be waiting for them with the camera. I intended to have my harpoon shaft fixed to my shoulder, so I would have it when I needed it, and I would carry a spare harpoon head with coiled cord in my breast pocket. If one idiot fish was not enough I would tie the second cord to the rock and spear another fish from the crowd that would be circling me.

The following day, at eleven o'clock, we were anchored once more at the same spot. Bill, who happened to have a day off, had come along. This time we had taken along a glass-bottomed box through which he would watch me from the boat. If I sat down on the top of one of the coral fortresses he would just about be able to see me.

Garlanded with my equipment like a Christmas tree I floated down. From my chest dangled the underwater camera and my underwater exposure meter; in my right hand I held my spear to which two cords were fixed, a long one which I intended to fasten to the coral and a short one which held the shaft to my shoulder. I soon found a clump of coral which looked like an armchair. I made sure it was not upholstered with stinging moss creatures and sat down in it.

In accordance with my plan of campaign I fastened the line to a projection on my right. The exposure meter showed me the correct stop; I set the focus at 2 m.—I was hoping the sharks would come that close. Secretly I was also hoping that one of the sharks might take a bite out of the fish wriggling on my line. If I succeeded in taking a picture of it at that moment I would be a good deal nearer to my dreamed-of objective of a research ship. A picture like that would not only be published everywhere and bring in some money, but it would also impress the film distributors on whose interest my next project depended.

In accordance with my programme a shoal of idiot fish approached. I chose the fattest of them, but I was a little over-confident, and struck too soon and too short. Alarmed, the fish made off. They returned, circling me at a distance of six to ten feet, but did not approach any closer. As I was not alone but had every one of my movements watched through a glass box from above I was doubly mortified by my failure.

In order to attract the attention of the creatures once more I rose from my seat and began to perform all kinds of contortions. Bill told me subsequently that Mahmud and O-Sheik had been absolutely entranced with these. The fish, evidently, also liked my performance. But they did not come any closer.

At long last my patience, or really impatience, was rewarded from another quarter. From a distance appeared two large bayards playing with each other. They were making straight for me, and although the larger one must have weighed at least forty-five pounds I speared it cleanly without a moment's hesitation.

It raced away and the usual turbulent struggle followed. I was still so angry about the idiot fish that I quickly fastened my second line to my belt, fitted the harpoon head and thrust it through the nearest specimen. Before I knew it the creature had pulled me off my clump of coral. My left fin was caught in the other line, the one in which the large bayard was wriggling, and I found myself floating on my back, with two powerful fish pulling me in opposite directions. Water had got into my mask and the exposure meter was pinching my breathing tube. If any sharks or barracudas arrived now they would be able to take bites off me as they pleased.

Together with the wriggling fish I sank twenty-five feet to the base of the coral. I was completely entangled in my various lines and was desperately trying to get my knife out of its rubber scabbard. In consequence I was unable to adjust my breathing valve. My fall and the resultant change of pressure had completely collapsed my breathing bag and I was suffocating. An infinitely empty feeling was rising from my stomach into my chest, which started to twitch convulsively. At last I had got my knife out and cut through one of my fetters. My mask was full of water and I could hardly see anything. I thought I could make out a shark and desperately thrashed about me. I had to press the valve several times before I realized that my bottle was totally empty and no more oxygen was getting through. This meant that I was now too heavy by a good many pounds and had to fight my way back to the top. I bumped hard against the rock, but just then felt my trapped fin freeing itself from the second rope. My camera had slipped over to my back and was strangling me. But now only one thing mattered—to get to the surface. I felt so hot that I started

Right: *On a reef slope in the Maldive Islands Dr Eibl and I killed some fish and hid them among the corals. It took some sharks which were swimming 100 to 130 feet away a minute or two to perceive the smell. Then they approached purposefully, fought over the morsel, but took no notice of us although we were standing quite close without any cover. Shipwrecked sailors, too, have found that sharks invariably direct their attacks against persons already injured. In our experiments we never used steel cages since only direct contact can yield valid information about the sharks' real behaviour towards humans.*

trembling all over. At last, after an eternity, I could see light around me. I pushed through the surface, whipped off my breathing tube and my mask, sagged below the water again after a vigorous breath which almost made me faint, surfaced once more and with my last ounce of strength struggled over to the reef. There I hung on, totally exhausted, until the boat arrived to take me aboard.

'That was really wonderful,' were Bill's first words. 'I have never seen anything like it.'

From a bird's eye view my performance must have looked like a glorious battle. Breathlessly Bill told me about two sharks which had swum quite close to me and had likewise 'watched' me. Lying flat on my back in the boat I recovered only very slowly. I had swallowed a great deal of water while ascending and I felt as sick as a dog. My heart was thumping as if it were going to burst. When I closed my eyes I saw swarms of fish gyrating around me, above me and below me.

Not until after lunch in the boat did I feel like getting into the water once more. The two lines with the baits were still down among the corals. As Mahmud established by peering through the box, the line I had cut had also got tangled up again in the coral. Both disappeared under the rocks and there was nothing to be seen of the fish at the ends of them.

As the spot was only about sixty feet deep I could, at a pinch, get there without breathing equipment. At about forty feet I stopped and swallowed; this relieved the pressure and I was able to carry on. If one's ears are in good order, and provided one's Eustachian tube is not blocked by catarrh, depths of sixty-five and even eighty feet can be reached with two such stops.

I first cut the line that was fastened to the rock and which held the bayard. At my second attempt I succeeded in dragging the fish out of a hole at the foot of the coral. Barely half of it was left; the rest had been consumed by a moray eel or some other fish.

While I was trying to free the other bait too—it had swum through several holes before the line got entangled again—I observed a number of barracudas in the deep water. I quickly went back for the camera and dived down towards them. At a short distance from them I stopped motionless, and soon they turned and came closer, enabling me to take a few good shots. I returned to the boat, loaded a colour film, and repeated all the shots in colour.

Then I had enough.

By nightfall we were back in Port Sudan. On my bed was a large official envelope. It contained a very formal invitation from His Excellency the British Governor-General to attend his reception in Khartoum in six days' time.

The King's Birthday

I was seeing sharks every day now and repeatedly had the opportunity of photographing them. It really seemed as though they had been away somewhere and were now returning to their normal neighbourhood. Especially towards evening, when the light under water assumed a strange chalky hue, I could hardly fail to encounter some of them. It would happen that I inadvertently turned my head and there behind me would be a shark. But even when I started at their sudden appearance I always enjoyed seeing them. No other marine creature can compare with a shark in beauty of shape or movement. Dolphins seem restless and unharmonious under water; tunnies look like robots chasing along pointlessly, merely because someone has wound them up; rays invariably seem like eerie mis-shapen monsters. But the sharks and the water around them are one; the shark moves with perfect grace, just as if propelled by the water.

Just as I had been extending my exploration to greater and greater depths, so I was now conquering the hours just before nightfall. The lower the sun sank, the more lively the sea floor. Shoals upon shoals of fish would rise up from the deep water; at times it seemed as if the fish were jerking one way or another in a kind of dance, but in fact they were merely chasing the small organisms floating in the water. Long slim lajangs sailed past in silvery squadrons, their gills puffed out. The ghostly silhouettes of unicorn fish were motionless against the dark background of the deep water in their hundreds and thousands; huge giant perch hung motionless in the open water like buoys.

More than once was I gripped by fear at the sight of the large black rocks around me and the realization of my own position. But it was not because of the sharks that I sometimes admitted defeat and escaped from the deepening darkness. On the contrary, at this nocturnal hour there was nothing more beautiful and seemingly less dangerous than a shark appearing out of the uncertain shadows, assuming shape, and gliding past with sovereign assurance. What was eerie was the uncertainty of the black shadows from which some terrifying beast might emerge at any moment.

The evening before my departure for Khartoum we were sailing home along the Wingate Reef just before sunset when I saw two flabby fin tips at play above the surface, keeping a steady distance of about fifteen feet between them. It was the same spot as before. And this time the water was clear.

We lowered the sail and rowed across cautiously. I loaded a particularly sensitive film, praying all the while that I would get there in time. The sun was at the upper edge of a black bank of cloud and in the next ten minutes would disappear behind it.

When I slipped overboard the fins were no longer to be seen above water.

I swam towards where they had last surfaced. The water was bottomless. Suddenly the sun plunged behind the cloud and there was total darkness. But there was just one small window left in the cloud and the sun's red disc was slowly moving towards it. This might give me another two or three minutes' light.

I was swimming about irresolutely when suddenly, far off to my left, I was aware of a commotion. It was as though some gigantic butterfly were cavorting about under the waves. At that moment the sun moved into the blessed window of the surface. As fast as I could I swam towards the butterfly. As I had surmised, it turned out to be a giant devil ray. I had not realized that these huge monsters occurred in the Red Sea; they are the biggest rays in existence and reach a wing span of up to thirty feet and a weight of three tons.

Never, except for the graceful play of some sharks, had I seen a creature so obviously enjoying itself. With its gigantic wings flapping up and down—it had been the extreme wing tips that had appeared above water, either alternately or simultaneously—this devil ray was dancing about in small circles, evidently just as much absorbed in its own enjoyment as those pug fish which are frequently seen near the reefs chasing their own tails and spinning about like tops from sheer exuberance.

Just then it spotted me. It stopped. It turned. It regarded me. It became restless. It curled its projecting horns. And then, on a sudden impulse, it came straight at me.

I forced myself to keep calm and focused the camera. In the middle of the huge swinging shape was a gaping square hole—its mouth. To both sides and a little above were the horns, which were now extended and rigid. Half way it suddenly turned and swam around me in a large arc, continually watching me with one of its eyes and getting closer on a spiral course. It still seemed to be in a good mood and as it swam curled its strange horns.

These horns are in fact two thick lobes projecting from either side of its mouth and clearly designed to close it, if necessary, rather like a double door. The large mouth of this creature is somewhat misleading—in spite of its enormous size the devil ray is harmless and, like many whales, feeds on small creatures suspended in the sea. Minute shrimps and strombs are the kind of delicacies this giant butterfly pursues. The fact that it is nevertheless hated and feared by the fishermen is due to a misunderstanding. What happens is that various small parasites establish themselves on the inner side of the horns. To deal with this irritating itch the devil ray has its own way of seeking relief. Whenever it passes a fishing vessel riding at anchor it will take the chain between its horns and race along it until the troublesome parasites are all scraped off. Unfortunately it will frequently rip the anchor from the bottom and this will

115

get caught in the ray's head. In panic it will then race out to sea, towing the fishing boat behind it. Many a fisherman is said to have found himself in this dire predicament. Small wonder this ray is known as 'the devil', and not just because of its horns.

I clicked my shutter, wound on, clicked again . . . and by then the ray was so close that its wings nearly touched me. As on its original appearance it suddenly took fright. I was seized by a powerful vortex and whirled aside. The thin black tail tip glided past me and the sun was extinguished. No stage management could have worked better.

The following day, at 4 p.m., Ahmed took us to the station, where a large number of white-shrouded figures were crowding along a train with white carriages. The windows were comfortably tinted against the glare of the desert. Bill and I went aboard and the train moved off in the direction of the mountains.

It was dark when we arrived in Khartoum. A friend of Bill's met us with a car. He was putting Bill up at his place, but for me a room had been booked at the Grand Nile Hotel which looked much like the Red Sea Hotel except that it was bigger.

I was still in my bath when Bill telephoned. He was disconsolate, but the party he had been asked to consisted of twelve guests and the hostess would on no account have a thirteenth at table. Attempts to find a fourteenth lady for me had failed. He was going to refuse and spend the evening with me.

I urged him not to consider me. I was dead tired and delighted to hang my dinner jacket back in the wardrobe. The following morning at 11 a.m. Bill collected me and we had coffee at his friend's. Then a state carriage with red plush seats appeared outside and carried us away.

At noon sharp we entered the Governor-General's Palace and were conducted up to the first floor where Lady Howe greeted us. Presently the Governor-General appeared, accompanied by two aides and by the Governor of Aden. We strolled into a tall room where numerous gloomy portraits gazed down on us from the walls. The menu differed in no way from that at Bill's place, except that the fried fish and roast mutton was followed by delicious doughnuts and finally by some cheese which was so hard that we cut wafer-thin slices from it. I sat on the right of His Excellency, and as he had been at the Embassy in Peking for a number of years we found a few interests in common.

Over coffee on the terrace Sir Robert looked at the underwater photographs I had brought along and I took the opportunity to tell him about my idea of a somewhat bigger expedition. After a few questions His Excellency promised me his support. I was to address the visa application for the members of my party to him personally, and as for the customs formalities, I was to send in a detailed inventory of all equipment and apparatus we would take along. He would then sponsor our application. He very cordially shook hands with me when we took our leave.

In the evening Bill and I, wearing dinner jackets, entered a long room which resembled the oriental stage set of a cheap suburban theatre more than the dining-room of a well-to-do Sudanese. The walls were hung with pictures painted on cloth and above the front door were stained glass windows. To the right behind the long, laid table was a pantry, and behind a screen was a cheap wash-stand. To the left, a number of Sudanese were squatting on broad sofas in front of small Turkish tables, puffing away at long hubble-bubbles.

After a long wait for the last guests we sat down at table. There was watery soup with bits of bread floating in it, then fish mayonnaise which tasted neither of fish nor of mayonnaise, and finally roast mutton. This was put before our host in one piece and he thereupon tore off large chunks and put them on his guests' plates. After four weeks in the Sudan I regarded myself as a connoisseur of mutton, but this was by far the toughest I had ever tried my teeth on. The finishing touch of the meal was a synthetic fruit jelly. Since I had not understood a word of the animated conversation I was glad to be out in the street again without having lost a tooth.

'Normally the Sudanese eat with their fingers,' Bill explained in the car. 'The host kneads a small lump of rice and gravy and places it in the mouth of his guests of honour.'

'And will it be like that at Tony's?' I asked.

'Oh no, Tony is quite different,' Bill assured me. 'He's a Greek, and his parties are the best in the Sudan. He owns all the cinemas and knows how to spend his money elegantly.'

We had stopped in front of a house from which came the sound of dance music and women's laughter. Through the door we saw a small bar at which our host was just pouring drinks for some ladies. When he caught sight of Bill he opened his arms and came to meet us with a blissful abandon which at first I attributed to the champagne bottle in his hand but which I subsequently realized was the normal reflection of his happy nature. Each of us had a glass thrust into his hand and very soon we were part of this truly carefree circle. There was dancing in the garden between flowering shrubs under the light of the moon; in between dances one would meet at a buffet which, in addition to sucking-pig, roast on the spit, lobster and caviar, included the choicest Greek delicacies. Bill and I exchanged rueful glances at having filled our stomachs with tough mutton and synthetic jelly. Tony was the ideal host. He appeared wherever a glass was empty or the conversation was flagging.

At six in the morning the hotel servant shook me awake. At seven-thirty

Bill and I climbed aboard the small aircraft which operated the service to the coast. By half past nine, after a restful snooze, we were circling over Port Sudan.

Below us the sulphurous clouds of a sand storm were gathering. There were still a few clear patches through which the ground was visible, but these were rapidly shrinking. As we were subsequently told, the pilot very nearly decided to return to Khartoum. He had circled three times and then decided to plunge down through the last clear hole in the cloud. No sooner had the machine come to a halt than the scene around turned into yellow-grey mist.

Out of this mist appeared Ahmed, the driver and a police officer who made his report to Bill in the car. Back home we had breakfast, then Bill picked up his attaché case and drove to his office.

'Life goes on,' he said sourly. His mood was once more at zero point.

A whole Swarm of Monsters

I was sitting in my bath, reading the bunch of letters which had at last arrived. Lotte was writing anxiously that she had got hold of a new Leica, but there were difficulties about an export permit. Besides, she wrote, there had been no letters from me for three weeks and everybody thought I was dead. There was a letter from a newspaper urgently asking for a report. An agency wrote to say I could not have an advance. A letter from home said would I for heaven's sake write to them. But what interested me most was a parcel from Mr Millword. It contained a book by Crossland and his own brochure about the pearl banks of Dongonab, north of Muhammad Qol.

I read it with mounting interest. When I had finished it I was determined to go diving there at all costs. I immediately started all preparations for a trip to Muhammad Qol, and four days later, accompanied by Mahmud, I left Port Sudan on top of a loaded lorry.

Muhammad Qol, our stop for the night, was an ancient fort surrounded by a few miserable wooden huts. Dongonab had even fewer huts, and these consisted more of spaces between planks than of planks themselves. A few fishermen welcomed us with a cordial handshake and invited us to step into the 'rest hut' of the village—a low room with a few bunks along the wall.

The only available boat turned out to be a very narrow dug-out canoe with, at best, room for three sitting behind each other. Nevertheless I hired it, put on my breathing apparatus and, fins on my feet and spear in my right hand, sat down in the middle. Mahmud paddled at the rear and the owner of the craft in front. After a good distance we stopped and the fisherman—a man with exceedingly intelligent features—explained to me in gestures that at this spot I would find as many shells as I wanted. The two leaned over to one side while I climbed into the rather muddy water over the other side.

Minute jelly creatures were whirling around me everywhere. I kept descending. Only when I could no longer see the surface did the bottom become visible below me. It was flat and sandy and gently sloping. When I reached it I saw that it was extensively covered with green growth and low clumps of coral.

It was some time before I discovered the first pearl-oyster. But after that I kept finding them everywhere. They were not very large and most of them stood upright, their shells slightly open. Sometimes there were four or five of them in a cluster. Most of them were growing on corals or stones.

My knife drawn, I swam from one to another, and before they had time to close I had cut through their muscles and was pulling the halves apart. I was seized with the fever of a treasure seeker. With trembling fingers I probed the flesh of each oyster, looking for a pearl. Behind me trailed a growing swarm of fish, fighting over the dead oysters. If a shark had come at that moment I feel sure I would not have noticed it.

After the first quarter-hour I calmed down a little. I began to examine the incidence and growth of the oysters and no longer expected to find a magnificent eardrop-sized pearl at my first try. In a few of the oysters I really did find small pearls, but they were firmly attached to the shells and therefore worthless. In the end I did succeed in finding one sizeable pearl which was attached to the shell at only one small point.

I could hardly believe my eyes when a shark suddenly appeared before me. It was pale grey with a pointed nose, rather fat and certainly over ten feet long. Under its belly swam two large shark suckers. I started guiltily, like a boy caught raiding the larder. And this, in turn, frightened the shark. It jerked round and was gone the next moment.

The disturbed sand in the water, now slowly settling again, marked the spot where the shark had been an instant before.

I remained submerged until my oxygen was used up. Having seen a part of these oyster banks I could well imagine the rest. There were spots where I knew in advance I would find an oyster. It was just like looking for edible fungi in a forest, when an expert knows in advance under what tree or shrub he should look.

Only during my ascent did I realize that I had got considerably deeper than I had thought. In the cloudy darkness I had lost all orientation. I surfaced a good distance away from the boat. Mahmud and the fisherman appeared to be sleeping. When I called to them they sat up and paddled over to me.

Far more profitable and of greater scientific interest than my visit to the pearl banks of Dongonab was my experience near the small island of Om Grush, south east of Dongonab on the edge of an atoll. The name of the island meant 'mother of sharks', and when I informed the fisherman that we would take our canoe there the following morning he accepted my instructions with a stony face. Mahmud, too, wore a rather odd expression.

Om Grush turned out to be a semicircular heap of rubble, no more than thirty yards across, with a small stone pyramid at the centre and surrounded by pounding surf. The only place to make fast the boat would be on the leeward side, where the waves from right and left overlapped in an area of turbulence. I do not know what Mahmud was thinking about, but close to the island we very nearly capsized. An opposing wave spun us round, the sail whipped across, a huge breaker struck our side, and a cascade of water came over the gunwale. At the last moment the canoe righted itself and we reached what little shelter the island offered. After some fierce paddling we got to the spot at the edge of the reef where the waves from the two directions met behind the island. But since these wave trains never arrived simultaneously the boat was being tossed to and fro.

I jumped out on to the shallow flat of the reef, secured the anchor more firmly, and through the waist-deep water hurried to the island. It consisted entirely of coral detritus washed smooth by the waves, with a few fine pieces of red organ pipe coral between them.

I took the mask and dived under the spray of the surf. As soon as the view cleared I saw countless brilliantly red fish hovering over the projecting green corals. A little further down were eighty or a hundred idiot fish. The astonishing thing was that looking down over the projecting corals I found myself gazing into a bottomless abyss. There was no sign of a reef face further down. It looked as though the island was freely floating in the sea—even below it there seemed to be blue water.

In fact, of course, the coral in the surf zone had formed an overhang of several yards, and not until I dived underneath this overhang did I see the the vertical reef below. The small island, on this side at least, resembled a tower rising from the deep like the stalk of a mushroom. It was possible that an elevation on the sea floor was enough to give rise to such a structure. If it had not assumed the shape of a pyramid but had risen with vertical walls, this might be due to the fact that the corals on the fringe thrived more than the rest and in consequence formed an overhang. Wherever they were smothered by corals on top of them they would die off and the overhang would crumble, leaving a vertical wall.

I had just been pursuing this idea when an uncertain feeling warned me to

120

turn my head. Behind me a giant of a shark had appeared—certainly some thirteen feet long. Like a gleaming projectile it was barely moving through the water, looking in my direction, ready to strike. I quickly focused and photographed it. Then I race to the surface, pushed through the cover of foam, breathed quickly, wound the film on and dived again.

But I was not to get a second shot. The shark had turned and was now making straight for me. And not—as lesser sharks had often done—out of curiosity or exuberance, intending to turn away again at close range, but with the unmistakable intention of attacking me.

It was beating its fins with increasing speed and its entire body was now one single movement directed towards me, with the sickle-shaped mouth showing clearly. I swam towards it but I knew instantly that this beast would not be scared off by this manoeuvre. I had only one other weapon: with a shrill cry I expelled air into the water.

I was flung back by a surge of water. In spite of its speed the shark had veered round shortly before reaching me and—just as those in the Caribbean had done—was racing downwards with alarmed fin beats. But almost at once it about-turned and came up for a new attack. Since I had no air left for a second yell and since moreover it was extremely doubtful whether such a yell would help a second time, my only salvation lay in a hasty retreat.

With a supreme effort I covered the few yards which separated me from the boat and flung myself in over the side. Mahmud caught my kicking legs and pulled them in. My head had landed straight on the charcoal brazier. There was a commotion under the surface and the shark struck the boat.

Mahmud seized an oar and thrust it into the water with the same determination that I had observed in him at Port Sudan when he was fighting another felucca-owner who had offered me a cheaper boat.

The shark dived under the boat to the other side. It was evidently annoyed at having lost such a tasty morsel. I raised no objection when the old fisherman untied the boat without awaiting my orders.

I knew that there was no absolute safety with the 'tigers of the sea'. I had known it since our expedition to Greece, where not even yelling had been effective because the sharks were accustomed to the burst of bombs which were unlawfully used there for fishing. This time my yell had just about saved me. Some measure of risk, obviously, would always attach to this method of marine exploration. The chemical means developed by the U.S. Navy for the protection of baled-out airmen were certainly no defence against sharks attacking with such speed and determination, and even if some special explosives, rockets or poison weapons were to be developed for killing sharks, this would merely be going from the frying-pan into the fire. A dying shark, lashing

121

about, would certainly attract other even more furious ones within seconds.

Our voyage out to the atoll had taken five hours and our voyage back was taking another five. Dusk had fallen and Muhammad Qol was already in sight when we passed a stretch of water with countless little pointed waves dancing on its surface. On closer inspection these waves turned out to be small pointed fins. No fewer than forty devil rays had assembled here in a gigantic swarm.

I leapt overboard and from the distance saw two large white bellies turning towards each other. But it was too late. Below water it was too dark for photography or observation. As I clambered back into the boat Mahmud assured me with a gesture that these devil rays would certainly still be there the following day.

I tossed about sleeplessly all night. The following morning the sky was overcast. The sea looked like a sheet of lead without the slightest wave. A fisherman was cleaning his dug-out canoe, and a few women were strolling out into the desert. The village was awakening. I lay down again and slept the sleep of the dead. At nine o'clock Mahmud called me and we got ready to sail out again.

We dragged the boat ashore on a sandy island, near the spot where we had seen the rays. Mahmud thought this was the best place for observing their reappearance. While he and a small boy were lighting a fire I strolled about the island, keeping an eye on the sea and collecting a few pretty shells.

I was getting fidgety. Where were those devil rays? Mahmud explained that they would not appear till about noon.

My companions meanwhile were drinking coffee. They urged me to join them and thrust into my hand one of those small cups without handles. Mahmud was offering round some sticky roasted dates. His right leg was stretched out sideways and tied to his big toe was a fishing line leading into the shallow water. I only noticed it at the moment his toe was jerked.

Hopping on his other leg Mahmud followed the line, and a moment later we saw a large creature thrashing about in the shallow water. This must be some kind of ray. Mahmud pulled with all his strength—then he reeled back and the line was slack again.

I had my mask handy and raced into the water. A trail of disturbed sand clearly showed me the way the creature had taken. Suddenly, in about six feet of water, the trail ended.

What had happened to the creature? I looked more closely at the sandy bottom and discovered a pair of eyes barely visible above the sand. And now I could also see the outline of the creature which had skilfully buried itself. It was a 'halavi', a guitar fish—a creature halfway between a ray and a shark.

I was about to get my harpoon but changed my mind. Cautiously I approached the spot where three fins showing through the sand betrayed the position of the longish tail. A swift movement—and I had got it. The guitar fish wriggled and thrashed about but I held on to it. I had to watch out, though, to avoid being bitten. Projecting from its head was a jelly-like transparent shovel-shaped nose which was striking out in all directions. The fish was dragging me down while I was trying to drag it ashore. At last it was overcome and I pulled it into the shallow water where Mahmud received it with great joy.

There was still no sign of the devil rays. At a good distance away we noticed some birds flying about over the water, always in the same spot. It struck me that I had seen just such birds above the devil rays the night before. I quickly ordered all our stuff to be loaded back into the canoe and we paddled off in that direction.

It took us over an hour. Slowly we were approaching the devil ray area. The whole sea seemed to be seething. By their screeching the birds made it clear that we were not welcome. Everywhere small fish were leaping up over the surface and were being snatched and devoured by the birds. And every-where below the surface were the huge mouths which devoured everything that crossed their path.

I took a number of pictures from the boat and then slipped into the water. At first I only saw innumerable fish streaking one way or another in excited swarms. They were being chased not only by the devil rays and the birds, but also by mackerel and some long silvery fish. Then the wall of fishes on my left divided and a large devil ray came swimming straight towards me.

It did not seem to see me at all. Blissfully flapping its wings it came closer. I clicked my shutter several times, shortening the focus, took a picture of the rectangular mouth, but the giant continued unconcerned. Its eyes rigid and glassy, it simply passed over me. In doing so it touched me—and at the same moment rolled over, whipping its wings and dealing me a terrible blow across my back. I thought my spine was broken. Although the creature's mouth is not dangerous—I had seen its sparse row of teeth in its lower jaw at quite close quarters—the movements of this giant when alarmed certainly were. To have knocked me out even for a brief moment would have been enough. Below me was a watery abyss.

Most of the devil rays were brown, but a few were pitch black. One had a strangely discoloured area on its back. They were swimming singly, in pairs, or in entire families of three and four, making a clean sweep among the fish and countless strombs which were floating in the water. The disproportion between their terrifying mouths and the minute size of their quarry was as grotesque as that between an elephant's trunk and the lump of sugar one feeds it. Like fantastic giant birds they were moving through the water with regular beats of their wings, at times extended forward and at times flicked across their mouths in order to trap some creature.

There were two of them which I could identify by external characteristics, and it was clear to me that, after the third or fourth encounter, they recognized me. I had never observed anything of the kind in bony fishes although these stand higher on the evolutionary ladder than cartilaginous fishes. It is an interesting fact that the cartilaginous fishes such as rays and sharks seem to surpass all others in intelligence.

I just about flung myself aside as a totally wild pair of devil rays raced past me. I had a good idea now of the kind of scene in a shoal of devil rays at mating time. Even the brief love play I witnessed was so tempestuous that the two beasts simply ran down anything that crossed their path.

Back in the boat—which was now following the shoal—I loaded a new film, and then I got into the water once more. Everything I experienced was so fantastic that I very nearly wondered whether I was not just dreaming. I had never felt fitter than at that moment. I had no fear whatever, and the emanation of so many waving bodies swept me along as if I belonged to the swarm myself. It was like a fever, a delirium of assurance, such as I had not previously experienced. I scarcely noticed my brief moments of surfacing to fill my lungs.

Later, as another devil ray was swimming at a depth of fifteen feet, I pushed forward over its back, between its flapping wings, and got right to the edge of its mouth with my camera. The beast did not notice me until I had taken my photograph. I rolled up into a ball and let the commotion pass over me.

I next loaded a colour film and repeated my shots. Then I took the film camera and shot a long sequence of the mouth of a devil ray coming straight at the camera. I had now been among them for a couple of hours and they were beginning to disperse. One of the creatures, with a misshapen swelling on its head, was acting oddly. It was shaking itself as if trying to get rid of something and also tried to scare me off by swimming straight at me.

I suddenly wondered whether, in order to investigate this monster, I might not kill it. If I fixed my harpoon head to the boat with a long rope and harpooned the devil ray through its wing, so that in trying to escape it would be obstructed at one side, my plan might work.

I knotted up all the lines I had with me into a strong rope with our anchor rope. If I was successful I might sell the ray's skin to a museum. The creature was certain to weigh over half a ton—but at that moment nothing seemed impossible to me.

I did not have to wait long by the boat before the black fellow hove into sight again. A little to my right it dived; I followed it and thrust my harpoon right through one of its wings. In the next instant the steel shaft had been bent to a right angle and the rope was being pulled away at great speed. On the surface I saw the boat suddenly turning and moving off. Mahmud, the old fisherman and the boy screamed and gesticulated. It looked as if it had suddenly been fitted with an engine.

Then it halted and began to turn. The devil ray clearly wanted to descend vertically and Mahmud was trying to grab the rope and pull it up. Since the main weight was to the fore and the ray was pulling downwards, the canoe's bows dipped deep while its stern rose out of the water. And since the devil ray was clearly racing around in a circle, the boat, too, was spinning round as well as rocking up and down.

I made for the boat as fast as I could, determined to work my way down the rope with my knife. But this was not to be. I saw a shark swishing past, also in the direction of the boat, and almost simultaneously the devil ray leapt out of the water quite close to the craft. Mahmud tried to haul in the rope, but just then it was snatched from his hands. There was a jerk, a report like a shot, and the rope had parted.

'Big shark!' Mahmud grinned happily as I clambered into the boat.

'Big *baksheesh*!' I replied in excellent spirits.

I did not yet feel the exhaustion that would come later. I had swum among the devil rays for more than two hours and taken photographs of anything worth photographing. I had every reason to be satisfied. These pictures were certain to guarantee our future expedition. Her sails filled, I could see my hoped-for research schooner heaving into sight.

I had ordered a farewell dinner for Bill and myself at the Ramona, the pleasantest restaurant in Port Sudan. We sat at one of the tables on the pavement, and we worked out that I had arrived in Port Sudan thirty-seven days ago.

The next morning Bill took me to the airport where Mahmud, whom I had generously rewarded, had turned up with his four children to say goodbye. There was nothing for it, I had to give each child a separate *baksheesh*. When I returned, he assured me, I could rely on him entirely.

We shook hands. 'In three months then?' Bill asked.

'Yes, in three months. Mid-April at the latest.'

He told me he would postpone his leave until July. I thanked him once more, boarded the machine and we took off. I saw Bill waving his hand and Mahmud's four children waving handkerchiefs. Then we rose in a wide circle above the chequer-board plan of the town and over the white lines of the off-shore coral reefs. Flying down the coast I had a last view of the islands of Mukawwar and Mayatib and tried to make out the atoll with the small island of Om Grush. Then I lay back in my seat and closed my eyes. Behind me lay an adventure more beautiful than any I was likely to experience again.

Shortly after my return to Vienna, Professor Storch, the Head of the Zoological Institute, organized a lecture for me in the Great Hall of the University. I was to speak about my adventures. About twice as many people turned up as there was room for. In the front row I recognized the Minister of Education.

Without much reflection I began as follows: 'Ladies and gentlemen. Before I speak to you about my expedition to the Red Sea I should like to thank those whose financial help made this journey possible. These include several forms of Vienna girls' schools, but, more particularly, I. K., the Mystery Man.' I should explain that there was a tradition in Vienna of catch-as-catch-can wrestling matches being held in the grounds of the Vienna Skating Club. Lately these had taken a sensational turn. An unknown man, wearing a mask and calling himself I. K., had been challenging the best wrestlers in the competition. This man was supple as a panther and, with some peculiar hold, succeeded in flooring one massive contestant after another. At first the public's sympathies had been with the Mystery Man, but when he defeated a great public favourite there had been some trouble and a good many seats had been smashed. As these contests were highly profitable the Skating Club did not want the police to ban these fights, and the biggest Vienna tabloid daily had therefore published a letter from I. K. to the effect that he had wrestled all that time without getting a single penny. He had, however, suggested to the Skating Club that in lieu of payment to him they might make a donation of 10,000 Austrian Schillings for some educational purpose. He proposed that this sum should be assigned to Dr Hass's next diving expedition. And in fact this human panther had personally handed over to me, in the ring, an envelope containing this sum. I distinctly saw the Minister of Education wincing at my mention of my mysterious benefactor. The next day a gentleman from his Ministry rang up to say that they would be pleased to discuss some official support for my work.

But although a most welcome amount was in fact authorized by the Ministry, this came nowhere near solving our financial problems.

I could see no other means of raising the enormous sum necessary for a new ship than by making a successful film. But in order to shoot such a film I would have to take four or five men to Port Sudan with me and allow a shooting time of about three months. Moreover, a ship would have to be hired. My photographs of the coral reefs, and especially those of the devil rays, were published by the leading illustrated periodicals of most big countries—but

Will man one day adapt to a permanent aquatic existence and enjoy underwater performances in submarine theatres? Will he be subjected, immediately upon birth, to a surgical operation—performed in a submarine hospital—to enable him to move freely between the surface and a depth of 6,600 feet? This prediction has been seriously made. However, biological and economic reasons alike completely rule out such a course of development.

A thirteen-foot tiger shark attacking. It took us years to discover a specimen of this dangerous species of shark. Eventually, in 1951, we spotted two of them off the Cocos Islands. One of them swam at me slowly but purposefully. I struck at its head with the point of my shark spear. It turned away but later made two more attacks. Then it disappeared.

Over: A sixteen-foot grey shark in the Aegean; behind its tail fin is Alfred von Wurzian. There are also large sharks in the Mediterranean, except that one hardly ever catches sight of them there. The one in the picture was attracted by detonated dynamite.

Above: *A brittlestar on a gorgonian at a depth of 210 feet. Its camouflage colour—a matching red—is surprising in view of the fact that, because of the absorption of light by the water, all reds appear as grey from one hundred feet down.*

Right: *A strange clam I discovered on a sandy bottom in the Nicobar Islands. It turned out that the highly developed eye belonged to a female octopus (Octopus aegina) which had laid its eggs between the empty shells. Its tentacles with their suction pads adhered so firmly to the shells that it was able to open and close them just as their original owner had done.*

On long voyages our scientists had to take their share of watch duty. At the helm of the Xarifa is Dr Ernst Gerlach, a marine worm specialist and an enthusiastic yachtsman.

even the considerable sum they yielded was not enough to meet our budget.

I negotiated with a Viennese distributor who showed interest in my project. Herr Schuchmann was anxious to help but explained that the market for documentaries was limited. 'It would be different, of course, if you could work in some kind of plot.' He turned his eyes on Lotte, my secretary, who was with me. 'Why don't you take Fräulein Lotte with you?' And that was how Lotte's wish came true. She had joined my Institute in Vienna as a scientific assistant and secretary two years before, but with the secret intention of taking part in one of my expeditions. I soon disillusioned her—not because I doubted that a girl might have the necessary ability, but because I foresaw all kinds of tensions. Lotte accepted her fate, or at least pretended to. As I subsequently discovered, she had been training in a Vienna swimming-pool three times a week, before coming to the office in the morning, and once, while I was away lecturing, she had borrowed my underwater camera and taken some very creditable photographs of fish and algae in a backwater of the Danube. The water had been icy and therefore very clear. Under the heading 'Expedition into the Vienna Polar Sea' she had published an illustrated report in an Austrian magazine. All that had occurred even before my trip to the Red Sea. The distributor's idea was not therefore too far-fetched, and I suddenly realized that the only way of raising the necessary money for my project was by a mixture of documentary and feature film. In this manner I might eventually get a new ship. I agreed.

Lotte has described her experiences in a book of her own (*Girl on the Ocean Floor*, Harrap, 1972). The voyage was not exactly smooth and successful. What I had not foreseen was the fact that with her participation we would gain a really first-class diver and an incredibly courageous one. I had merely intended to take her along, willy nilly, in order to shoot a few pretty sequences with her in the shallow water. But things were to take a different turn.

In addition to my film hopes I also had another iron in the fire. There was a chance of getting my ship through some commercial marine research. All my observations so far had suggested that fish recognized each other by the nature of their fin movements—especially in dark or opaque water—and that therefore the recording of these vibrations and their artificial propagation in the sea might open up new possibilities for the fishing industry. Among fishes living in shoals the individual is first attracted to and then held within the shoal by the vibrational melody emitted by the shoal. If one were to succeed in radiating this sound artificially, then fish such as herring could be induced to form shoals around a loudspeaker and might thus be easily guided into a net. The fishes emitting particular vibrational melodies in their love play might similarly— in the interests of commercial fishing—be misled by the artificial production of such vibrations. Furthermore, predators which recognized their prey by its fin movements might be trapped by the emission of such impulses. It was probably this last possibility that would be the easiest to realize. In our experience sharks suddenly emerged from the deep sea whenever a speared fish wriggled on the harpoon head. It should be possible to record this wriggling on magnetic tape and then retransmit it, amplified, under water. If we succeeded in doing this we should be opening up very real new opportunities both for commercial shark catching and for anti-shark measures near bathing beaches.

I had taken out appropriate patents and got some specialized firms to manufacture an underwater microphone and an underwater loudspeaker for me. Philips had put a studio tape recorder at my disposal for my investigations. A special recording technician was to accompany us to operate the equipment. Admittedly, we needed a ship in the Red Sea, a ship which we could anchor at the spot where big fish could be speared and sharks attracted. Finally I would have to find a mobile generator there. But these endeavours could well form part of the film story. I therefore combined these two possible sources of income. As a setting for the film story the abandoned town of Suakin seemed to me particularly suitable, or rather the coral reefs which had strangulated the harbour of this once flourishing trading centre. The main theme of the film was to be our search for the devil ray, that terror of the natives. Lotte, as the first girl ever to dive in the Red Sea, and the luring of sharks were to be further elements of the plot. As for the rest, that would have to work out in accordance with what befell us once we were there. I suspected that the Red Sea still had a lot to reveal to us, a lot which had remained hidden from me on my first visit. I was to be proved right.

Right: *The coral cod* (Cephalopholis argus) *also display magnificent colours in the tropical seas. They almost invariably keep close to the grottos they inhabit.*

FILM-MAKING AGAINST THE ODDS

Riding a Shark

The sea is reluctant to reveal its secrets. We have often been asked how, on our skindiving expeditions, we managed to face up to the great marine creatures. But in fact this was considerably easier than finding them. Some of them we sought for many years in oceans all over the world. We dived at spots where the natives watched us fearfully, at spots where they predicted certain swift death for us—and nothing happened. We had to search huge areas before encountering any legendary monsters at all.

One such rare encounter was on 7th May 1950.

We were at the start of my second expedition to the Red Sea. We had set out from Suakin early in the morning, and the flat desert coast with the lonely silhouette of the ancient ruined city had dissolved behind us in the mist. We were about eight miles offshore, sailing over a mirror-smooth surface which blended into the sky with virtually no skyline. The minute droplets of mist suspended in the air made the low sun appear like a blurred Chinese lantern behind a frosted window-pane.

There were five of us in the boat—Wawrowetz, Gerry Weidler, Lotte, Mahmud and myself. Somewhat sleepily, the men unshaven, we were keeping a sharp look-out. We expected at any moment to see the sickle-shaped wing tips of the giant devil rays appear on the surface.

During my first stay in these waters I had succeeded in swimming close up to these creatures and photographing them underwater. My pictures had made the round of the world's illustrated magazines, and these creatures were now to be the principal actors in our film. Lotte was beside me in the bows, her camera ready for action. Behind us, neatly laid out, were diving masks, harpoons, breathing equipment and underwater cameras.

The sea was utterly lifeless. We could see deep into the clear water but there was no trace of a fish anywhere. Just small strombs floated past us. I scooped up a few of them with my hand. In the water on my palm they continued to flutter merrily, like minute butterflies.

'That's not a bad sign,' I said to Lotte. 'It was just the same last time. These strombs seem to be the favourite diet of the devil rays.'

Soon afterwards we saw a line of foam in the distance, with numerous birds rising and dipping above it. We sailed closer. We saw a blurred black shadow under the disturbed water. The line of foam slowly moved on. Suddenly the birds panicked and streaked away. The foam subsided. By the time we reached the spot there was nothing to be seen.

We crossed and recrossed the spot, staring into the clear water. But all we saw was strombs. Meanwhile the birds were collecting over a new spot, a short distance away. We followed them. About five minutes later Mahmud excitedly gripped my shoulder.

We looked back. A little way behind us, at almost the precise spot we had just patrolled, there was a tall black triangle on the surface. It looked like the dorsal fin of a shark except that it was much bigger. It could be a piece of wood that had risen up to the surface. But where would it have come from? The sea here was 1,600 feet deep. Besides, the triangle was slowly moving over the water.

We turned and sailed back. It was becoming increasingly clear that what we had before us must be a creature of exceptional dimensions. Through the calm water we could clearly make out a shadow which seemed to have no end to it. A few hundred yards from it I had the motor cut and slipped on my fins.

Mahmud rolled his eyes and started to chatter excitedly. He bent down as if taking a heavy burden on his shoulders, then lifted it like Atlas carrying the globe, and then let it crash down on one side. He repeated this act several times, rolling his eyes all the while. He seemed quite desperate at my failure to understand his meaning.

'Should we follow you in the boat?' Gerry asked.

'Yes, do—but row cautiously and quietly.'

'It's got some patches or stripes,' Wawrowetz said.

I hung the underwater camera around my neck and slid into the sea. My harpoon was fastened by a loop to my shoulder. In this way I had my hands free for swimming and taking pictures, but could grab the spear any time I needed it.

The water was pleasantly warm. Below me lay an abyss without parallel. I started swimming towards the fin. It was moving only slowly over the surface. Its rear edge was frayed.

The closer I got the more difficult I found it to control my fear. No real danger is quite so bad as something one does not know and cannot see, something that one's fancy invests with fantastic details. Above water the mysterious fin was already almost within reach but I still saw nothing below.

Nothing but the empty, blue, bottomless sea. The silver darts of the sun-rays were my only companions. In throbbing bundles they pierced the water from all sides, converging far below me, at the exact point marked by my own shadow.

At last I was able to make out the first vague outlines. Then the veil lifted completely. What I saw was so exceptional that I remained hovering in the water motionless. Before me was a shark at least twenty-five feet long. Its entire huge body was covered with hundreds of white dots.

It was hanging under the surface, almost motionless. Only the large, crescent-shaped tail fin was slowly moving to and fro. Near its head the spots were small and numerous, towards the tail they were larger and arranged in rows. Between them ran projecting edges. The strongest of these terminated in the root of the tail.

The most unusual feature was the creature's mouth. In contrast to all other sharks it was not on the underside, a short distance behind the nose, but right in front at the foremost point of its head. It was slightly opened and had lips. In spite of its enormous size the creature looked good-tempered and harmless. Like a bed of ox-eye daisies the giant was floating below the surface.

I instantly recognized the shark from reproductions I had seen in scientific works. I had even seen a stuffed specimen at the Natural History Museum in London. It was a whale shark, the largest of all the sharks. Since it was first described by a South African zoologist in 1849 it had only been sighted by ships about a hundred times. It lives in the tropical seas—in the Indian Ocean off the Philippines, and off the coast of Lower California. Some of the observed creatures had the incredible length of sixty-five feet and a weight of up to ten tons. Most of them had swum calmly and slowly just below the surface. They were quite harmless.

Just like the largest rays—the devil rays—these whale sharks feed on plankton, which they filter out of the water with their feathered gills. The American research worker William Beebe had met a whale shark nearly forty feet long on his Zaca expedition, and one of his men had harpooned the creature from the boat. The shark had dived away but had reappeared a quarter of an hour later, when attempts had been made to sink further harpoons into its body. But its skin had grown taut and turned into an armour against which the steel harpoon heads had been bent. Beebe had fired two revolver bullets into the shark's head at close range, but the giant had calmly continued on its way. The line of the first harpoon had then been made fast on the expedition ship, but the resistance had been too great and its point had torn out of the shark's body. With regular flips of its tail the monster had slowly made off.

The American Williamson had approached a whale shark with his diving craft and had filmed its spotted skin through the observation window. But to the best of my knowledge no human swimmer had yet observed this creature under water.

The shark had meanwhile noticed me. It still seemed suspended under the surface by its dorsal fin, watching me with its small eye. My closer approach did not seem to worry it in the least.

I was so excited that I wasted my first few exposures. I had forgotten to set the range and I had forgotten to allow for the parallax of the viewfinder. None of these shots was subsequently any use. I was terrified by the thought that the creature might take fright at me and suddenly dive away. But the giant showed no alarm and continued on its way quite slowly, with a wonderfully relaxed movement.

Whenever I surfaced I heard excited shouts from the boat. Everyone wanted to know what I had seen. Gerry was standing in the bows, his spear at the ready, yelling across to ask if I needed help.

I called back that the shark was totally harmless but that Gerry should come in just the same. I was now less than six feet away from its body. To my astonishment my presence did not worry the creature in the least. I swam alongside it and touched its skin. It was rough, like medium-grade sandpaper, and the white spots looked as though they had been applied with a rough brush. Between the spots were narrow white wavy lines which might be taken for the rippling reflections of sunlight. Slowly the body glided past me and the huge tail fin swung over towards me. I felt reckless. I grabbed its upper end with both my hands. Immediately I was being pulled through the water by a calm, assured force. I was being towed along in a big snaking motion first ten feet to the right and then ten feet to the left. But the movement was clearly getting more irritable and rapid.

I hurriedly let go. I seemed to have alarmed the good-natured fellow after all. But its movements instantly slowed down again and a moment later it was swimming as calmly as before.

A little distance away Gerry was hovering below the surface. He was a good swimmer and had joined my expedition from love of adventure. But he probably had not expected that within three weeks he would be swimming alongside a twenty-five-foot shark in a bottomless sea. I motioned him to come closer and we took the shark between us.

I now succeeded in taking a number of shots showing the creature against a human scale. I had recovered my composure and was working with concentration. I systematically photographed the shark from all sides. As we subsequently discovered on examining the pictures, ideas about the shape of this shark's head had not been quite correct. Most drawings had reproduced it as though it had a raised forehead. It is probable that the drawings were made after the creatures had been dragged ashore, dead, when the head had sunk down to the ground under its own weight. My whale shark had no trace of such a 'thinker's forehead'. Its back ran in a perfectly straight line from its upper lip, while its belly curved up towards its lower lip by way of a bulging 'gorge'. Its mouth in consequence was directly below the surface of the water,— a most useful arrangement since that is where most of the plankton is found.

The shark had now caught sight of the boat and was approaching it in a wide arc. Our little cockleshell was a hive of activity. Lotte and Wawrowetz were climbing over the thwarts, changing films and lenses. Their first shots too—as we discovered later—all turned out useless.

I swam across and got the cine-camera.

I yelled across to Gerry to come and swim alongside the shark but not to touch it.

"From in front or from the side?'

'Obliquely from behind!'

A moment later we were under water. I held my breath—in my viewfinder was the picture of a lifetime. In front was the shark, just like a submarine—and alongside it the tiny human being approaching it.

The camera's clockwork purred—and abruptly came to a stop. I turned the handle, shook the camera—to no avail. I hit it with my fist—but the mechanism was dead. The film must have jammed. With a curse I swam back to our boat and thrust the camera into Wawrowetz's hand.

'Use this one in the meantime,' Lotte said, passing me our second cine-camera. I grabbed it and swam back to the shark.

It was a grotesque situation. Our second camera was fitted with a telescopic lens. We used it for close-ups, chiefly to fill the frame with small fishes. And now I had this unique giant creature, in especially clear water and brilliant sunshine, and in my hands was a camera with which at best I could get only one-third of the monster into the frame. Even if I retreated to the limit of visibility I only had about half its body in the picture.

The shark had descended a little and was now swimming at a depth of ten feet. I first aimed the camera at one of its eyes. It was small and very mobile. It reminded me of the eye of an elephant. In both cases there is a huge mass of flesh covered with a thick skin, and in it a tiny peep-hole through which the creature's personality gazes out into the world. The expression of the shark's eye was intelligent and understanding. It seemed to watch me with interest as I closed in on it and simultaneously adjusted the focus. I halted and allowed the shark to swim past me. While it was doing so I could see that its eye continued to be fixed on the camera and was twisted right back. It was like the eye of a passenger in a submarine vessel looking out of a porthole and watching me curiously.

I quickly rewound the camera and swam a little way ahead of the shark. I started my next sequence once more from its head, but this time I kept the focus at five feet and panned the camera straight down the creature's back to the tip of its tail. Even though I could only get part of the creature into my picture with this camera, the sequence would nevertheless show the scale of the giant. Once more I rewound the clockwork and swam ahead of the shark. Although it was moving slowly it was by no means easy to overtake it—especially as I had to surface from time to time like an out-of-breath dolphin. And now for the mouth.

In front of its half-opened jaws were a dozen small pilot fish moving in and out of the dark opening as though this were the most natural thing. A few of them advanced a short distance into the clear water, but when I came closer with the purring camera they escaped into the shark's mouth. There is a widespread belief that these fish guide the shark to its prey—that is how they got their name. But in fact we have nowhere observed this, and in this particular case it would be technically impossible. Certainly the small fish could not guide this shark to its food, the plankton.

What then did they want of it? What were they seeking in its mouth? I assumed that this situation was similar to that with the devil rays, in whose wide-open mouth I had also observed pilot fish which fed on small parasitic crustacea there. This is a case of genuine symbiosis, an arrangement for the mutual advantage of both parties. The pilot fish clean out the mouths of the devil rays and the whale sharks, removing parasites which have settled there, and as a collateral these giants permit them to live in their mouths without swallowing them. The great advantage to the small fish is the plentiful food they find there and the protection they enjoy against their enemies.

I dived under the shark's belly and filmed a few slender shark-suckers which were swimming there, pressed close to its skin. Suddenly I saw one of them making a quick sortie out into the clear water and snapping for a small fish. This insignificant incident provided me with the answer to a question which had long baffled us.

It used to be assumed that these shark-suckers attached themselves to sharks and other large marine creatures by means of a suction cup on their forehead in order to gain a free ride and feed comfortably on the food refuse of their host. But we had frequently observed to our astonishment that in fact— at least during the day—they seemed not to be making any use of their suction cups at all. Although they kept close to their host's skin we had never seen them actually attaching themselves.

Indeed, I had been able to observe this on my own body. Small shark-suckers had frequently come and joined me and had swum along with me, just as if I were a shark. They had kept under my stomach and if I disturbed them there had moved between my legs. In this way they had accompanied me over great distances. But never once had one of them as much as touched me with its suction cup.

The shark-suckers evidently use the large marine creatures for protection and concealment. They swim along pressed closely to their bodies and are thus able to approach lesser fish unnoticed. These small fishes, as we have often observed, do not seem to be afraid of the very large marine creatures.

'Camera ready!' Wawrowetz called out to me as I surfaced again. I quickly swam to the boat and collected it. I had lost all sense of space or time. As through a mist I saw Wawrowetz leaning over, taking one camera from me and hanging the other one around my neck. In spite of the strain I did not wish to make the smallest pause. When one has waited years for such an opportunity one finds one's system capable of quite an exceptional performance.

Gerry meanwhile had disappeared and I had to wait for him to surface again.

'We are repeating the sequence!' I yelled.

'What?'

'Dive down, swim alongside, but don't touch!'

'O.K.'

For the second time I had the thrilling experience of a unique sequence. The camera ran for two or three seconds—then its hum rose to a higher pitch. I felt like crying.

My effort counted for nothing compared with my helpless despair. This time the perforation of the film had torn and the sprocket was spinning without moving it. That was why it was running faster and at a higher pitch. The camera had to be opened and the film reloaded.

It took all my self-control to remain calm. I swam over to the boat and climbed in. I dried my hair and hands on Lotte's towel. Then I opened the camera myself in order to put it right.

The shark meanwhile came quite close to the boat. Perhaps it wanted to see what had happened to me.

But that was not what it wanted. It pushed its head immediately under our keel and began to scrape its skin against it.

Mahmud excitedly hopped from one side of the boat to the other, and I suddenly understood his earlier strange gesturing. These whale sharks, it seems, approach fishing vessels to rid themselves of troublesome parasites. They scratch their skin against them. And if a shark is particularly large or particularly

135

vigorous it may well happen that it lifts up the whole boat and overturns it. Thor Heyerdahl once told me that he had had a similar anxious moment in the Pacific when a large whale shark got under the *Kon-Tiki* and rubbed its back against the raft's rudder.

The camera was now open and I carefully loaded the film. But the perforation tore out again. I loaded another cassette—and just then came a shout across the water. Gerry, who was swimming a little way off, seemed to be quite beside himself. 'Another! Another!' he screamed.

I left the troublesome camera, picked up the telescopic camera again— Wawrowetz had meanwhile reloaded it—and was back in the water.

True enough, a second whale shark was approaching. It was a little smaller and was coming along quite confidently, just as if wanting to visit its friend under our boat. At a distance of about thirty yards it calmly turned and took another course. I pursued it, but it was shy and swam faster. Although I did my best to drive it back I had to give up after 200 yards. It had clearly taken fright and disappeared into the distance.

Could the two creatures belong together? Sharks perform a genuine copulation whereby the male twists itself round the female's body. I found it difficult to picture these good-natured giants in a state of excitement—racing through the vast spaces of the deep ocean, chasing each other and terrifying all other fishes by this spectacle.

Nothing is known about the age of these whale sharks. With bony fishes it is possible to calculate their age from the rings on their scales and the layers of their otoliths, but this is not possible with sharks. As a general rule the giants of the animal kingdom reach a very high age—simply because it takes decades to build up such a large body. Giant turtles reach an age of 300 years and the giant whales are similarly credited with over a hundred. Since the whale sharks are plankton eaters and do not find particularly plentiful supplies of food in the tropics, it is likely that they too take a long time to reach the size necessary for sexual maturity.

I swam back. The first whale shark was now hovering about ten feet away from the boat. Gerry was sitting on its back, reclining comfortably as if on a couch. I also saw a number of rough red stripes which I was sure had not been there before. These ran diagonally across its flank. As he saw me approaching Gerry triumphantly waved his harpoon. The steel shaft at its head—a moment before all rusty—was gleaming bright. Gerry had cleaned it up against the shark's skin. The rust red stripes were a further testimony to the creature's wonderful docility.

Mahmud was quite beside himself. In a kind of rapturous St Vitus' dance he hopped about in the boat as the two of us now climbed on to the shark's back. We held on to the stiff leathery dorsal fin, riding astride the shark. Anything I had experienced in fourteen years of skindiving paled before this incredible reality.

There is an ancient Hawaiian legend about two shipwrecked fishermen who at night clung to the dorsal fin of a huge shark and who, over the next few hours, were drawn by it close to an island. After our experience this seemed to me entirely possible.

'Now look,' I said to Gerry. 'You swim above its head, and the moment you hear me filming you pat its snout.'

'O.K.'

I swam a short distance ahead and then, camera running, I aimed straight at its mouth. I raised the camera towards Gerry who thereupon tapped the shark's snout with his flat hand. The obliging animal opened its mouth wide and I concluded my sequence with an internal view of its whitish fleshy throat.

Writing about this sequence later the film critic of the *New York Times*—whose verdict otherwise was very favourable—observed that this shot must have been made with a camera lowered into the sea. I should like to assure Mr Bosley Crowther at this belated moment that he was wrong. The sequence was shot in exactly the manner described.

I must equally reject the suggestion of a German fisheries biologist who claimed that we had first stunned the whale shark with dynamite. This suggestion is easily refuted, for if we really had used explosives then surely I could not have filmed the pilot fish in front of the shark's mouth or the shark-suckers under its belly. They would have been the first to have been killed by any explosion.

I knew that other sharks took fright if one screamed at them under water. I tried this out on our whale shark but it did not react in the slightest. We next took one of the small oxygen cylinders from our breathing apparatus and released the gas straight at its head at a pressure of 150 atmospheres. The shark turned aside a little—but that was all. A plankton-eater does not require sensitive perceptions—certainly not a giant of this magnitude who cannot have many enemies and who, moreover, is protected by a highly effective armour.

Lotte, Gerry and I slipped on our breathing apparatus in order to study the creature at leisure, but we only got there in time to watch its departure. Gradually the huge body began to move. The time for its visit was over and some invisible clock suggested to it that the moment of departure had come. It dipped and moved off at an oblique angle.

We gazed after the huge creature with a sense of reverence. There was something majestic and solemn about the gradual disappearance of the giant. In the vastness of the empty sea it was getting visibly smaller. It shrank more

137

and more, it faded and got paler, until only its flicking tail was discernible far away in the deep blue depths. Then that too melted into the infinite void and the sea was once more empty.

Three days later I was diving with Lotte at the harbour mouth of Suakin. It was Sunday. We had sailed out every morning before sunrise and had searched vast regions for whale sharks—in vain. Now, on Sunday, everyone was free to do what he liked. Wawrowetz and Gerry had got hold of some camels and wanted to ride out into the desert. Xenophon, back from Port Sudan, wanted to overhaul our equipment, which was showing considerable traces of wear. Lotte and I had sailed out with Mahmud. I wanted to show her how fish could be speared by the old and now almost forgotten method.

There were plenty of fish by the reef where we anchored. But I could not do a thing right. I was out of practice. My arm was slow and the fish invariably dodged my spear. The moment I dived they warned each other with their fin beats.

Lotte watched me for a while, then she swam into the shallow water and there hunted with a light catapult. Obstinately I continued my efforts. Among some tall corals, hard by the edge of the old channel, I caught sight of the caudal fin of a snapper. I dived down to the bottom a short distance away and cautiously crept up towards the coral.

At that moment the fin vanished and in its place appeared a slim brown shark.

I expended all my anger in a thrust which did not miss its target. The next moment I was being pulled along behind the shark. It was exceedingly small— only about my own length—but full of energy. The harpoon head had come off and was lodged in its tail but one of its barbs was projecting through the skin. It could tear out at any moment.

Without much hesitation I pulled myself up by the line and seized the shark by its caudal fin. Since sharks cannot as a rule turn their heads round to their tails this seemed an entirely safe spot. But my shark was the exception. It flung its head back and at the same moment I felt a stinging pain in my right fore-arm. As fast as I could I struggled up to the surface. I raised my arm complete with the shark's teeth sunk into it up into the air. That made it let go. My arm looked as if it had got into a meat mincer. The muscle was severed right to the bone and a large trail of blood was spreading around me.

I yelled across to our boat which was bobbing on the waves some 300 yards away. Mahmud had anchored it and had stretched himself out to sleep. As the wind was against us he could not hear me.

'What's the matter?' Lotte called out, swimming over to me rapidly.

'Stay where you are!' I shouted. I was afraid that the blood might attract bigger sharks. I too swam towards the shallow water, still dragging the shark behind me by the harpoon.

Lotte cast one alarmed glance at my arm then she swam alongside me, both of us yelling as loud as we could. Fortunately my wrist had protected the artery, otherwise I would have bled to death. Only when we had got quite close did Mahmud hear us. He leapt to his feet, quickly raised the anchor and came rowing towards us.

I do not know why I did not let go of the harpoon. I gave the shark to Mahmud who dragged it into the boat and beat it to death with a stick. Lotte and I clambered aboard at the other end. She gave me her thick Turkish towel and I tied it firmly around my wound. But within a minute the towel was coloured red. Mahmud took the starter cord of our outboard motor and tied off my arm at the shoulder.

Now of course we lacked the cord for starting the motor. After a great deal of confusion we at last got moving. Twenty minutes later, as we approached the rest house in Suakin—one of the few surviving buildings in this virtually abandoned city of ruins, and situated right at the waterside—we saw three strange figures waving to us from the terrace.

After my bad luck I was now exceptionally fortunate. It was the harbour master of Port Sudan who had made a Sunday excursion to Suakin with his wife and a friend of hers. One of the women was a trained nurse. The three packed me into their car at once and drove me to the wound-dressing station at the next village. When the wound was found to be serious they immediately drove me on to the Port Sudan hospital.

As one can never be sure what a shark has just eaten, a shark bite invariably involves the risk of blood poisoning. But my shark bite, fortunately, was entirely sterile. I was stitched up and—since I did not develop a temperature—discharged with a huge bandage the following day. But for the next three weeks I was not allowed into the water.

It was a new heavy blow for our expedition. With my good hand I typed my first report for an illustrated magazine to which we were under contract. What I wrote did not sound exactly credible. Within four days I had held two sharks by their tails. The first one—twenty-five feet long—had shaken me off, but we had subsequently ridden on its back. The other—barely six feet long and weighing thirty-five pounds—had nearly killed me.

The White Death

Let me say it at once: we never encountered any legendary giant octopuses.

No doubt octopuses and squids in general do grow to considerable size—huge specimens have been found in the stomachs of sperm whales—but these live at great depths and do not presumably come up often to regions reached by divers. Most tales of men wrestling with octopuses are no doubt the kind of tall story told by all fishermen, and those giant octopuses in American films are made of rubber and are artificially moved.

In our experience the most dangerous marine creatures are the sharks. Even though their aggressiveness has been greatly exaggerated, they certainly have been responsible for a sufficient number of grave injuries and deaths. Their teeth are amongst the most terrifying murder instruments in the animal kingdom. A twelve-foot shark can cleanly bite off an arm or a leg; a twenty-foot shark can bite a human body in two.

The teeth of a shark are described as a 'revolver set'. Just as bullets are automatically replaced in a revolver, so a shark's teeth are replaced in its mouth. They are arranged in several rows one behind the other, and if one row becomes worn out the next one takes its place.

The embryos of certain sharks show how these teeth have originated. They are ordinary skin scales which have grown into the shark's mouth across the edge of its jaws, from above and below, and have there developed more vigorously than on its body. Both layers of the skin are involved in this formation—the lower skin produces the core of the tooth and the upper skin then covers it with an exceedingly hard enamel. As the scales are arranged in rows, so are the teeth in the shark's mouth. And because the shark can convert scale structures into fully grown teeth again and again, its teeth are permanently renewed. It is the view of scientists today that the teeth of bony fishes, amphibians, reptiles and mammals—and hence also our own teeth—go back to these shark teeth. In the long line of our direct and indirect ancestors it is likely that teeth were first evolved by creatures belonging to the shark family. They have been taken over by all higher vertebrates and adjusted by them to each species' particular requirements, according to its way of life. Thus ultimately even the large tusks of the elephant derive from the so-called 'placoid scales' of the shark which cover its skin with thousands of minute teeth.

The idea that man, the crown of creation, should include in his ancestry the 'ugly' shark may be distasteful to some. But there is other evidence clearly supporting such a descent. The embryonic development of many animals repeats the features of their ancestors. Such reminders of a remote past are evident also in man. Thus the human embryo, in its fourth week, develops four gill arches which are subsequently back-developed and converted into other organs. The present-day diver, equipped with heavy breathing apparatus, may occasionally regret this loss.

The shark's teeth—that strange link between them and us—are interesting also in that they represent the best criterion for distinguishing between different species. The white shark, the most dangerous of the lot—also known as 'white death'—has large triangular teeth with sharp serrated edges like a saw. The equally feared tiger shark has curved and asymmetrical teeth. In the Australian grey nurse shark each tooth has been developed into a long two-edged dagger.

As sharks have no bones, their skeleton consisting of perishable cartilage, their teeth are the only part that is preserved of them after death. These are found in large numbers in the deep-sea mud—both of surviving and of long extinct species. Some of them are of alarming size. In the Cretaceous period—about 130 million years ago—there lived an ancestor of our white shark which, judging by the size of its teeth, must have reached a length of 100 to 130 feet. It would have been able to devour animals the size of an ox at one single bite.

It is possible that these ancestors still exist. The findings of the *Challenger* expedition suggest that their last appearance was not very long ago in terms of geological history. After all, the ancient coelacanth had been regarded as extinct for 60 million years until 1938 when a fishing vessel off the South African coast unexpectedly hauled up a living specimen from a depth of 230 feet.

At that time we were not particularly careful. In fact, thinking back to this second expedition to the Red Sea, I blame myself for a good many things.

When my arm had healed up we started diving near a sunken ship off Ata. I had known about this ship from my first expedition: about sixty years ago she had struck a reef in a storm and sunk in fifty to eighty feet of water. Although the bows had been completely shattered, her stern and mid-ship section were well preserved. The deck was almost horizontal and over the years had turned into a magnificent coral garden.

I examined the various species, some of which had grown faster than others, and just as if it were a coral reef filmed the fishes living in the wreck. Lotte helped me with the photographic camera while Gerry stood by with the harpoon to protect us against unwelcome surprises. All three of us wore our light-weight oxygen equipment which allowed us to spend an hour at depths of up to sixty-five feet.

When my film ran out I signalled to my two companions to wait for me and surfaced. I reloaded the camera. I descended again and found Lotte on her own. She was crouching on a large steel plate, looking rather dazed. As soon as she caught sight of me she gestured that she wanted to surface immediately. I swam up with her. Up by the boat we had to help her take off the breathing equipment. With a sigh of relief she climbed on board.

'What happened?' I asked. 'And where's Gerry?'

'He'll be back in a minute. He saw a fish and chased after it.'

'And you?'

'Oh, nothing special. I'm feeling much better now. But at the time I was so scared I could hardly move. As I was watching Gerry swim away the thought flashed through my mind: I hope no shark will choose just this moment to make an appearance! I turned my head—and there was a shark. I think it was about ten feet long. And with terribly vicious eyes! It moved straight above me and turned left to watch me with its left eye. I couldn't have moved even if I'd wanted to. Everything in me seemed frozen rigid. But perhaps it only wanted to inspect me.'

'Well, you've passed your baptism of fire,' I tried to reassure her and to apologize for ourselves.

She smiled a little. 'Yes, but I felt rather cold at the time!'

I thought of Lotte's parents who had entrusted their daughter to me for this unusual voyage, and I too felt a little shivery. I had not intended to let her dive with breathing apparatus just yet, but during the very first days one of our men dropped out because he could not stand the heat, and his apparatus therefore became available. And as Lotte had proved a skilful skindiver I yielded to her entreaties. Time and again she suprised us by her courage and perseverance.

On our arrival in Port Sudan I had said to her, 'From today on you are a man!' She understood and acted accordingly.

Apart from the sharks what worried us most were poisonous creatures. The greatest care is always necessary before touching anything at all on the tropical sea bed. There are poisonous corals which cause painful stings—such as the elkhorn coral belonging to the hydrozoa. Then there are sea urchins and starfish with very dangerous spikes. And finally there are numerous fishes which have developed often highly poisonous stings at the root of their tail, on their gills, or in their dorsal fins.

Whenever we speared fish which then escaped into a hole in the corals we avoided simply reaching into that hole. With a little bad luck there could be a moray eel lurking inside.

On the other hand, we found the notorious barracudas to be fairly harmless—with rare exceptions. Breder in his book *Marine Fishes of the Atlantic Coast* believes that these large pikes have been responsible for many an accident attributed to sharks. We were unable to confirm this either in the Caribbean or in the Red Sea. True, large solitary specimens approached us menacingly, but at a range of twelve or fifteen feet they invariably turned away and then followed us over great distances like faithful dogs. Sometimes they opened their teeth-studded mouths—but that was all. Even in shoals they mostly behaved timidly.

My first picture of a large shark: July 1939 off the south coast of Curaçao. Everyone thought we were crazy to be diving in those waters. It turned out, however, that it was far easier to ward off the sharks than to approach them. Only exceptionally do these notorious predators attack humans.

We were the first to use skindiving apparatus for filming and research purposes. In the waters off Greece in 1942 we explored submarine grottos and studied fishes, rays and sharks by turning ourselves into aquatic creatures.

Above: *A sting-ray weighing 220 pounds.*

Right: *A shark amidst a silvery shower of dead fish. The evil practice of dynamite fishing is causing a great deal of damage. Within seconds of the explosions sharks appear on the scene to participate in the banquet. These sharks do not react to yelling: their perceptions have been dulled by the explosions.*

Above: *It has been said that the whitelip shark (Carcharhinus longimanus) attacks every diver. This has not been our experience: this shark behaves no differently from other species.*

Left: *If one places mirrors in a coral reef one discovers that many fish regard their own mirror image as their worst rival for food—a member of their own species.*

Right: *Lotte proved to us that women are just as courageous as men. The outcome of her first voyage with us was that we got married.*

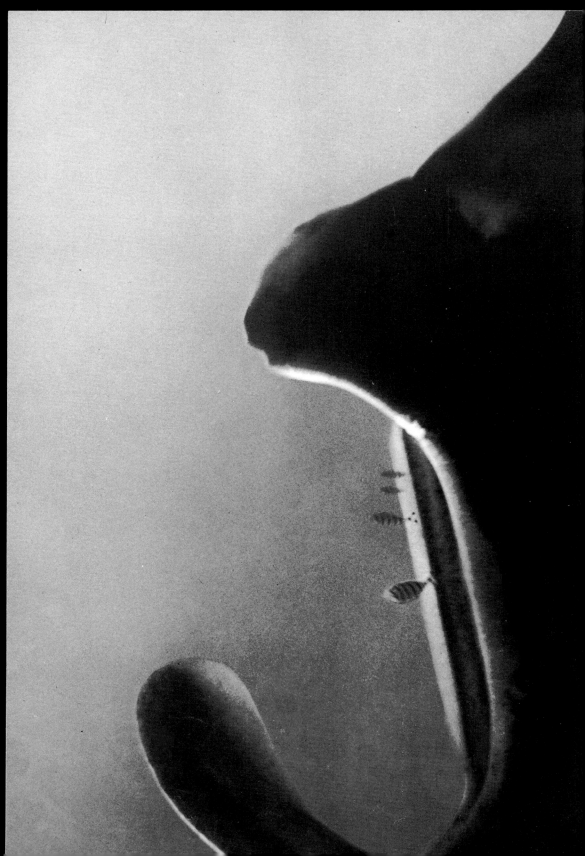

I was very anxious to shoot a sequence showing that these creatures were not dangerous. The opportunity for this arose when I encountered a shoal of forty or fifty barracudas in the passage between two reefs; they were hovering in the water, rigid and motionless. They were evidently sated and merely snapped up some small delicacy here or there from the current. When they caught sight of me they stared at me in their characteristic menacing way and one by one they awoke from their immobility until the entire shoal was surging inquisitively towards me.

I swam up to the boat and collected Lotte. She was to wait for the shoal to come close to her and then chase it away with her hands. Since she had just come up from an hour's diving her breathing apparatus was not ready for action. Xenophon gave her one of our spares.

'It's a bit on the big side for you,' he said, 'but it'll be all right.'

She strapped it on and we descended together. The barracudas were still in the same spot. I led Lotte to a coral on which she was to sit and hurriedly swam off a short way to gain the necessary distance for my shot.

The barracudas obliged and repeated their recent manouevre. In serried ranks they were approaching Lotte. Through the viewfinder I could see her glancing first at me then at the barracudas and then towards the surface—and suddenly she was furiously finning upwards.

I just about managed to catch her before she reached the top. I pulled her down by one leg, pushed her back to her coral and motioned her to sit still. When the barracudas were close enough she was to chase them away by moving her arms. As Lotte had in the past shown too much rather than not enough courage I did not understand her sudden fear. These barracudas were merely being inquisitive.

Lotte tried to explain something but there was no time. The barracudas were returning. I pushed her down on her coral, raced away, wound the camera and turned back. And I saw Lotte again racing to the surface with furious kicking motions.

Up in the boat we discovered that her action had nothing to do with the barracudas at all. In the hurry Xenophon had omitted to tighten the joints of her breathing tubes.

In our breathing apparatus the exhaled carbon dioxide was absorbed by a chemical in the bag carried on the back. Originally this chemical was caustic soda, but this was dangerous to the diver if water got in. We had therefore changed over to absorbent lime, as also used in submarine escape devices; this was entirely harmless although it had a slightly bitter taste.

Lotte's breathing bag was full of water. She was spitting and shaking herself. 'Ugh, that tastes frightful! It began coming through as I was descending, but I didn't want to spoil the sequence and so I swallowed the water. But then I got this bitter gravy in my mouth! And when you pulled me down again I just couldn't swallow fast enough. . . .'

Some skindivers who visited the Red Sea after us have described sharks as unpredictable. I would not endorse this judgment without reservation. It is, of course, true that they do not behave in exactly the same way everywhere—in Australia, in particular, we were to encounter some surprises—but on the whole the behaviour of the various species is fairly consistent.

As we frequently dived among the same reefs we came to know the sharks living there. Just like those in the Caribbean, the sharks in the Red Sea have their definite territory in which they are encountered time and again. Some of them had special characteristics, and these we recognized easily. As a rule they would appear the moment we started work, watch us for a while, and then vanish for the rest of the day. If we wanted to film them we had to do so during the first half-hour. Sharks are like an ocean police force. With their delicate senses they perceive the noise of a boat casting anchor or a person getting into the water, even over considerable distances, and turn up to see what is happening.

We have occasionally known lesser grey sharks and brown sharks suddenly racing up and circling a diver at very close range. Anyone experiencing this for the first time would inevitably regard this as an attack—but in fact it is merely playful behaviour by the young of the species. This is how a young shark tests its strength, and no doubt it derives some pleasure from frightening other creatures. I have seen them pounce in exactly the same way on shoals of fish and on turtles, certainly not with aggressive intent but because they enjoyed the reaction they produced.

It was on our very first encounter with sharks in the Caribbean in 1939 that we had discovered that even large specimens can be turned to flight if one swims straight at them without hesitation. A shark is used to seeing all other creatures flee before it. Hence if that strange species, man, comes swimming straight at it its reaction will be to escape and perhaps even to experience fear.

Our second discovery of those days—that sharks can be scared off by yelling at them at close range under water—was much derided at the time, but skindivers in various parts of the world have since successfully used our method. In 1943 it saved the lives of three survivors of a German U-boat off the West African coast. When they were attacked and bitten by sharks they remembered my report at the last moment, and by putting their heads under water and yelling they succeeded in driving the sharks away. The official American Air Force report *Airmen against the Sea* also advises aircrews who have come down in the sea to use yelling under water as an important means of defence against sharks.

Admittedly, we have also experienced exceptions. Many sharks—as for instance a species we encountered off the Azores—do not react at all. There are also regions where the sharks are insensitive, such as the waters off the Greek islands. We observed there in 1942 that the sensory perception of sharks had been blunted by the fishermen's use of dynamite. Much the same is probably true of sharks near open bathing beaches and therefore familiar with human voices, and of those which follow ships and get accustomed to the noise of propellers.

I had an exceedingly dangerous encounter with a shark at the time we were moving our headquarters from Suakin to Port Sudan. From there we were investigating the nearby reefs. On the morning in question we were sailing to Sanganeb Atoll, about eleven miles away.

Bill Clark had decided not to go to the office that day and had been fishing all the way out. By the time we reached Sanganeb, about 9 a.m., he already had several large fish in the boat.

We made fast along the wooden pier which linked the steep reef face with the lighthouse on the reef plateau. While the rest of us climbed the lighthouse in order to film a few sequences from the top, Bill went on with Xenophon to the northern edge of the atoll. Soon afterwards they returned, chuckling cheerfully. In barely an hour and a half Bill had caught twenty-three more fish, altogether about 260 pounds in weight. I asked him for some of the bigger ones, carved them up and flung them into the sea from the end of the jetty. The lighthouse keeper had told us about two hammerhead sharks which frequently turned up when refuse was thrown into the sea. To film some hammerheads had been my greatest wish for many years. I was hoping the smell of the blood would attract them. Of course I realized that diving under these circumstances would not be without danger.

We arranged that no one was to follow me, and half an hour later I went into the water with breathing equipment and a cine-camera. I descended close to the vertical rock face. I was being watched by several pairs of eyes. Directly

Preceding pages: *My first successful shots of devil rays were made in the Red Sea in December 1949.*

Left: *A specimen with a sixteen-foot wingspan. These giant rays are accompanied by pilot fish; in the event of danger these fish withdraw into the ray's mouth. This is a case of symbiosis: the fish clean the devil rays' mouths and, protected by them, find ample food for themselves.*

above me, on the upper edge of the reef, which came nearly up to the surface, Lotte and Leo were lying on their stomachs in the shallow water, peering down at me. A short distance away to one side, immediately next to the black outline of the projecting jetty, hovered the silhouette of our boat, and next to it was a white circle with a dark shadow in it—Xenophon watching me through the glass window of the observation box.

Immediately below the jetty, at a depth of twenty-eight feet, a black-tipped shark was floating; it was a good ten feet long. It was snapping up bits of flesh which had caught on the coral. Below me the reef face dropped vertically into a bottomless sea. There was no trace of any hammerheads. I chose a clump of coral on a bastion about forty-five feet below the surface and sat down astride it.

The shark soon noticed me. It swam over to me a little nervously and inspected me. At ten feet it turned and swam away. It described an arc and returned. Once more it turned away at ten feet. It repeated this manoeuvre four or five more times. As an object for my film sequence this shark was ideal. It invariably approached the camera from the front, and whenever it swam away I had just enough time to rewind.

I was sitting on my vantage point, my whole attention focused on the black-tipped shark, when I had a strange sensation at my back. Immediately behind me was a huge shark.

It had come up from the other side, along the reef face. From its shape and colour I recognized at first glance the kind of shark it was.

It was the white shark—the white death.

Normally these creatures live in the open sea and are only rarely seen on the coast. For an unforgettable moment I saw its broad head approaching me. Around its mouth there was a vicious, tense expression. All kinds of thoughts flashed through my mind. My spear was hovering above my shoulder but it was too late to reach for it. It was over six feet long and the shark was within five feet of me. I yelled and made a movement towards the attacker. Calmly and unimpressed the mouth was moving closer. The creature evidently intended to tear a chunk off me. Perhaps it regarded me as a lump of flesh. It had almost certainly fed on something already and the taste of blood was in its mouth.

Among all my confused thoughts was also one which struck me like an electric shock—I had only my bare hands to defend myself with.

On no account must I strike at the shark's nose. For in that case it would simply open its mouth and my arm would land between its teeth. Only when its nose was quite close did I strike out with my right hand, past its mouth, against its gills. I could not have hurt the creature, but the unexpected contact alarmed it. I felt the pressure of water—its body had turned on the spot, the shark was swimming away.

It made a circle and returned. By then I had grabbed my harpoon and struck it against its head. The point scarcely penetrated the skin but the shark once more turned away. Just then I saw that the other shark—the one I had filmed—was now also attacking me.

With all my strength I turned my spear to the side and hit it. Then I swung my weapon back and struck the other. But I could not possibly defend myself on two sides simultaneously. The shaft was too long and offered too much resistance; I could not swing it about fast enough. There was only one thing left to me, the most dangerous course of all—escape.

As fast as my fins would take me I raced up along the reef face. The sharks hesitated for a moment then they streaked up behind me, their tails thrashing. I kept them at bay with my harpoon. But as I had to look down below me during my escape I twice struck my back and shoulders hard against projecting corals. Then I was at the top. Hard beside Lotte and Leo. I pulled them along with me and threw myself into shallow water. And already the sharks were there too. They halted, hesitated, and swam excitedly up and down the reef edge.

Holding our spears in front of us we awaited their attack. But they merely looked at us menacingly and calmed down again. The white shark made another turn and then slid downwards. The other moved off in the opposite direction.

With shaking knees we climbed on to the jetty. If the water had been deeper our adventure might have had an ugly ending. Here we had encountered a shark which meant business. The other probably only attacked me from envy—rather like two dogs when one of them finds a bone. This time I very nearly was that bone.

I have never met a large white shark since. I have read several reports by other divers who encountered white sharks, but I am not convinced that in all cases the identification was correct. If all white sharks behave like my specimen then certainly one must watch out for them.

My experience had also taught us that one's harpoon shaft must not be too long. The ideal length is four feet.

Well then—are sharks dangerous or not? The incident I have recounted was really an exception among more than a thousand encounters with sizeable sharks. It taught us that one must never be over-confident, that it is very dangerous to dive when the smell of blood is spreading, and that one must always and everywhere be prepared for any surprise.

The Language of Fishes

I was swimming along a steep rock face against which there was a considerable surf, when at a depth of about forty feet, a good distance ahead of me, I saw the tail of a large grouper showing behind a stone. The creature was totally screened and only its gently moving caudal fin was visible. While looking towards it and evading a spray of froth I involuntarily splashed a little at the surface. Down below the fish immediately spun round. Its head appeared and it looked up at me inquisitively. There was no doubt that it had noticed me. In spite of the crashing surf it had perceived the slight noise produced by my clumsy movement.

We may be sitting in a concert hall, immersed in a thousand sounds—and a door creaks. We hear it in spite of the large number of sound waves. Clearly this is not just a performance of the ear but a performance of a registering brain. The same kind of thing may have been true of the grouper. Amidst its familiar music of the surf my own movement was like a creaking door.

Fishes do not have ear openings on the outside of their bodies; they have no need of them below water since the tissues themselves are excellent conductors of sound. Moreover, the swim bladder appears to play a part in the perception of sound. Fish have been trained to react to certain notes—one note being associated with food and another with a blow with a glass rod. They soon learnt to differentiate between the two notes. Then gradually these notes were brought closer together. In this way it has been established that carp, for instance, have an acuteness of hearing rather similar to that of humans, being capable of distinguishing intervals down to a quarter-tone.

The only question is whether musical notes can be equated with the water movements caused by a swimmer, i.e. whether fish actually 'hear' such vibrations in the water.

Fish have minute sensory cells—perceptors—at numerous points of their bodies; these are particularly numerous along their so-called lateral lines. They are situated there on the base of a mucus-filled canal which communicates with the ambient water through numerous orifices. From each perceptor a minute sensory fibre projects into the canal. Sharks, moreover, have special sensory grooves on their heads, the so-called Laurentian ampullae. All these organs have long been known but their functions are not yet clearly understood. As a rule they have been rather vaguely described as organs for the perception of water currents. But since the nerves of these sensory cells lead to particularly well-defined areas of the fish brain, it may be assumed that these organs are of rather greater significance.

In a number of books I have seen the suggestion that the lateral line system provides the fish with the kind of remote sense of touch that bats are known to possess. These, too, move in the dark without colliding with anything, and this ability was a mystery for a long time until two scientists discovered that while in flight the bats uttered short ultrasonic cries. These cries are reflected by the objects about them—like the rays of a pocket torch when we shine it on an object in the dark—and this reflected echo is perceived by the bats with their highly sensitive ears. In this way they interpret their surroundings as if by radar and recognize all obstacles without being able to see them with their eyes. But since our own ears do not perceive ultra-sound we cannot hear these shrieks.

I thought that it might be similar with fish. By their swimming motions they emit vibrations in the water and these are reflected back to them by stones and other bodies, and possibly intercepted by their lateral-line nervous system. In this way they might 'see' the objects around them even in totally opaque or dark water—not by means of light rays but through mechanical vibrations reaching their sensory organs along their bodies sooner or later, and in this way they might be able to form in their minds a spatial, three-dimensional image of their surroundings.

This sounds complicated, but only because we cannot easily picture something that lies outside our own sensory perceptions. Man has been likened to a dark sack with a few holes in it. Through these 'holes'—our senses—we see and recognize the world. There are plenty of animals with other senses, other 'holes' than ours; they see and interpret the world differently. Whereas our principal sense is sight, a dog does its 'seeing' mainly with its nose; its picture of the world is probably not imaginable by us. The same thing applies even more to many insects which possess sensory functions totally beyond our comprehension. And it might well be the same with fish and sharks. Since their eyes are of only limited service to them in frequently dark and opaque water, it is possible that they build up their image of the world mainly from the impressions transmitted to them by water vibrations.

This would also explain the fact that fishes and sharks adopt a sideways-on position when observing us. Such a position would be due not so much to the lateral placing of their eyes as to the lateral location of their vibration-sensitive organs. The further apart these sensors are spaced, the clearer the three-dimensional impression obtained by the creature—just as we artificially increase the distance between our eyes in a stereo-telescope in order to intensify our three-dimensional vision. This would lead to the interesting conclusion that fishes, including sharks, have a better long vision and spatial concept the larger they are, and the larger, in consequence, is their area of perception.

I had reached this point in my reflections when we made our highly interesting and strange observations off the Curaçao coast in 1939.

On that island's tempestuous northern coast with its numerous sharks these creatures invariably appeared whenever we had speared a sizeable fish. They appeared within ten to twenty seconds although until then there had been no sign of them as far as one could see. Had they been attracted by the smell of blood? Hardly. Since visibility under water was 130 feet, they must have come up from distances of 140 to 1,000 feet. But no smell could possibly spread that far at such a speed. What else could have attracted them? We assumed that it was the frightened wriggling of the speared fish that they 'heard'. Or, to stick to the picture we have been using, 'saw'.

On one occasion we missed a fish but it took great fright and thrashed about violently; a shark instantly appeared. So it was certainly not the blood. At the next opportunity—I have mentioned it before—I dived down to the bottom at the same spot and beat my foot fins as hard as I could. We waited, but no shark appeared. A little later we speared a fish and several sharks appeared instantly.

Either my theory was wrong and it was not the wriggling that attracted them—perhaps it was some scream of the fish that was inaudible to us—or else the sharks were able to distinguish between the wriggling of a distressed grouper and the vibrations produced by my foot fins which were meaningless to them.

This second possibility gave me much food for thought. Since the various species of fish are very differently shaped and have very different fins, it seemed reasonable to assume that they would each emit in the water a different 'vibration melody' which would be typical of the species concerned. It might also be assumed that identical fish would perform very different movements according to their mood—a healthy fish would differ from a sick one, and a hungry one from one about to mate. Was it not feasible that sharks, and also other fishes, might perceive such differences? Was it not possible that they recognized one another in this manner in opaque water or in the dark?

I thought of fish I had seen swimming close past the mouth of a shark without anything happening to them. Perhaps they sensed from the shark's movements that it was sated and not hunting for food. Or take fishes in their love play. We had noticed with numerous species that the partners had swum around each other with rapid fin vibrations. Was this really the expression of their excitement or was it not perhaps vice versa? Perhaps fish used these movements to get one another into readiness for mating. Perhaps their fins performed a kind of declaration of love, similar to the mating call of the birds.

Think of deep-sea fishes. Many of these have organs of luminescence by which the species probably recognize each other. It seems hardly likely, though, that a pursued fish would light its path for its pursuer. Since all deep-sea fish are predators the discovery and identification of prey is the greatest problem. Perhaps they too recognize one another by their characteristic fin melodies.

If these suppositions were correct, then the silent world of the sea would suddenly be full of sounds, even if our ears do not perceive these fish 'voices' any more than they do the cries uttered by bats. Even the terrifyingly black sea depth would then be 'bright' and 'friendly' for its denizens—'illuminated' not by sun rays but by water vibrations.

The problem of the 'live bait' would then also appear in a new light. I am referring to that cruel practice of using live fish as bait. The hook is carefully put through the fish's back to make sure it remains alive as long as possible—and this kind of bait will catch more fish than a dead one. Why? Because living flesh tastes better to the predator? Could it not be that the predatory fish—just like the sharks—are attracted by the bait's wriggling? That they are attracted from great distances by the agony vibrations of the tortured fish?

William Beebe made a very interesting observation on his Zaca expedition. He reports how he held a captive fish on his line and simultaneously observed through his viewing box the behaviour of two sharks and one sea perch. Whenever he pulled his line and the fish began to wriggle the predators approached 'like dogs snapping'. When he let go of the line and the fish was once more swimming normally, the sharks and the sea perch immediately lost interest. Only the wriggling, the unhealthy element, aroused their interest. Beebe believed that it was a law of nature that the abnormal provokes predators into destroying it.

There were obvious possibilities of a practical exploitation of my observations. If fishes and sharks really had a 'language', a particular method of communication and mutual recognition, then it might be possible to record these vibrational melodies by means of an underwater microphone and re-broadcast them through an underwater loudspeaker to deceive their own species and other fishes.

Some fishes live in shoals. How do they find each other in opaque or dark water? According to my theory the individual hears the melody emitted by the shoal and is attracted by it. It might be possible, by emitting this shoal melody, to create an artificial shoal and guide it. Then there are certain predators which follow the shoals. Presumably they, too, find these shoals by the vibrations they emit. Might it not be possible to trap them with the sound of the shoal? And finally, in the case of marine creatures at mating time, would it not be possible to deceive their partners by the emission of the water vibration produced by them?

I published my observations in *Jagd unter Wasser* ('Hunting under water') in

1939 and in *Unter Korallen und Haien* ('Among corals and sharks') in 1942. After the end of the war I took out world patents for my idea. Among the many possibilities the attraction of sharks seemed to me best suited for our first series of experiments. All we needed was the recording of a wriggling fish. If we succeeded in recording these vibrations and in re-broadcasting them, this could be of considerable importance to commercial fishing. Shark fishing so far has been a paying proposition only on a small scale—simply because not enough sharks had been found. If, on the other hand, it were to prove possible to attract them, then it would be far simpler to hunt them with nets or rods or by new electrical techniques. A catcher might sail along the coasts, process their skin and blubber, and turn the rest into manure. Moreover, the method might be used at shark-infested bathing beaches—such as on the Australian coasts—for dealing with this constant danger.

At Port Sudan we got hold of a large portable electric generator. We staged our first experiments in the Suakin lagoon. What we needed now was a ship which would take us with our plant to spots where sizeable fish might be speared in front of the microphone and where there were also sharks to enable us to test the effect of these transmissions. It did not seem a great problem but in fact it nearly cost us our lives.

We were looking for a motor boat but could not find one that was for hire. We were referred to the ancient sailing cutters in Flamingo Bay, once the proud sovereigns of the Red Sea but now half-rotted wrecks enveloped in swarms of flies. The stench hit us even as we approached. The few craft which were still seaworthy were used for catching oysters and trochus shells, and this not exactly sweet-smelling merchandise was auctioned in Flamingo Bay.

We were told the best ship was owned by a wealthy Arab named Tachlowe. We inspected his craft and I sent him an invitation to visit us at the house we had rented. Before very long a huge car arrived and an exceedingly fat man emerged from it, followed by an interpreter. We agreed that I should have his ship for £50 a week, including his Arab crew of ten. Mr Tachlowe would have the *El Chadra* specially cleaned for us. Two planks were to be laid across the entirely open hull of the ship. The slightly raised after-deck, which was protected by a sun awning and measured sixteen by thirteen feet, was to serve us for sleeping, living and working accommodation. The crew lived on the fore-deck.

Two weeks later we were bobbing along the coast, just like passengers a hundred years ago, under a high, picturesque sail. The big generator had been installed in the hull and our tape-recording equipment was stowed away in waterproof crates. Life could not have been more primitive. Bill Clark had lent us a folding camp bed for Lotte; the rest of us slept on rubber mattresses.

We were full of enthusiasm. We bore the heat and the stench of mussels, we bore the small flies which loved crawling into our nostrils and the huge cockroaches which consumed our generously scattered insecticide powder and seemed to thrive on it. Lotte's raised bed was better ventilated, but it suffered from the disadvantage of being directly below the boom on which the cockroaches conducted their evening stroll. Whenever a terrible scream snatched us from our dreams it would be because one of them had dropped on Lotte's face.

On waking in the morning we saw the crew, wearing only loin-cloths, kneeling on the planks, lowering and raising their upper bodies in the direction of the rising sun. They were all good-natured and friendly, except for our helmsman who had savage eyes. Mahmud told us he had occasional fits. Then he would go all rigid and incense had to be burnt under his nose. This would revive him. The captain was stolid and reserved. I have recently learnt that three years after our voyage the *El Chadra* sank in a storm and the entire crew was drowned.

I soon had trouble with the captain when he did not want to anchor at any of the places I favoured for our experiments. He wanted to spend each night in one of the muddy bays on the coast. We, on the other hand, needed sizeable fish in clear water, and that meant anchoring near a coral reef in the open sea. After three days I assumed personal responsibility and we anchored just above the wreck of Ata.

It had been arranged that Bill would follow us in the car, and so I sent my two assistants ashore in the dinghy to ferry him out. The boat had been out of sight for half an hour when we saw a broad glistening strip of water approaching us. A few minutes later we were buffeted by a violent storm which broke with incredible fierceness. Although it was five o'clock in the afternoon, everything was as dark as night. The heavens opened and a flood came down upon us.

The sea rapidly grew rougher and the *El Chadra* was bobbing about like a cockleshell. Through the wall of rain we could see the crew in a state of great excitement dropping two further anchors, but their ropes broke one after another. In a gesticulating tangle the men produced one more special anchor from the hull. This was fixed to doubly strong ropes and appeared to be a sacred object to be used only in a supreme emergency. It dropped at the very moment that the last of the other anchors parted. If this one broke loose as well that would be our ticket to eternity. All about us was darkness. Soaked to the skin we sat on deck, pressed close to one another, and I had ample time to reflect upon the captain's arguments. He had mentioned sudden storms—but my mind had been on fishes and microphones and I had swept away his storms with a casual gesture. I was telling Lotte some kind of nonsense, yelling into her ear to distract her attention from the terrifying roar behind us. As a result of our various manoeuvres we were now barely forty yards from the reef which was being lashed by the enraged waves with a monstrous din. The storm was forcing us straight towards the reef. Our boat was on shore but it would have made no difference if we had had it with us. Over a radius of six miles the sea was intersected by coral reefs in all directions. Whether on board the *El Chadra* or in the dinghy or swimming—anything here would be instantly ground to pulp between breakers and reefs as if between millstones.

We now viewed the wreck below us in a new light. On its deck, now a pretty coral garden, figures had no doubt crouched one day as miserably as ourselves. Perhaps they, too, had placed their hopes on their last anchor.

Slowly, very slowly, the night passed. In ever-renewed gusts the howling storm swept over us. Only gradually did it run out of breath. The lashing, drumming rain subsided. In the first pale light of the morning we looked at ourselves and at the battlefield that had been our deck. The sea, a dirty grey, had been smoothed by the rain, and rose and fell in a strong swell which swept heavily over the reef. The sailors were lying in the hull as if dead, sleeping. All night long they had hung on to the rope, compensating its movements to prevent it rubbing and breaking at a sudden jerk. Creaking and groaning the *El Chadra* pitched and rolled. She was a hundred years old and she made it very clear that she did not think much of me or my decisions.

Towards ten the dinghy arrived with Bill. He had already caught three fish. They had spent the night partly in and partly under the car. At the captain's request we dived for our lost anchors and with a good deal of difficulty knotted the ropes together again. We set sail at noon and returned to Port Sudan.

As our next objective I chose the island of Mukawwar, sixty miles to the north. We would be able to anchor there in the shelter of the island, we would have clear water and probably enough fish. Once again we were slowly rocking along the coast. But our engine was packing up. We had to send it back by lorry from Muhammad Qol to Port Sudan. This meant that we now only had a rowing boat for our experiments.

We intended to stage these at the tip of a reef off the southern side of the island. Our sailors nearly pulled their arms out of their sockets trying to row the *El Chadra* against the wind to this spot. I had promised the captain we would anchor for the night in the calm bay off the mainland.

At long last, towards noon, we reached our spot. While Wawrowetz was operating the equipment on deck, we took the microphone and the loudspeaker down to the bottom. Gerry would spear the fish while, simultaneously, I was to try to hold the microphone in front of it. Leo was carrying the cine-camera and Lotte the photographic camera. We left the loudspeaker on the sea bed near the ship, in under forty feet of water, and swam down a gently dropping valley where there was no shortage of sizeable fish.

Unfortunately none of them seemed prepared to let itself be speared for the sake of science. Our procession was arousing their suspicion. In particular, the long microphone cable curving up to the surface seemed to frighten the fish. We have known similar reactions when swimming with a harpoon whose line led up to the boat. It is said that certain South Sea islanders carry a rolled-up tape with them when swimming and release it when there are sharks about. The sharks are said to swim off because they believe the strange creature to have such a long tail that it must be exceptionally large. I do not know whether this is true, but certainly fish do show this kind of reaction.

When we realized that we were getting nowhere we hid the cable among the corals and I posted myself against a roughly three-foot-high ridge beyond which the reef dropped down steeply. If I wanted recording to start I was to scratch the microphone with my nail—Wawrowetz would thereupon switch on the tape recorder. At the end of the recording I was to call out 'End of recording' and he would switch off. We waited among the corals, each at his or her post. There was a lively traffic of fish over the ridge—except that they all continued to avoid the microphone. I signalled to Gerry and he swam off over the barrier into the deep water in order to spear a fish there. Admittedly this would not help our recording, since our fish had to be speared immediately in front of the microphone, but I was hoping that Gerry's wriggling fish might attract others which would be less shy.

We heard the clank of metal and saw the fish wriggling—and six seconds later we spotted the first shark. Another followed. Gerry hurried back and freed the speared mackerel from the harpoon head. Another two sharks were approaching from the other side. Within barely forty seconds there were altogether six sharks swimming up and down behind the barrier. It was a splendid confirmation of my theory but did not advance our present endeavours.

From under the block of coral on which I was standing a five-foot moray eel was calmly emerging to pick up the fish thrown away by Gerry. This moray eel was about the only creature we could not use for our purpose. As it had no fins it could hardly emit effective vibrations. Lotte and Leo came closer, photographing and filming, and then the eel withdrew into its hole and we all returned to our posts. Three of the sharks were still swimming up and down behind the ridge. The fish were as shy as before.

Suddenly we heard music. The whole sea was full of it. Wawrowetz had found his wait too boring and was testing our underwater loudspeaker with a jazz record. The idea that music sounds distorted under water is quite incorrect. The sounds came through prefectly clearly and without interference; it was an incredible experience to watch the rhythmical oscillations of the underwater world suddenly accompanied by rhythmical music. The fish took no apparent notice of the sound.

As it seemed pointless to wait any longer I put down the microphone and swam back to the loudspeaker, at which a few fish were nibbling. Whenever a particularly shrill note came through I observed some slight reaction. Then the disc was at an end. The next item was a Viennese waltz.

That, too, made no impression on the fish. But while I was watching them the water next to me suddenly darkened and I witnessed an astonishing performance. No fewer than 300 large silvery jacks were approaching in tight formation and began to circle me and the loudspeaker. They kept about ten feet apart and performed what looked like a round-dance. The waltz tune—it happened to be Johann Strauss's *Roses from the South*—had almost certainly nothing to do with this performance, which was due to sheer curiosity. At the most the sounds may have attracted the creatures. But the effect of this fish waltz was so perfect that I later included it in our film just as I experienced it.

I could not foresee that this waltz would earn me some rather dubious laurels. When an American version of our film was subsequently produced in Hollywood the American film editor placed the waltz at the centre of the action. Our experiments with inaudible water vibrations did not impress him much, and so he modified the plot and made us emit all kinds of strange noises into the sea. Only when cow bells, revolver shots, children's crying and other sounds had failed to make any impression on the fish did I—in this version of the film—conceive the brilliant idea of trying a Viennese waltz. And now the fish grouped themselves into pairs—the editor used for this purpose the shots we had made of fish in love play—and soon everything was swimming and dancing to the waltz tune. We had reserved the right to reject alterations during production, but we were only shown the version just before the New York première, when it was all finished. There was nothing left to us but to point out the error in interviews and to accept with good grace the congratulations heaped upon us for proving that fish were musical creatures.

In the course of further experiments we found that the movement of the cable produced clicking noises. We therefore moved it as little as possible, but still experienced other kinds of interference which we were unable to eliminate. The magnetic tapes also dissolved along the edges under the heat, and when we listened to our underwater recordings there was a clacking sound which was certainly not identical with the recorded fin beats. In the end we had to concede that the difficulties facing us on board this primitive craft and in this climate were too great. On our *Xarifa* expedition to the West Indies we continued these experiments with improved equipment, but the short time at our disposal again prevented us from arriving at useful results. However, a biological station in Florida subsequently proved that we had not been chasing any will-o'-the-wisp. The scientists there succeeded not only in attracting sharks by the emission of such vibrations but even in artificially producing vibrational patterns of particular effectiveness.

In Cairo, where we stopped for a few days, I asked Lotte if she would marry me. We were both utterly exhausted from the past few months, we were emaciated, and we were both suffering from boils. Having left this dreadful heat and humidity behind us we now both plunged back into a new life. With a charming smile and appropriate hesitation she agreed.

We were married at Küssnacht near Zürich, and apart from her parents the only persons in the know were the two witnesses we needed. We went to the registry office straight from the film-printing works and very soon returned to the cutting-room. The problem now was to turn our vast footage into a successful feature film. The printing works made the choice easier for us by spoiling a considerable part of our sequences through faulty development. It took me weeks to get over this disappointment. I thought of the infinite pain I had taken to re-spool each of those films in an improvised dark room, of the care with which we had protected them against damp, of how we had stored them in the ice plant of Port Sudan to keep them safe from the murderous climate. And now a large part of our yield had been spoiled through the faulty operation of a machine! The man responsible for it regarded us impassively: 'Most regrettable, to be sure. But unfortunately there's nothing to be done.'

I was glad I had repeated so many sequences. The zoologist, whose ambition it was to equip a modern research vessel, was now being forced into the role of a film producer. Many of the ideas I had hatched under the humid haze of the Red Sea had come off. But others had not. Sequence by sequence we built up the film story. There were no models for us to follow because until then documentaries had been in a category of their own (shown as matinées on Sundays) while feature films had been in another category (shown as the ordinary evening programme).

Eight months later, at the Venice *Biennale*, we received for Austria the International First Prize for documentary films. The representative of the Ministry of Education beamed, and we beamed likewise. Lotte took one print to Paris in order to negotiate there with the president of one of the biggest American firms of distributors. It turned out that he was most anxious to acquire the film—not from us, however, but by way of an American producer. I do not want here to go into the difficulties we experienced in the further course of events, or talk about the usages of the film industry. Suffice it to say that our film was so successful that it carried us like a big wave over all our problems. During the next few years it was shown in nearly every civilized country—and in a lot of uncivilized ones—and a portion of the admission money handed over by spectators of every shade of skin colour eventually, and after a great many deductions, came to us. But this wealth did not stay in our pockets for long. In Denmark I bought the steel hull of one of the biggest sailing yachts—a vessel built in a British shipyard for Mr Singer, the sewing machine king. He had sold his yacht before the war and she had passed through several hands, and then during the war, stripped of her keel and masts, she had been used to carry coal. It required a good deal of imagination to buy this steel hull in order to rebuild it into a new ship. All our revenue henceforward flowed into this project.

On my return it was suggested to me that I should set up my planned 'International Institute for Submarine Research' not in Vienna but in Liechtenstein. I gladly accepted the proposal. With normal taxation our project could never have been realized. In Liechtenstein I was not entirely exempt from tax but I was able to conclude with the Government a favourable agreement for an annual bulk payment. We found a suitable house in Vaduz and settled in. It may have been a little unusual to establish an oceanological institute among snow-capped mountains, but perhaps this was symbolical of our enterprise. One needs a certain distance to overcome ingrained concepts. One of these views was that specialist scientists—who were not as a rule outstanding sportsmen—could not possibly be transplanted to the sea bed in shark-infested regions in order to study there the growth of corals, or worms, or crustaceans, or fish or anything else. We gave our ship her original name, *Xarifa*, which is Arabic for 'The Beautiful'. We were told that this was lucky.

I had the hull transported to Hamburg for fitting out. If I had then known the eventual cost I should probably have given up hope. Fortunately I did not know. In Hamburg, a city of sober businessmen, few believed that we would survive financially. A sea captain who offered us his services as an adviser began his helpful activity by having all brass items on board stripped and selling them privately. He talked me into buying a new engine which did not fit the ship at all but which earned him a handsome commission. At the last moment I succeeded in cancelling this transaction. I now sent Xenophon to Hamburg. He was well informed on all practical shipping matters and I knew I could rely on him and his judgment. He became virtually the soul of the ship, and he was to stick with her for many years. We also enjoyed the help of Frau Thea Schneider, an elderly lady who had spent all her life looking after research scientists. She approached countless firms, and many of them proved willing to supply us with their equipment at reduced cost or free of charge. I do not

In 1950 we photographed our first whale shark under water. This biggest and most good-natured species
of sharks grows to a length of sixty feet. Like the devil rays and whalebone whales they feed on plankton.
One can get close to them and touch them without any trouble. We also held on to their tail fins. In the
picture I am filming its small eye.

Over: *Gerry Weidler approaching a whale shark.*

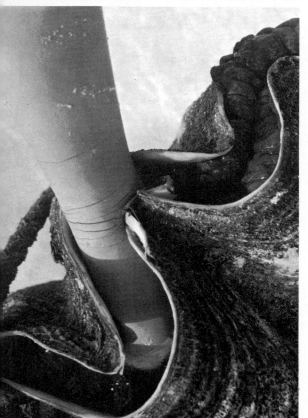

The world's largest shell, the 'murderer' or giant clam (Tridacna gigas), can weigh up to 440 pounds. It is said that divers who get an arm or a leg caught between the opened shells have been held fast and have lost their lives. We tested this by thrusting a plaster leg into such a clam. It snapped closed very quickly and held the leg in an iron grip. The edges of the shells had cut into the plaster to a depth of half an inch. Only back on shore were we able to cut through the closure muscle and free our dummy leg.

Right: A thirteen-foot hammerhead shark over a flat sandy bottom off Green Island (Queensland). It passed underneath me and did not notice me until its dorsal fin nearly touched me. It turned, and one side of the 'hammer' eyed me. This made me jump—and my jerking frightened the shark which promptly raced off.

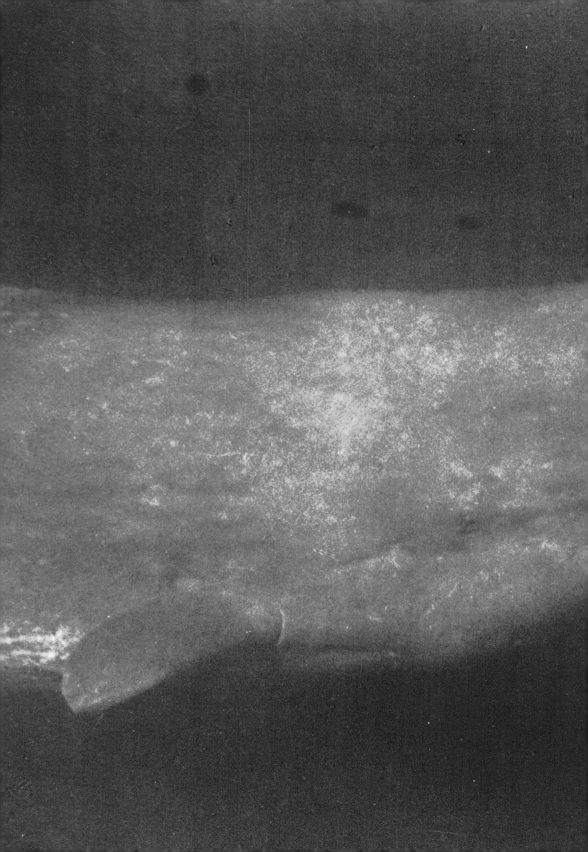

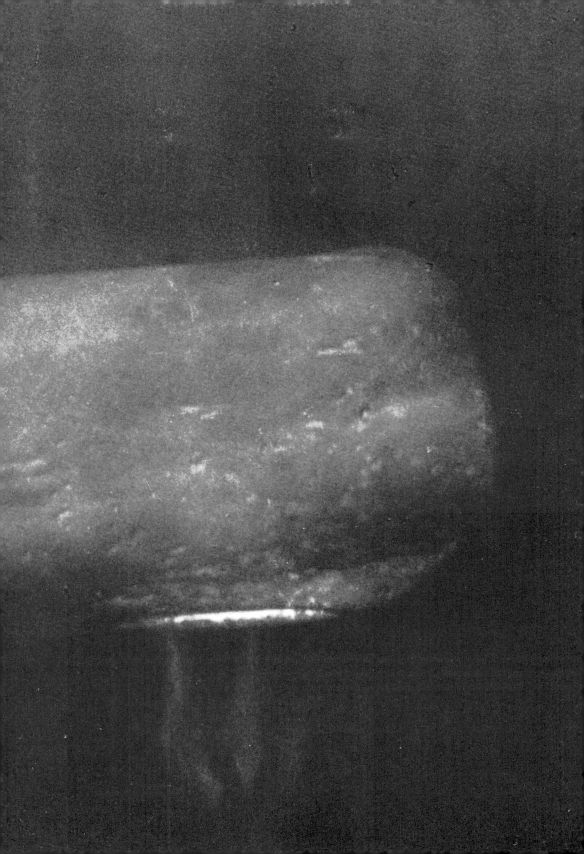

believe that any research vessel had ever been brought to life in such a manner by non-experts.

Meanwhile the American version of our film had been completed in Hollywood and the distributors invited us to attend the premières in the major cities in person. We were to take our diving equipment and underwater cameras with us in order to show them at television interviews.

'Do you know what this means?' I asked Lotte.

'Well?'

'It means that we can get as far as San Francisco free of charge—and with all our equipment.'

'So?'

'So we don't have to pay a lot more to fly on to Australia. This would be a unique opportunity for visiting the Great Barrier Reef. . . .'

The main guidelines for the fitting out of the ship had been laid down and our presence was no longer indispensable. Frau Schneider and Xenophon would keep an eye on everything. We had put off our honeymoon for an indefinite period—now or never was our chance to have it.

A DREAM COMES TRUE

Voyage to the Great Barrier Reef

Ever since I had started diving the Great Barrier Reef had been the Mecca of my dreams. The world's biggest coral reef, it extends for some 1,250 miles along the east coast of Australia, and in some places reaches a width of over ninety miles. What few reports there were of professional or pearl divers all spoke of unparalleled magnificence and wonders. This was also the habitat of the world's largest shell creature, the legendary murderer clam, said to have cost many a diver his life. I wanted to see all this for myself.

What interested me particularly was the outer edge of the huge barrier; as far as I was aware no one had previously dived there. We could make our headquarters at Cairns, a small town in Queensland. Not far from there were also the historical places associated with Captain Cook's voyage.

Time and again I had to think of his small ship—shorter than the *Xarifa* though a little broader in the beam—which had sailed these seas in 1769 and very nearly foundered on the Great Barrier Reef. I was fascinated by the astonishing voyage of the *Endeavour* and wanted to follow in her tracks.

Captain Cook's first objective had been the island of Tahiti, where he called according to plan and where an astronomer in his party studied Venus's transit across the sun. Then, in accordance with secret orders, he turned south-west, into unexplored waters, in order to search for the legendary *Terra Australis Incognita*, that fifth continent according to certain theories believed to be at that part of the globe. But all he found was an infinite ocean. Eventually he reached New Zealand, already discovered by the Dutchman Tasman in 1642. In five months of conscientious work he surveyed its coasts and then set sail for the north to regain the familiar sea lanes. Suddenly, on 21st April 1770, his first officer, Hicks, spotted land ahead. In Botany Bay, so named by Cook, his men stepped on Australian soil.

Cook subsequently depicted this bay in such glowing colours that the first British settlers, arriving on board eleven ships eighteen years later, were somewhat disappointed to find themselves gazing upon rather desolate scenery.

They followed the coast down and discovered one of the world's finest natural harbours, the present-day Sydney. Cook had sailed past without examining it closely, merely naming it Port Jackson. After his two years' voyage Cook was anxious to return to Batavia as quickly as possible and thence to England around Africa. He followed the newly discovered coast towards the north, but more and more reefs and small islands barred his way. His men were plumbing the depths day and night, and most of the time Cook's ship was preceded by a pinnace. No one on board suspected that they were sailing into a funnel that was getting progressively narrower—into the channel formed by the Great Barrier Reef, from where the open sea can be regained only with the greatest difficulty. . . .

The inquiries I made the very next morning confirmed me in my intentions. As the airlines flying to Australia by the eastern and western routes were in fierce competition, the fares were relatively low. The flight from San Francisco to Sydney, although the same distance as Zürich to San Francisco, cost only half as much. Our only problem was the *Xarifa*, whose fitting out was just then entering a vital stage. But we could lay down all the details in advance and leave the supervision to our trusty Xenophon.

Our aircraft touched down in Sydney and the engine noise died away. At the foot of the gangway was a large number of press photographers, their cameras poised. As we descended flashlights went off—and behind us a young lady was nodding her head in all directions. The welcome was for Miss Australia returning from the United States.

As I could not find my vaccination certificate the quarantine officer took me into another room and vaccinated me there and then. They do not waste much time in Australia. In the foyer, after our baggage had been checked, we were met by ten hefty men. One of them stepped up to us, shook hands and made us honorary members of the Underwater Spearfishermen's Association of New South Wales. He was Dick Charles, its President, who told us that in Sydney alone the club had over 1,000 members.

'Normally membership is strictly confined to men,' he said to Lotte. 'But we're making an exception for you.'

Preceding pages: *The twenty-foot head of a fifty-two-foot bull sperm whale. The eye is minute and lies thirteen feet back down the side. I could not make it out under the water, but it is discernible in the photograph.*

Left: *Lotte behind the tail fin of a sperm whale. All whales are descended from terrestrial vertebrates; their dorsal fin is a hardened skin fold, unsupported by any skeletal structure.*

161

The representative of the American film distributors, who had likewise turned up at the airport, brought over one of the journalists who were crowding Miss Australia. The moment the word 'shark' was uttered he ran over to his colleagues and brought them to us.

The following morning we saw our names in bold type in every paper. For the first time we were in a country where sharks really were a national problem, where each year several people were injured, and often killed, by sharks, and where the Government had set up a special Shark Control Department. That anyone could refer to these creatures in friendly terms, or that we imagined we could scare them off by swimming straight at them or yelling at them was a sensation. In the *Daily Telegraph* the well-known Australian naturalist T. C. Roughley said that he could not see himself ever describing a shark as a beautiful creature. A Brisbane paper speculated about our expectation of life and said they would put it at a fortnight. The *Courier Mail* had a half-page cartoon showing me facing a huge shark under water and yelling at it. Written across the shark was 'Income tax' and the caption read: 'But this one you cannot boo away!'

We received a lot of letters and telephone calls from well-meaning people warning us. Dr Coppleson, a leading surgeon, insisted on showing me all his frightful clinical photographs of people whose limbs had been bitten off. They were mostly corpses, many of them lacking very large crescent-shaped chunks. The bite lines were as clean as if drawn with a razor.

'Maybe elsewhere the sharks are harmless,' Dr Coppleson said. 'They certainly aren't in our waters. I'm giving you here a dossier of over a hundred proved cases of men being attacked by sharks. As you'll see, eighty per cent were fatal. There are six species here which attack humans—the white shark, the tiger shark, the hammerhead, the grey nurse shark, the whaler shark and the mako shark. The white shark fortunately only rarely comes near the shore. Most of the incidents are probably due to whaler sharks and grey nurse sharks.'

I had asked Dr Coppleson to have lunch with us and I had considerable difficulty in preventing him from showing his pictures to Lotte as well. 'You may be interested to know,' he was saying to her, 'that many people believe that the consumption of human flesh is positively harmful for a shark. A few years ago a ten-foot tiger shark was caught for the aquarium in Coogee. Immediately after its arrival it vomited up a human arm and shortly afterwards died. Although the arm must have been in its stomach for several days it had hardly been attacked by the digestive juices. As the police subsequently established, it was the arm of a missing person who had probably been murdered and thrown into the sea.'

Captain Young in his book *Shark! Shark!* reports a similar case. When he opened up a thirteen-foot brown shark caught near Key West he found in it a human arm, some other lumps of flesh and a scrap of blue cloth. Young photographed the hand and showed the picture to all those who doubted that sharks really ate human flesh.

Dr Coppleson warned us against taking these matters too lightly. His statistical analysis showed that accidents had happened in good and bad weather alike, in shallow water as often as in deep water, and in a clear sea just as often as when the water was cloudy. Most of the attacks had occurred between December and April—i.e. during the Australian summer—and mostly after 3.30 p.m. Lone swimmers had been favoured by the sharks, and once a shark had attacked a person it had usually returned to its victim a few more times. The first bite would be aimed at the legs or the buttocks, the next would be at the person's arms as he defended himself. People hurrying to help the victim— and there had been quite a few helpers—had not been injured in any of these incidents; the shark had invariably bitten the person already wounded. The victims had included both white and black people.

This last point is of particular interest as it is widely believed that sharks do not attack dark-skinned people. Many negroes consider themselves immune and, for extra safety, paint the palms of their hands black. Captain Young also pointed out that newspapers he had thrown into the sea had attracted sharks, and that the sharks off Hawaii would go for a dead horse dragged out into the sea more quickly if that horse was a grey. No doubt a light-coloured body is visible in the water over a greater distance than a dark one, but the Australian accident statistics show that one should not rely on this too much.

We were still thinking about Dr Coppleson's account when, together with thousands of other people, we swam at Bondi Beach that afternoon. On a raised platform stood a lifeguard on the look-out for sharks. He told us the beach was regularly fished and sharks of twelve to sixteen feet in length were frequently encountered. More recently aircraft had been employed for shark spotting, and attempts had even been made to fight sharks with depth charges. It was exactly a year to the day since the Australian surfing champion, Francis Okulitch, had been killed by a shark just over 200 yards offshore.

On the Sunday, our last day in Sydney, Dick Charles drove us out in his car to Botany Bay, where the skindivers were having a picnic. There were a dozen large tents on the beach and countless diving figures were moving in the greenish water at roughly the spot where Captain Cook first stepped ashore to plant the Union Jack on this continent. One man was just landing a strangely coloured shark—a 'wobbegong'. The whole body of this creature is covered with irregular patches, presumably for camouflage; its head is broad and flat, and its whiskered mouth contains exceedingly sharp teeth.

163

'They lie among the seaweed and the foam, so you often don't notice them,' Malcolm Fuller, one of the club's best divers explained to us. 'The other day a fellow was diving under a rock where a wobbegong was lying, and the shark took fright and bit his face. The poor blighter was in a sorry state. We've harpooned wobbegongs over six feet long.'

We too went into the water, but it was cold and rather murky. I genuinely admired the courage of these Australians who went skindiving in decidedly poor visibility in waters known to be shark-infested.

The following day we flew to Brisbane, found that our supplies of absorbent lime and oxygen cylinders had arrived, and paid a visit to Dr Tom Marshall, the well-known ichthyologist, who gave us more tips and good advice. We continued our journey by air, and ten hours later, rather exhausted, arrived at Cairns. A small bus carried us down a bumpy road to an old-fashioned beach hotel. Under the heavy heat of the night we lay awake for a long time. Dr Coppleson's statistics had left their mark on us.

The next morning there was a fresh breeze and the sun was shining from a cloudless sky. All gloomy prophecies were swept away. We were at our destination. Before us lay the legendary coral sea, and barely twenty miles offshore, beyond the horizon, was one of the world's great natural wonders.

The Great Barrier Reef

The Great Barrier Reef of Australia is the largest construction built by living creatures on this globe. No human achievement can even compare with it. In order to gain some scale of comparison we estimated the cubic capacity of this huge rampart, 1,250 miles long and often over ninety miles broad, a rampart with a sheer drop of over 6,000 feet on its outer edge. The figure we worked out was the colossal total of 567 million million cubic feet.

On the basis of this figure the Great Barrier Reef is eight million times the size of the pyramid of Cheops, 100,000 times the size of the Great Wall of China, and 2,000 times the size of the city of New York.

It is thought that the eastern side of Australia was once considerably higher and that the Barrier Reef was formed by a gradual sinking of the land

Central section of the Great Barrier Reef. Between the outer slope and the coast the sea has a maximum depth of 165 feet. As the tide levels differ by up to twenty feet, considerable currents run through gaps in the outer reef chain. Within the vast enclosed lagoon the water is often opaque.

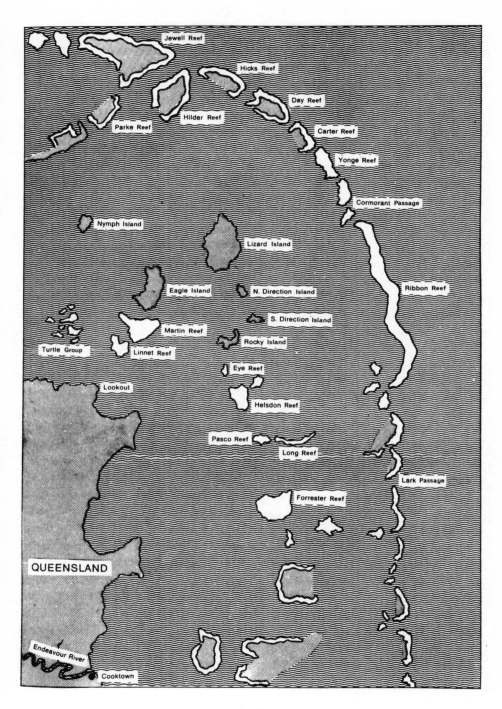

Jewell Reef

Hicks Reef

Day Reef

Carter Reef

Hilder Reef

Parke Reef

Yonge Reef

Cormorant Passage

Nymph Island

Lizard Island

Eagle Island

N. Direction Island

Ribbon Reef

S. Direction Island

Martin Reef

Rocky Island

Turtle Group

Linnet Reef

Eye Reef

Lookout

Helsdon Reef

Pasco Reef

Long Reef

Lark Passage

Forrester Reef

QUEENSLAND

Endeavour River

Cooktown

165

below the sea. Originally it was probably a fringing reef along the coast, which subsequently grew at the same rate as the land sank, and in consequence moved away from the coast. In the progressively widening canal new reefs were formed so that nowadays the entire vast area is criss-crossed with coral ranges.

The survey ships *Fly*, *Bramble* and *Dart* have begun to map this huge area, but the task has not yet been completed. The first comprehensive zoological work was Saville Kent's *The Great Barrier Reef of Australia*; its above-water photographs of the parts of the reef visible at low tide provided the first impressions of this wonder of the world. We had the book with us, and C. M. Yonge's *A Year on the Great Barrier Reef*, in which the leader of the British Barrier Reef Expedition of 1928-9 sums up its findings in a very striking manner. Both these books were valuable signposts to us in the short time at our disposal. Above all, they were our source of information on the fauna encountered here.

Fred Williams and Captain Barns, the harbour master, helped us find a suitable motor launch. As it was late December, the beginning of the cyclonic period which precedes the rainy period, the fishermen were just about completing their voyages to the reef. A ship that is caught in a cyclone is lost. No matter how well she is anchored, the whirlwind will nonetheless force her under water. In 1899 an entire flotilla of pearl-fishers' cutters suffered this fate. All thirty-seven ships sank and more than 300 men lost their lives. In 1911 the 1,800-ton steamer *Yongala* was caught in a cyclone and vanished without trace, with 140 persons on board. The wreck was subsequently spotted by an aircraft, lying on the bottom in a hundred feet of water, broken in two.

Hardly a year passes without several cyclones sweeping over Queensland, and numerous towns, including Cooktown, have been devastated. For us, however, this dangerous period had an important advantage. Throughout the rest of the year a regular trade wind blows from the south-east, so that powerful waves are cast against the Barrier Reef. Only during the cyclonic period—between sudden rainstorms—are there some fine sunny days with no wind at all. That was the weather we were hoping for. Only if we had such weather could we successfully dive along the outer edge of the Great Barrier.

We eventually found three boats whose owners were ready to take the risk. We decided in favour of the twenty-foot motor launch of a Mr MacDonald, who had been engaged in commercial fishing in the Barrier Reef area for twenty years and who seemed to us most reliable. On a magnificent cloudless morning we put out of Cairns and sailed up the coast in a northerly direction. We passed steep inhospitable mountain slopes covered with primeval forest. At dusk we reached the minute Low Island, at the centre of which stood a tall lighthouse.

Here the British Barrier Reef expedition had had its headquarters for a year. As we approached we saw a light shining through the bushes and heard noisy music on the radio. A family and a bachelor were living on the island in contented solitude. The children received their schooling by radio; food and mail arrived once a week. We circled the island in the dark and then sat on deck under our small swinging lantern, eating one of those inventive salads the Australians are justly famous for.

The next morning we left Low Island behind. It was a sultry day and the mirror-smooth sea rose and fell in an infinitely vast gentle swell. Towards noon we reached our first destination—the famous Endeavour Reef on which Cook had foundered.

Ever since the last century countless divers have searched here for the six cannon jettisoned by Captain Cook. To the Australians these are sacred national objects, and every schoolchild knows the story. But so far no one had succeeded in finding them. Cook's data are not very precise, and the reef is in fact considerably larger than might appear from the chart. In a flat arc it stretches over five miles, and it also has a number of secondary reefs lying outside it. The area within which the *Endeavour* is known to have foundered is therefore rather extensive.

Lotte and I were looking somewhat glumly at the dimly visible ranges of reefs. The water was so opaque that there was no point in attempting a dive. MacDonald explained that the water here was nearly always cloudy but that this was a particularly bad day. We therefore put off our intentions and moved on to Ruby Reef, one of the bastions of the outer barrier.

'Over there, look!' Lotte suddenly exclaimed.

Not far from us a large coiled snake was floating on the smooth surface. It was a brilliant yellow with a dark pattern. I wanted to stop the ship but MacDonald assured us that we would see several of these every day. I believed him—and have regretted it ever since. Throughout the rest of our stay we never saw another.

Shortly afterwards we witnessed an astonishing natural phenomenon. In the direction of the Barrier a tall white wave crest abruptly rose above the barely visible horizon and there, with lightning speed, moved from left to right across the sky. This spectacle was repeated several times, and we were to witness it frequently in the future. It was a mirage, the reflection of the surf beyond the horizon being projected on to the sky and there magnified on a grand scale.

We were standing at the bow, watching for the outer surf to come into sight. Because the water was so still we did not see the leeward side of Ruby

Reef until we were quite close to it. Large light-coloured patches were visible below the surface—circular coral towers of sixty-five to a hundred feet in diameter, rising absolutely vertically from a dark depth. We reduced speed and moved closer.

The water here was again rather cloudy. In the shadow alongside the boat we identified pinhead-sized medusas in their millions drifting through the water like snow.

Judging by the colour of the water, the sea seemed to be a lot clearer round the near-by Pearl Reef. We sailed across. There were again the same coral towers, and we secured our craft to one of them. Wearing breathing apparatus Lotte and I went into the water.

Our first impression was overwhelming. The flat roof of the tower, about ten feet below the water, was like a magnificent flower-studded meadow over which the strangest fishes were fluttering like butterflies. Along the sheer side, on the other hand, down which we were descending, the water grew increasingly opaque and there were only a few living coral. The dark shadows of grottos and overhangs seemed like evil monsters staring at us. Soundlessly fish appeared from the misty green, moved past us, inspected us, and just as soundlessly vanished.

We stopped at a depth of about forty feet and, as if in a box at the theatre, perched below an overhang. Here, too, countless minute jellyfish were drifting through the water. I was looking at Lotte and she was looking at me. We were afraid.

We were afraid of sharks suddenly emerging from the cloudy water; we were even more afraid of some other surprises which we could not foresee. Among these were, above all, the legendary 'sea wasp'.

We knew that no human eye had yet caught sight of this creature. Most probably it was a small medusa, but even those who had fallen victim to this sinister creature had not seen it. A typical incident was that of a young man of nineteen who was bathing in chest-deep water about forty miles south of Cairns in January 1937 when something suddenly stung him. He dragged himself ashore, collapsed, and was dead within seven minutes. A soldier in the Australian Army who suffered the same fate was dead within three minutes. We had spoken in Cairns to Dr Flecker, who had investigated these cases, and he assured us that with all other victims death had invariably occurred within ten minutes. All these accidents had taken place between 13th December and 10th April. The cause had definitely not been Portuguese men-of-war (physalia), since their striking blue umbrellas would certainly have been sighted; besides, these creatures cause severe stings but not death. Dr Flecker suspected a relatively small creature, probably a carybdeid medusa, living on the sea floor and rising to the surface upon reaching maturity. Its poison was more effective than any known snake poison.

We were squatting on our ledge, mesmerized, gazing on the twilight activity before us. When a particularly strange fish floated past with a curved projection on its head I took a picture of it. Lotte seized my arm. From a crack at our side appeared a huge wrasse which had a ball-shaped bump on its head. At the very spot where Lotte was leaning against the rock I saw a long hairy worm creeping out from a crevice. We swam up to the surface.

'Not very beautiful here,' I said when we were back in the boat, in bright sunlight.

'No—it's not worth the effort. The corals here all look dead.'

We would have sooner bitten off our tongues than admit to the fear we had felt.

In the evening there was a blood-red sickle moon in the sky. We had anchored in the lee of Ruby Reef. MacDonald and our cabin boy were pulling one red perch after another out of the dark water with landing hooks. From the outer edge of the reef came the steady rumble of the breakers. We were at our destination and we were feeling small and miserable. This gigantic sinister reef was depressing us. We suspected that it would be very difficult to get at its secrets.

The following morning a strong wind was blowing. Shoals of hunting bonitos were driving glittering clouds of fish over the surface. The water was a deep blue and there was a sparkling spume of sunlight from every wave crest. We sailed back to Pearl Reef and made fast at a spot where an entirely enclosed brilliantly blue lagoon lay within the wide flat top of the reef.

Swimming against the current we crossed the reef and entered a veritable fairy landscape of corals. The lagoon was thirty to forty feet deep, and in this relatively sheltered water tall delicately ramified coral trees had developed. Countless brilliant blue and yellow fish were swimming around a tall bouquet of corals in the centre. Two small grey sharks approached quite close, inspected us and disappeared again. Wherever we looked we discovered astonishing coral formations, and among them swarms of large and small fish. Here too we saw our first giant clam lying on the bottom. It was over three feet long, and between its half-opened corrugated shells the thick mantle protruded like brightly coloured flower petals.

We inspected it reverently. We knew from Yonge's book that these mantle lobes were a kind of vegetable garden in which the creature cultivated minute algae of the kind that also floated about freely as plankton. These settle on the skin and in the tissues and represent an additional source of food for the clam—a rare case of food provision within a creature's own body. The clam also equips each one of its larvae with hundreds of these symbiotic algae. As these algae need sunlight the giant clam is invariably found in the brightest light and with its mantle turned outwards.

Lotte got a little too close with her hand. With a jerk the clam closed—at first only partially to enable it to draw in its mantle—and then the wavy shells shut firmly.

'What do you think?' I said to Lotte back at the surface. 'Should I put my foot in one? I don't believe it could hold me.'

'Better not risk it. Perhaps we can get hold of an artificial leg. Let's play it safe.'

We explored the entire lagoon and took a great many photographs. Then the current turned and the water became cloudy, so we sailed over to the first Ribbon Reef and anchored on its leeward side. Here I went into the water on my own, with breathing apparatus.

The reef formed a veritable labyrinth. The gorges were twenty feet deep and terminated in an underground chamber which received its light through a large opening at the centre. Further ravines and grottos radiated from the chamber. One of the passages led to the interior of the reef, divided there, grew narrower, and finally ended in a deep hole. Another, after much twisting and turning, opened out into a valley overgrown with magnificent corals. As I had good all-round vision in this system of grottos I felt completely safe. I probed my way yard by yard, and gradually regained my confidence. I gave each grotto a name and called the central chamber, in whose corner I discovered a strange pile of empty shells, the 'Mausoleum'.

It looked very much as if this was the lair of a large octopus and the empty shells the remains of its meals. There were also remains of the armour of dead crayfish. I searched every nook and cranny, but found no trace of the creature responsible for these banquets.

While Lotte spent an anxious hour waiting for me in the boat, I was sitting in the opening of a passage leading to the coral valley, enjoying myself watching the fish. A whole number I already knew from the Red Sea, but there were others, some with strange patterning, which I had never seen before. Lightning-fast wrasse were rushing about; a large porgy hung in front of me motionless while a small worm-shaped fish was cleaning its gills; a pufferfish was gyrating comically; high above me a squadron of pencil-shaped garfish was sailing past; a couple of triggerfish were elegantly courting over a huge brain coral; indefatigable parrot fish were nibbling the blue, reddish and yellow coral tips; a spotted moray eel was peering out of one hole, while a small grey ray with pale blue dots was sleeping in another. Whichever way I looked, there was a confusion of colourful life, and it was exceedingly difficult among the multitude of impressions to observe anything more closely.

I concentrated on the large porgy and the little fish which was cleaning its gills. The porgy was solemnly keeping its thick-lipped mouth open and the small worm-shaped fish was busily swimming in and out of the porgy's mouth as well as through its opened gills. I felt a stinging pain on my ankle. I had slightly grazed my skin there, and another worm-shaped fish was now nibbling my wound. Calmly it pulled off a scrap of my skin. I chased it away but it returned instantly. Especially when I kept still in order to take a photograph it immediately renewed its attack.

In the evening both Lotte and I found our backs badly sunburnt. MacDonald put on some liquid which he said would work wonders but meanwhile burnt like hell. He and the boy spent the whole evening at the radio, trying to get the meteorological service. He maintained that in the cyclone which had passed over Cooktown a piano had been lifted 150 feet into the air. At sea, he explained gloomily, one never experienced more than one cyclone. But nothing could spoil our mood that evening. We had had our first glimpse of this great wonderland; we had gained a foothold. In our dreams we kept seeing giant clams and thousands of strange fish gyrating around them.

The weather left a great deal to be desired. The following morning the sky was overcast and there was a tall dark cloudbank towards the mainland. We sailed out to the fifth Ribbon Reef, but it was too windy and we sailed back again. Across the flat top of the reef I gazed out longingly towards the great breakers. Would I ever get my wish and dive out there, on the outer edge?

We anchored near the 'Mausoleum' and I conducted Lotte through all the passages I was familiar with. Now there were considerably fewer fish about. We had made the same observation before. Whenever a human enters a new region he disturbs its ecological balance and it takes days for its inhabitants to settle down again.

Once inside the grottos we felt we belonged to the reef, as if we were just two of its innumerable denizens, all living in the shelter of its countless niches, as if we were guests at some large hotel. We also sensed that the reef was asleep during the daytime. Only in the dusk of the grottos did we see the opened buds of the polyps; in bright light all coral polyps withdraw into their calcareous shells and do not open again until nightfall.

What is the reason for this behaviour? In spite of their obvious greed these polyps with their bud-studded tentacles live a comfortable life. Their main diet is the zooplankton, and these organisms shy away from direct light. The light is too strong for them and can even kill them. For that reason these minute creatures float up and down in the sea in huge clouds. At dawn they

171

are on the surface and as the light gets stronger they descend to greater depths. At nightfall they again rise to the surface and during the night they float about at random in all directions. That is the time for the coral flowers to open. Then they feed enough to rest once more during the day.

The sun disappeared behind a cloud and our grotto was plunged in complete darkness. We waited a little longer and then ascended. The sky had clouded over. The dark cloudbank over the mainland had grown considerably. It was raining there. MacDonald made it clear to me that he was no longer feeling happy at our anchorage.

We nevertheless stayed for the night but the waves were getting bigger all the time. The strong wind was whistling over the water and we were spattered by fine spray. The next morning the whole sky was grey. We dived once more in a small enclosed lagoon, but there was a strong current and the water was rather cloudy. MacDonald was impatient to leave. He had not heard any weather reports for a whole day and was uneasy. With a heavy heart I agreed and we set our course for the Hope Islands, two small densely wooded islands a good way inside the channel. There was an excellent anchorage between them, MacDonald assured us.

From the distance we saw thousands of white spots among the tall trees. They were pigeons. MacDonald had a gun on board. Half an hour later we were creeping through the thick undergrowth among the giant trees and soon were sitting on the beach in the dark, plucking the birds we had shot.

Pitch-black clouds were closing in from all sides. The water had fallen totally silent and the air was vibrating with electricity. MacDonald secured the ship with a second anchor and showed me on the map that we were now lying protected in a pocket of several coral reefs and that the weather could now only hit us from the north. He was going to bake a pigeon dish called 'pantaloons'. Just as he was getting down to this praiseworthy activity the storm broke.

The sky opened its floodgates and cascades of water poured down on us. There were continuous flashes of lightning and equally continuous claps of thunder from all sides. MacDonald had stowed away everything, but suddenly he stood before me all pale. The storm had veered and was now striking straight from the north. This meant that, in spite of the total darkness, we had to raise our anchors, sail out of the narrow channel into the wind and round the island in order to seek shelter on its other side.

Now we saw that we had made the right choice of ship and captain. Apart from the compass our only point of reference was the snow-white silhouette of the island as it appeared for a fraction of a second in each flash of lightning through a thick curtain of rain. It was a masterpiece of navigation to have got us, in those conditions, through the reef and to a sheltered spot on the other side of the island. We helped as best we could and were all soaked to the skin and exhausted. The thunderstorm continued noisily through the night. Nevertheless we insisted that our poor Mr MacDonald should produce his 'pantaloons'.

The next morning was so calm, sunny and cheerful that it almost seemed as though the thunderstorm had just been a bad dream. There was a particularly marked low tide and the extensive reef plateau south of the island was entirely above water. We strolled about through the small pools, turning over stones and finding magnificent snails. We also discovered two cone snails which must only be touched at the ends of their shells since they have a poisonous sting which is suddenly shot out of the orifice. Since all the clouds had now disappeared we quickly returned on board and again sailed out to Ruby Reef.

For the first time we saw the outside of the Barrier relatively calm. True, there was still a slow swell rising and falling, so that we could only approach the edge, which was marked by extensive areas of foam, to within thirty or forty yards, but it would have been technically feasible to dive there. I would have had to get into the deep water in the open sea, however, and swim to the reef underneath the clouds of foam, and the boat would have had to circle around and would not have been able to come to my aid if necessary. MacDonald and the boy cast out drag lines and we sailed along Ruby Reef, across to Andersen Reef and thence along the outer side of Escape Reef. I was on the look-out for a more suitable spot but had to give up my search. In the present conditions the enterprise was too dangerous and we would surely find a better opportunity before long. With a heavy heart I gave instructions to turn back.

MacDonald was telling us that enormous sharks had frequently appeared when he had been fishing off the outer edge.

'There was one I saw,' he said, reeling in his line, 'that was so large you wouldn't believe me. But it's true. I'd been fishing at that spot for a couple of hours, and some other sharks were about too, and just then this monster emerged from the depths. I never saw anything like it. I can't even estimate its length. It was gigantic and enormously fat.'

'What colour?'

'Dark. The only thing I noticed were its enormous gill slits. The water was fairly calm and I saw it quite clearly. It was rising slowly, a veritable monster, and quite plump and ponderous, and then it turned and disappeared. But it was certainly over thirty feet.'

It could have been a basking shark, the second largest species after the whale shark. It lives in the northern seas, also feeds on plankton and is distinguished by its particularly long and conspicuous gill slits. That it should have appeared in tropical waters seemed unusual.

Cheerful and good-tempered as MacDonald normally was, that day he and the boy were getting increasingly fidgety—and we knew the reason why. The next day was Christmas Eve, and the day after that was the most important holiday in Cairns. But we had expressly agreed that if the weather was good we should stay out over the holiday. We now lay along the inner side of Ruby Reef, and Lotte and I swam out from here to a brilliantly blue lagoon which I had spotted from the roof of the deck house.

What surprised us most was the size of the creatures found here. Not only were the corals and clams strikingly large on the Barrier Reef, but all other species also seemed to be represented by particularly big specimens. There were pale yellow sea cucumbers which looked like marrows, and deep blue starfish which reached fifteen to twenty inches in diameter. On a coral face we spotted an ugly black lump. Lotte touched it with her finger-tip and the black skin was pulled back, revealing the most delicate white porcelain. It was a fist-sized white cowrie shell.

We turned over some clumps of coral and underneath them found tiger-striped cowries. Suddenly Lotte took my arm and pointed to a not particularly attractive but rather stunted thistle coral. She drew me closer and touched a tuber-shaped structure. It was something we had read about and talked about only yesterday. The tuber was actually the strange abode of the small crab hapalocarcinus, the female of which allows herself to be overgrown by the branches of a coral in a manner not yet understood. In so doing the coral leaves orifices large enough to admit the considerably smaller male. The young similarly slip out through these openings. I took my knife and carefully broke open the bladder. The small crab was cowering at the bottom of it, frightened, and made no attempt to escape. Its life's purpose was destroyed. An unusual situation: a female building her own cage from which she can never again escape.

When we surfaced an hour later we heard loud thunder and found to our surprise that the sky had completely clouded over and it was beginning to rain. With a show of regret MacDonald informed me that this break in the weather made it necessary to return to Cairns.

From sheer joy at getting back in time for Christmas the boy very nearly steered us on to a spur of the Undine Reef. There was a grinding noise, but at the same time we cleared it. Only another ten feet to port and we would have struck it full force. MacDonald, who had been getting a fishing rod ready, leapt to his feet and took the rudder himself.

We again spent the night at Low Island and reached Cairns the next

Preceding page: *The Rolleimarin camera I developed in 1951 is still being used by most top-rank photographers. Focusing is by ground-glass viewfinder—an advantage especially for close-ups taken with special lenses. All other adjustments are possible under water; so is the use of flash.*

Above: *Queen angel fish (Angelichthys ciliaris) in the Caribbean. To take this kind of picture one must patiently stalk the fish, one's mask pressed against the ground-glass viewfinder. Earlier scientific publications often represented coral fishes in the wrong colours. This was because they were painted from dead or captured specimens whose coloration had altered.*

Right: *Minute cardinal fish (apogonidea) among the feathered branches of a hydroid colony, taken with a close-up lens.*

The underwater photographer is a match for the surrealist painter. The blue ocean depths contain subjects every bit as bizarre as the wildest products of human fantasy. But only the flash camera reveals them: frequently the underwater photographer only sees what he has taken after developing his film.

Above: *A still life of feather-star, horny coral and sponge.*

Left: *A dragon fish* (Pterois volitans): *the spines of its dorsal fins are poisonous.*

South Sea idyll on Tillanchong Island in the Bay of Bengal. The island is mountainous, covered with jungle, and uninhabited. Places still untouched by human beings have become rare. We have spread all over the globe—and much has been ruthlessly destroyed. Not until our interests begin to suffer—as, for instance, through what is now recognized as 'pollution of the environment'—does public opinion support the idea of protection, a demand long raised by scientists.

Untouched fauna on one of the Galapagos Islands: a colony of sea lions. A number of nature's greatest wonders have been saved from destruction by the creation of animal reserves and parks; but so long as we talk about 'protection of the environment' we have barely come within sight of the real problem. Animals and plants were not created for Man: we ourselves developed from among them, we ourselves are part of 'nature'. That is why we should talk not of 'the world around us' but of 'our world', and why we should feel part of it.

Particularly threatened today are the fish of the littoral zone—mainly by the growing number of under-
water fishermen who hunt them with increasingly efficient weapons. Already the coasts of the Mediterranean
and many tropical coasts—such as those of Tahiti and Jamaica—have been 'hunted clean'. Unless skindivers
want to rob themselves of the pleasure of watching a colourful aquatic world, they must support the call
for a world-wide ban on all mechanical underwater weapons. Above: blue parrot fish (callyodon).

afternoon. Beside the bed in our hotel room there were no fewer than thirty empty beer bottles. The place, normally so dignified, was changed beyond recognition. Nearly all the guests had drunk a lot more than was good for them and hardly anyone knew who belonged in which room. Everybody was embracing everybody else and there was cheerful singing in the lounge.

At MacDonald's invitation we had Christmas cake at his home, and Fred and Peg Williams collected us there and drove us from one house to another. Everywhere we met new people and all of them told us stories about sharks. None of them believed that we had already dived by the outer reef.

The following morning Fred and Peg drove us in their car into the highlands, where we spent two wonderful days at Yongaburra. Everybody was saying that the rainy period would start early that year. And once it started raining properly it would not stop for a long time. In Cairns the water would then rise to fifteen inches in the streets and the shopkeepers would put sandbags outside their doors to stop the water coming in.

The moment we were back in Cairns I got in touch with the bush pilot whose small aircraft provided the link with remote localities. If we were to reach our destination in time we would have to study the unending reef ranges from a bird's-eye view, take aerial photographs, and decide in advance on the best spot for our work. The bush pilot agreed to fly us over the entire reef area from Cairns to north of Lizard Island. As his little aircraft was open on both sides we should be able to look down as much as we pleased and take photographs. We took off early in the morning and first flew out to Evening Reef, where we circled for half an hour. MacDonald, who had never flown before, accompanied us.

During my close study of Cook's diaries it had occurred to me that it was perhaps a mistake to assume that he had foundered on Endeavour Reef. Two hours before her accident the *Endeavour* had passed through shallow water which had rapidly dropped to seventeen fathoms. The general view hitherto was that these shallows had been the outermost flat end of Pickersgill Reef, but it could quite well have been a very slight elevation marked on the charts as Bonner Rock. If that assumption was correct then her course would have taken her not to Endeavour Reef but to Evening Reef. We circled over both reefs and I took several hundred photographs. We later patched them together laboriously into one mosaic and so obtained an accurate overall chart of the reef ranges as they are today.

We next flew to Ruby Reef, which we already knew from sea-level, and then on over the long chain of Ribbon Reefs which, from the air, looked like long strings of sausages. Each individual reef in the string was curved towards the sea at its centre with both ends arching back. On their inner side they were all flat and sandy, and along the deep-water line rose towers similar to those near which we had dived. Within the narrow passages small reefs had formed and were evidently still growing vigorously.

What interested us most was the outer edge. Here the long white chains of breakers washed over the reef plateaus and hard in front of them the sea was bottomless and black. At a few points—especially on the third, fourth and fifth Ribbon Reefs—we saw outside the reef edge a barrier which clearly did not come right up to the surface but which formed a longitudinal channel. I could not find an explanation for this and determined to get a closer look at these formations come what may. We flew over the Cormorant Gap and over the twelfth Ribbon Reef, named after Yonge, then over Carter Reef and Day Reef, between which Cook had safely regained the open sea. The endless range of reefs there makes a wide turn so that the last two run in a north-westerly direction. Of particular interest to us was the adjoining Hicks Reef. At its western end on its outer edge were some small and most promising bays.

On our drive home from the airfield Lotte suddenly pointed to a hosiery shop. Its window contained numerous dummy ladies' legs cover with silk stockings. We stopped the car, went in and to everybody's astonishment bought one of the legs. It was made of plastic. Back at the hotel I filled it with plaster of Paris. Here was something for the murderous giant clam to try its strength on. The comparison was not altogether fair since the dummy leg had virtually no ankle and, moreover, was much too hard. But at least it was a leg, and it was the best leg we could find.

At our Destination

On the morning of 2nd January I left Cairns with MacDonald. As we had been notified of the arrival of a new camera, Lotte stayed behind and was to fly out to Cooktown to meet us there. We first sailed to Green Island, where a gentleman from Cairns wanted to show us a giant clam over six feet long. But he spent three hours searching for it in vain. So we dropped him and sailed on to Pixie Reef, which we reached while the light was still good. This was a typical young reef, rising like a solitary dome from the sea bed 120 feet down. Its surface was covered with magnificent gardens entirely of stagshorn coral, through which flowed a current so strong that the fish seemed to be blown about between the coral trees as though by a strong wind. In an attempt to take photographs I clutched a coral branch with one hand, but the current swept me away and washed me right across the reef. As if in a river I was carried through ravines and channels, and everywhere there were fish fiercely

176

flicking their tails and struggling with their heads against the current. Two small sharks were streaking like rockets to and fro between the corals. Everything was caught in the stream; only the corals stood stiff and unconcerned. With majestic calm they raised their palmate branches and delicate stone buds into the turbulence around them.

We spent a wet and thundery night in the shelter of Cape Tribulation. By sunrise we had reached Evening Reef, which we had circled so often in the plane. With the aid of our patchwork charts I examined its outermost bastions. But these dropped so steeply that they could not be reconciled with Cook's data. If the *Endeavour* had foundered here she would have hung over the edge of a vertical wall.

So it must have been Endeavour Reef after all where the famous cannon were lying. Two hours later we were there. I had worked out seven zones through which the boat was going to tow me with my breathing apparatus on a criss-cross course. Nowadays there are far more comfortable aids for this kind of thing, but all I had then was a small plank on a rope, which I clutched at both ends and with which I steered my way up and down. I don't believe that I have ever since been so persistently afraid as I was that day and the next.

The water was so dirty that I could scarcely see fifteen or twenty feet. In the sea, especially when there are sharks about, that is very little. I kept close to the bottom and floated over incredible coral formations. It was like a huge field of ruins: at some spots the corals were piled on top of each other in colourful confusion to a height of several feet. A cyclone must have passed over this region fairly recently; tall towering blocks had sagged like giant trees in a primeval forest, and over them younger corals were already growing profusely in the strangest shapes.

Judging by investigations made in the Maldives and off Samoa, my search had very little hope of success. It had been established that over a span of a thousand years corals formed a cover eighty feet thick; by this calculation the reef would have grown some fifteen feet since the wreck of the *Endeavour*. On the other hand, from studies on sunken ships I had observed that the growth of coral did not proceed quite so rapidly on foreign bodies, frequently not even reaching one-tenth of the normal rate. On such foreign bodies, moreover, the corals form a very special association, involving far more different species than on a reef. Thus even if everything was totally encrusted there was some hope that the spot might be pinpointed in this way.

I gritted my teeth and at a speed of one to two knots glided over endless distances through the opaque water. Strikingly large giant clams lay massive among the coral debris. They seemed like eerie blossoms of the underworld, traps lurking amidst all this ruin.

A large mako shark was swimming straight ahead of my gliding path. Ponderously it moved out of the way and I did not see it again. Then, on my second tow, I was followed by two whaler sharks which showed the same kind of interest in me as pikes do in an angler's hook. I got so nervous that I cut short my glide and considered sailing on to Cooktown by nightfall. But I kept thinking of those coral-encrusted cannons of the great navigator, so I overcame my reluctance and completed our programme the following morning. I did not find anything, but at least I felt that I had done my best. Let the cannon continue to rest peacefully, entombed in this coral chaos.

The sun was setting as we entered the derelict port of Cooktown. Of this once flourishing gold-mining town nothing is now left. The mines have long been exhausted and the harbour has proved unsuitable for sizeable ships. Finally a cyclone destroyed a large proportion of the houses. At one time the town had numbered 20,000 inhabitants; now there were 350.

Lotte met us in a long deserted street with a few scattered tumble-down houses. She seemed greatly relieved to see us.

'I have taken a room in this rickety shed which calls itself a hotel,' she reported. 'Everyone's drunk here.'

MacDonald gave us a lantern in case we wanted to return on board for the night. He warned us against wild boars which were apt to attack nocturnal walkers.

The only hotel in town looked exactly like the boarded sheds one sees in westerns. The doors were crooked and a few not exactly confidence-inspiring figures were propping up the bar. A particularly unshaven giant rose as we entered. He vigorously shook hands with us, forced us to have a beer with him, and told us about a certain Mike Buzzarton who had been a tourist guide on Daydream Island.

To impress the girls this man had performed headstands on the masthead of his ship. If, when sitting at the bar, he was called away he would invariably take out his glass eye and place it by his glass to make sure no one drank his beer. His speciality had been fighting sharks with a knife. For this purpose he would choose an entirely harmless species with a thin skin, and with these he would stage terrifying duels. 'Until he made a mistake one day and found himself facing a grey nurse shark,' the giant concluded with a grin. 'That was the end of his shark fighting.'

The other beer drinkers seemed likewise to be informed about our plans from the newspapers. One told us about Otis Barton, who had dived off Lizard Island and had been attacked by a shark there. Quite recently a young couple had been eaten by sharks in the harbour of Cooktown. They all grinned and drank our health.

As it was still windy and overcast the following morning I asked MacDonald to show us the six-foot giant clam he had told us about. We anchored near the spot. He and the boy towed us about in our minute dinghy for two hours, staring at the bottom, only twelve feet below. But the clam was no longer there. Instead MacDonald showed us some mangroves on the coast, among whose roots small but very tasty oysters were growing. Since his whole cargo hold was full of ice, to enable us to preserve any fish we caught en-route, we enjoyed a delicious first course to our meal that night.

The following day, at long last, was fine again. There was still a strong south-easterly blowing but this would not affect our destination, Hicks Reef. Since the small indentations on its outer side, which we had spotted from the air, all faced north they were bound to be sheltered.

We anchored at the north-western corner and with my diving equipment I stepped into a scene of breathtaking beauty. Through a curving forty-foot-deep ravine I reached a veritable submarine temple. It measured over fifty feet in diameter, and its vertical walls were covered with blossom-shaped corals as if with fantastic ornaments. The ceiling was provided by the silvery waves; the floor was a flower garden glowing in all colours and hues. Moreover, fish from far and wide seemed to have assembled here. In fantastic swarms and patterns they were hanging almost motionless in the crystal-clear space.

I swam back for Lotte. She took the newly-arrived Rolleimarin flashlight camera and I took an underwater Leica with a telescopic lens in order to take close-ups of fishes. At the entrance to the temple we stopped as if before a work of art. It almost seemed blasphemous that we, the first human beings, should disturb this peace.

Then we swam in, right among the fish, and started work. I used my small spear as a yardstick for my photographs. In order to get sharp pictures with my telelens I had to get the range correct to within two inches. I focused to the length of my spear, held it to one side and clicked the shutter when a fish was at the right distance.

An exceedingly elegant shark, about five feet long, streaked twice across the chamber at breathtaking speed. Like colourful fireworks the shoals of fish scattered in all directions. The shark made a casual movement and disappeared through one of the ravines leading to the outer slope of the reef.

Meanwhile, I saw Lotte use her flash. Her first object was a grouper which took such fright when the flash went off that it escaped almost as fast as the shark and through the same ravine. She then took two shots of wrasse which, strangely enough, did not react at all. On the other hand, a near-by giant clam closed with a plainly audible jerk.

A coral towering in the middle of the chamber had an ugly lump on top of it. I prodded it with my spear. To our surprise it hopped down. It was the most poisonous of all fishes, the notorious stone fish. The spikes of its dorsal fin eject a nerve poison which is said to have lethal effect. The creature is so sure of its defensive strength that it rarely budges if one inadvertently touches it or steps on it. That is why it is particularly dangerous. Even with a well-trained eye it is almost impossible to distinguish a stone fish from its surroundings. We swam up along the opposite wall of the chamber across a small barrier and reached a neighbouring ravine whose walls dropped steeply some fifty or fifty-five feet to a sandy floor. Down there hovered a long grey shark of about ten feet with a smaller one swimming around it—perhaps a youngster circling its mother.

We descended some fifteen feet when the small shark noticed us and by some movement alerted the big one. The latter turned immediately and came up towards us by the fastest route at an oblique angle. By the shape of its tail, its short nose and its projecting teeth I at once recognized it as a grey nurse shark.

Behind us the ravine narrowed. I moved in front of Lotte and held out my spear towards the shark. It came so close with its head that I prodded it. It flicked back, described an arc and now returned from the other side. It seemed to have lost interest in me but to be making for Lotte instead. It was probably attracted by the reflector of her flashlight. Whenever I prodded it it opened its mouth like a large vicious dog. Everything was happening so quickly and unexpectedly that we did not realize the seriousness of the situation until afterwards. Suddenly there was a flash behind me and the shark raced off downwards at an incredible speed.

Lotte had triggered off a flash. Rarely have we seen a shark move so fast and straight.

Down below, at about a hundred feet, it about-turned and very quickly came towards us again. We had by now reached the upper edge of the rock face and slipped over the shallow barrier into the large chamber. There we climbed to its upper edge so that our heads were above water. We took our breathing tubes out of our mouths and yapped for air.

'Did you get him?' I asked Lotte.

'I've no idea. I just held the camera in front of me and suddenly the flash went off. Did you see its teeth?'

The sun was at the edge of a large black cloud. When we had calmed down a little we descended once more and swam down the passage leading to the outer slope of the reef. Carefully keeping against the rock face we rounded the corner.

We had reached our destination. Admittedly this reef was one of the few whose outer face was not struck by the trade wind but it was nevertheless undoubtedly the outside of the Barrier. Before us lay the boundless vastness and abyssmal depth of space. Under water it suddenly went dark. The cloud had moved in front of the sun. We were looking on the sombre and ghostly reality behind the mental picture we had so often painted for ourselves.

The reef face dropped down at an acute angle like some ancient rampart broken up by tracks and rifts and overgrown with flowering climbing plants. But here there were only small tough species of coral, adhering to the rock like clumps of moss. The formations were not nearly so magnificent as in the sheltered water of our temple. As the sun's diffused light had gone we were able to gaze down to a much greater depth. Lower down the coral formations were more slab-shaped. There, too, a large turtle was slowly paddling along.

We went a little deeper and examined all the corals and fishes we encountered. Towards the open sea a shoal of large king mackerel was sailing past. We saw them through a veil of lesser fish which were hanging in space like frozen falling stars. Generally speaking, the fish life along the Great Barrier was not particularly interesting. Nor did we encounter a single shark. As Lotte's manometer was showing only ten atmospheres of oxygen we cast one last look at this structure, thousands of years old, to which we had been the first human visitors, and swam back through the ascending passage into the now dusky submarine temple, and from there through the winding ravine back to our boat. For the first time we felt the equals of the Great Barrier Reef.

The weather became exceedingly close and sultry. The air was as heavy as lead and we could feel in every nerve that rainy and stormy weather was gathering around us. Only reluctantly did MacDonald agree to continue our voyage according to our timetable. Inland, only a few hundred miles away, a cyclone was raging. If it changed its direction it might hit us.

We reached the tenth Ribbon Reef over a completely smooth sea. Even so, there was a heavy swell at its outer edge. I was rowed to one of the small reefs which had grown up in the passage between the ninth and the tenth reefs, and there I developed a new method of diving.

Since there were unwelcome sharks off the vertical reef face, I went overboard in the shallow water over the reef plateau and there searched for one of those openings which communicated with the reef's system of grottos. Down there it was as if I were in a huge rabbit warren, with passages branching off in all directions and some of them emerging on the outside of the vertical wall at a depth of thirty to forty feet. Having carefully examined the grottos I ventured as far as the exits and sat down on the edge. I was quite safe there, knowing that behind me was a hole into which I could withdraw in case of danger, like a snail into its shell.

My impressions of that moment came back to me spontaneously five years later, in 1957, when I was writing the preface to a new book which was to bear the ambiguous title *Wir kommen aus dem Meer* (*We Come from the Sea*, Jarrolds, 1958). I wrote then:

As I was sitting at the entrance to this grotto with my small breathing apparatus, observing the fish and the fish in turn observing me, I suddenly had the impression that these eyes were in fact the eyes of the ocean. . . .

I suddenly saw the totality of all oceans as one single vast vibrating individual. . . .

Down here in the sea, at a moment in the distant past, was lit that mysterious spark which triggered off such a miraculous evolution on our cooling planet. . . .

Was not all life a kind of manifestation . . . a condensation and embodiment of the properties innate in the sea, produced by the energy of the sun? . . . And was not I, an air-breathing creature penetrating into this submarine world with artificial gills, likewise such a manifestation returning ultimately to the sea, though differently from a river or a raindrop?

. . . I suddenly saw the whole multitude of terrestrial animals and plants from the perspective of their origin. . . .

The various branches of the natural sciences are now certain that all manifestations of life are parts of one single immensely complex process which took its origin in the cooling oceans some 1,500 million years ago. . . . This miracle, far greater than a single act of creation of separate organisms, manifested itself somewhere in the womb of the sea. I have never since got rid of this idea. It has led me to view anything I have seen or experienced in the sea with redoubled reverence and redoubled interest.

The weather was getting increasingly threatening. MacDonald and the boy spent half their day at the radio trying to get the weather service. The wind turned almost every hour and sudden showers came down upon us time and again. On the morning of 10th January the sea was completely smooth as if before a storm. Tall black cloudbanks were piling up towards the mainland.

It was now or never. We sailed round the reef. On its outer side, too, the sea was entirely smooth. I dived close to the edge. What I saw was the most dismal sight of my life. I was gazing on an enormous slope dropping obliquely, with not a single sizeable coral growing on it.

The scene was reminiscent of a rocky coast in the Mediterranean. The enormous power of the waves and the swell had scoured everything smooth. The water was dark and not very clear, and apart from a few groupers a good way down I saw virtually no fish. I dived as deep as I could, continually turning around. If a shark appeared at this spot there was nowhere for me to hide on the bare slope. But no shark showed up. I investigated the slope as much as my nervousness permitted and was vastly relieved to get back into the boat. Now all we had to do was to sail over to the fifth Ribbon Reef and inspect the strange outer channels there.

During the next two days rain fell almost uninterruptedly. A cold wind was sweeping over the sea. We were lying in the shelter of the fourth Ribbon Reef and MacDonald was getting increasingly anxious for us to return. There was no doubt—the rainy period had started. Since heavy breakers were lashing the outer edge, I decided on the desperate plan of risking a sally right across the reef plateau in our minute dinghy. It was raining, and halfway there our small outboard motor packed up. I left the boy with the boat in chest-deep water and, wearing diving equipment and carrying a spear, struggled against the current as far as the breakers. After a number of falls I got through below them and really found myself in the channel.

Here everything looked just as dismal and deserted as at the ninth Ribbon Reef, except that there was another wide barrier outside the reef slope proper. I forced myself to swim across. It was just as smooth and devoid of living coral as the slope itself. There were no clues to the manner of its origin. But it must have been formed a long time ago.

In the end I lost my nerve after all. Although there really was no reason I chased back through the breakers in a kind of panic. Several times I struck sharp corals, had to spit out my mouthpiece and swallowed water. In a heavy rain-squall I staggered back into the dinghy. The boy helped me aboard and the current quickly carried us to the ship. I assured MacDonald that there was now no longer any obstacle to our return.

In the rain it was difficult to make out the reefs and we made only slow headway. We spent the night in the shelter of the second Ribbon Reef, in a violent storm. The next day the sky was totally black but it rained only intermittently. We reached Low Island and continued our voyage the next morning.

'Do you know what we've completely forgotten about?' Lotte suddenly asked.

'Well?'

'Our leg!'

She was quite right. We had been waiting for a particularly large giant clam and eventually forgot about our experiment. Now that the sky was clearing a little we sailed over to Michaelmas Cay, a large sandbank on which thousands of terns were hatching. On the leeward side of the reef, in rather cloudy water, we eventually found a few medium-sized giant clams. With one of these we now staged our experiment.

While Lotte was taking pictures I thrust the leg between the opened shells and—just as fast as a man who might have stepped in inadvertently—withdrew it again. Or rather, I tried to withdraw it. But the clam had already closed and was holding it. The more I pulled and twisted the more firmly the two halves of the clam closed. The creature certainly had no sinister intentions but merely reacted to the irritation of a foreign body and tried to shut itself in.

I waited until I noticed some loosening and suddenly jerked again. But again the clam was quicker. After thirty-five minutes we gave up, hauled the clam up by a rope and pulled it into shallow water. With a knife mounted on a stick I thrust between its two shells and cut through its main muscle. Only now was the leg released and we were able to inspect the damage. The edges of the shells had cut into the plaster from both sides.

So the stories about the murderous giant clam would seem to be true. If a native gathering sea cucumbers in chest-deep water stepped into a giant clam at low tide it was entirely possible that it would hold him until he had drowned in the rising water. Equally a diver reaching between the clam's shells could undoubtedly die a pitiful death.

Before returning home we paid a visit to Heron Island in the southern part of the Barrier Reef, some 600 miles from Cairns. Unfortunately the weather was bad here too, but we nevertheless dived among the near-by reefs.

Below fifteen feet we found most corals dead and silted up, but at the top, on the reef edge, there was a profusion of life. Once again we found confirmation of the law that the number of species diminishes in a cooler climate whereas the number of individuals increases enormously. In contrast to the exceedingly manifold formations near Cairns the reefs here were made up of a very small number of species but these were predominant over great distances.

Regretfully we said farewell to the Great Barrier Reef. We returned to Sydney where, in response to an invitation from the Royal Zoological Society, I spoke about our experiences. Two days later we were 3,000 nautical miles away, at Canton Island, whose parallel reef channels we had noticed while flying from America to Australia.

We were greeted by a cloudless sky. A few friendly Polynesians watched us stowing away our somewhat battered equipment in a car put at our disposal by the airline.

We drove a short distance across the atoll, which was overgrown with low scrub, and at a few places tried to reach the reef slope by wading through the shallow water of the outer reef plateau. The channels we had sighted from the air began in the surf region and were three to five feet deep. They had evidently been washed out by the water flowing back into the sea and offered a simple way of getting into the deep water underneath the breakers. One merely had to find the end of one such canal and fling oneself in; after that one was drawn out automatically and rapidly underneath the rumbling waves.

The outer reef edge sloped moderately at first and then steeply, not unlike the outside of Hicks Reef. A particular species of shark, with a black and white patterned dorsal fin, was common here. We saw up to ten specimens simultaneously. They proved to be sensitive to sound and were frightened off by shouting. On our third foray we were accompanied by Jim Beudecker, a Dutch employee of the airline, who until then had dived only in the shallow water of the inner lagoon. He later wrote to me that he had completely overcome his fear of sharks and sent me underwater photographs which he had taken, all alone, on the outer slope.

We stayed for three days, had another three days in Hawaii, and eventually flew back to Europe.

We were no sooner back than the problems of equipping our ship burst upon us. The next few months were among the most difficult but also among the best of my life. The plan I had been striving to realize for years was now step by step becoming reality. Our ship was more than merely a purposeful assembly of metal and wooden parts, of countless motors, special instruments and articles of use—it was a living organism which we were developing, piece by piece, towards functional capability. It did not consist of cells but it was nevertheless a kind of extension of our own bodies, a gigantic organ with the aid of which we would magnify enormously our own personal achievements. As a biologist I could not help comparing the development of our research ship with the evolution of animal and vegetable organisms. The required function dictated and indeed directed the necessary structure of this organ in exactly the same way as the functions to be performed by a fin, lung or leaf had in the course of evolution determined the structure of these organs. The parallel went a good deal further. Each organ not only had to perform its own function but had to meet certain 'internal' demands. The components of which it was made had not to obstruct one another but had to be mutually attuned and integrated. Any industrialist who builds up a firm is familiar with this problem. The problem of internal harmony is absolutely decisive. In our case it covered not only the correct allocation of shipboard accommodation and its equipment, but even more so the selection of the necessary members of the expedition. The *Xarifa* required a captain, two officers, one engineer, one cook, one steward, four full-time and two light-duty sailors. That was a total of twelve. In addition we had envisaged accommodation and working space for eight scientists and technical assistants. We needed a doctor and we needed a wireless operator. We found a good combination in Dr Heino Sommer; he was a doctor and a radio ham—thus combining two functions in one person. Likewise we needed an experienced sound technician for the continuation of our vibration experiments started in the Red Sea. Dr Georg Scheer was a professional zoologist who was also a physicist—again a fortunate combination of functions. I needed an accomplished photographer, but also a precision mechanic capable of repairing our countless instruments in the event of breakdown. Once we were in remote regions we had to be entirely self-sufficient. This vital double function was discharged by Kurt Hirschel, a graduate engineer. Professor E. Ankel, Rector of Giessen University, an experienced zoologist and a little older than the rest of us, was prepared to join us for at least the first part of our expedition. This was of particular importance as he was Adviser to the German Research Community, the authority most likely to finance the purely scientific activities of our voyage. As an outstanding representative of behavioural studies, this exceedingly important young science, we were fortunate in getting Dr I. Eibl-Eibesfeldt to agree to participate. As a cameraman I hired Konstantin Tschet, an old hand at feature films. As an experienced diver who would also be able to help me with underwater photography Lt-Cmdr Jimmy Hodges was to join us, an Englishman who had made a name for himself as a naval frogman and underwater cameraman. Each one of these picked members of our team made himself responsible for part of our overall organization and played an active part in getting our necessary equipment and spares together. At Hirschel's request I equipped not only a carpenter's shop but also a precision mechanic's workshop on board. As captain I enlisted Johannes Diebitsch, who had served as First Officer on board the training schooner *Grossdeutschland* and who made himself responsible for the selection of the rest of the crew.

A German film distributor declared himself ready to guarantee 300,000 marks for a film about our first voyage. This was the most vital financial contribution. Admittedly he stipulated that I should go even further along the road taken in my last film—if possible, I was to dispense altogether with a spoken commentary and shape the story-line entirely with the aid of dialogue, just as in a feature film. I agreed unhesitatingly—indeed, in my position I was prepared to agree to anything in order to overcome our growing difficulties. Not until later did I realize with some alarm what I had let myself in for. I was to ask the scientists and officers accompanying me to make themselves available as actors in a film plot. I—though no expert—was to write a scenario during our voyage, a film script that would be able to compete with ordinary feature films. In brief, laymen as we were—apart from our professional cameraman

Tschet—we were to join battle with a highly organized industry. Considering that our film was the first German Technicolor production and that it was shown in England at the Embassy Cinema in Leicester Square, where all the Royal Command Performances were held, and, what is more, as an ordinary evening feature, I am still amazed at our achievement. The fact that not all reviewers were favourably disposed towards our strange hybrid product is hardly surprising.

All my collaborators were immediately ready to accept this additional function. The one thing that mattered to all of us was our real purpose. We had no doubt that, after all this film work, we should still have enough time for our scientific work. We were all anxious to prove that this new method of research was not only feasible but could produce valuable results. That alone was what mattered.

ON BOARD THE XARIFA TO THE 'BEWITCHED ISLANDS'

Hunting the Sperm Whale

Six months later came the moment we had been working for. Her sails filled, our proud *Xarifa* was heading out to sea from Hamburg. She was to take us into the Caribbean and to the Galapagos Islands on an eight-month voyage. Thousands had come to see us off. There were few sailing ships of her size left in the world. The people who waved to us all the way down the Elbe to Cuxhaven in saluting the *Xarifa* were probably paying homage to a bygone age.

Our mainmast was just over a hundred feet tall and we carried 5,900 square feet of canvas. With our auxiliary engine we had a speed of up to nine knots; under sail we could touch twelve. We carried twenty tons each of fuel, oil and water; this meant a cruising range, with the engine, of 4,000 nautical miles (roughly from Hamburg to the Antilles), and water supplies for a maximum of five months, counting ten and a half pints per head per day. But as we were going to call at numerous ports en route we did not have to be too economical with water.

As soon as the last guests had gone ashore and the coast had vanished behind us, our normal shipboard routine began, a routine which was to weld twenty men and one woman into a community. After a brief stop in London, where we picked up our second cameraman, Lt-Cmdr Jimmy Hodges, we crossed the Channel and subsequently the Bay of Biscay in rough weather. Books on marine mammals and whaling passed from hand to hand. Off the Azores, our first destination, we intended to observe and film sperm whales under water. The more we read about these largest surviving beasts of prey, the more eagerly we were looking forward to our first encounter.

Their mode of living is one of the most unusual in nature. They dive vertically down into a lightless deep sea and there hunt for ten-tentacle squids which they seize with their serrated lower jaws. They then surface at top speed, breathe about seventy times on the surface, and once more return to the deep sea. When a cable was raised from a depth of over 3,000 feet a dead sperm whale was found entangled in it—evidence that these creatures frequent such tremendous depths. It is a mystery to divers how sperm whales manage to escape caisson disease.

A human who has spent half an hour at a depth of 200 feet has to make a number of stops, totalling ninety minutes, during his ascent. Unless he does this, the nitrogen dissolved in his blood under pressure at the lower depths will form bubbles and cause an embolism resulting in paralysis and possibly in death. The sperm whale—an air-breathing warm-blooded mammal like ourselves—dives ten times as deep and surfaces without intermediate stops. One theory suggests that the nitrogen is chemically bound by the sperm oil in the creature's head, while another suggests that this is achieved by nitrogenous bacteria. But since the sperm whale does not breathe below water, and indeed exhales before submerging, it could well be that the nitrogen content of its blood is not ever sufficient to cause an embolism.

Considering the difficulties the aquatic creatures had to overcome in order to adapt themselves to a terrestrial existence, it is astonishing that some of them should subsequently, under difficulties no less serious, have returned to an aquatic life. The dolphins and whales are descended from terrestrial beasts of prey which moved into the ocean some fifty million years ago. As warm-blooded animals they had to protect themselves against the cold of the water by a thick layer of fat, the blubber, and, since they could not restore their lost gills, had to content themselves with limited diving periods. Dolphins dive for twenty minutes; sperm whales can remain under water for over an hour. They owe this ability to small bundles of vessels distributed throughout their bodies in which they are able to store large quantities of blood and hence also a great deal of oxygen, which is supplied on a priority basis to the central nervous system when they run short of air.

The layer of blubber—originally a necessary aid—proved particularly advantageous. In the Arctic seas, where fishes and sharks find their activity restricted by the cold, the whales became superior to them thanks to their internal heating. In consequence, they were able to hold their own particularly well in the cold seas and it is probably from there that they have spread all over the world.

Mating of sperm whales takes place on the surface. They give birth to living young, usually only one. Like young dolphins, the whale calves are able to swim and breathe from the start; they are instructed by the mother animal and suckled under water. They live in herds and their migrations are subject to seasonal cycles. A young English zoologist, Robert Clarke, had been in the Azores a year before us and had told us that August was the best month for observing the whales. Unfortunately we had been unable to get there in time but we were hoping that we might still have good weather in September.

It was dark when we reached San Miguel. We anchored over a fairly steep bottom off La Capelas. In no time a procession of small lights was coming out towards us and circling us like a chain of glow-worms. These were fishermen setting out with carbide lamps. The first Portuguese words were exchanged, there was laughter, and bottles of beer were passed overboard. The boats stuck close to us and we watched them haul up their nets full of wriggling fish.

The following morning the scene had changed. Instead of a dark silhouette we had before us steep sunlit slopes covered with green vegetation, and on top of them the spotlessly clean houses of the small fishing village. Between the steep black cliffs of the coast we saw a minute port with numerous boats pulled up on the beach. I went ashore with Captain Diebitsch, but a sentry informed us that we had to report at Ponta Delgada, the capital. So we sailed the *Xarifa* round the island.

San Miguel is the largest and richest island in the Azores. Like the rest it is of volcanic origin. According to an ancient chronicle a high mountain is said to have stood at its western end and to have served the Portuguese discoverers as a landmark as recently as 1432. The mountain is said to have vanished in a tremendous volcanic eruption and to have dragged seven towns down into its three-mile-wide crater. We later visited this spot, the Sete Citades, the 'seven cities'; today it looks very peaceful. The vast circle is covered with magnificent flowering *Hedychium gardnerianum*, a lily-type plant of Himalayan origin, and at the bottom of the crater are two picturesque lakes, one of them green and the other blue.

As soon as we had completed all formalities at Ponta Delgada, we asked for the brothers Cymbron Borges de Sousa who ran the island's whaling business. Clarke had enjoyed their help, and we too were received in the most friendly manner. Whereas the first whalers, who arrived here from Brittany in the sixteenth century, settled in the north-east of the island, the centres of whaling nowadays are Ponta Delgada and La Capelas.

The whales would surface some ten to fifteen miles offshore and be sighted by lookouts posted at prominent spots on the island. Mr Pedro Cymbron assured us that he had two elderly men who could estimate the size of a whale at that distance to within three or four feet, simply from the way it blew its spray.

'When a whale is sighted we are notified by telephone,' he continued, 'and alert the boats from here. On the two sides of the island there are flotillas of two launches and six to eight whale-catchers each in permanent readiness. They are in radio-telephone contact with us and the observer posts in the mountains, and are directed to the whales in this way. Once they have closed in the motor boats are halted and the rowing boats try to overtake the creatures.

Under the aegis of the C.M.A.S. (Confédération Mondiale Activitées Subaquatiques) underwater
hunting competitions are being held, with prizes for whoever kills the most fish. The movitation, no
doubt, is man's hunting instinct and his desire to impress. But from purely selfish considerations all
underwater sportsmen should oppose this trend. Evidence that the stock of fish, and hence the magic of
the submarine world, can be wiped out in next to no time is already available.
Above: Black angel fish (Pomacanthodes arcuatus).

The sensation of weightlessness and three-dimensional locomotion is especially strong when one visits sunken ships. One circles the masts and superstructures, much as the birds used to, one glides over the deck into the cabins. The picture shows my wife at the rail of the Umbrea, which went to the bottom off Port Sudan. As the ship carried a cargo of ammunition, the danger of spontaneous ignition persists to this day. Large quantities of Maria Theresa dollars are said to be locked up in her strongrooms.

*In the Nicobar Islands we discovered the wreck of a British warship, whose lamp-room was still intact.
The ship had been under water for thirty years, but when we had cleaned the lamps they were almost as
good as new. Here Dr Eibl and I are inspecting our share of the 'salvage operation'.*

Konrad Lorenz has shown that the striking colours and patterns of coral fish have a signal function addressed to the other members of their own species. The signal means: 'This is my territory. If you approach any closer I will fight you!' This 'intra-species aggression' ensures that members of a species are very regularly distributed over a suitable living area, and that this space, therefore, is optimally utilized.

We are accustomed to seeing each animal and each plant as an individual, as having a purpose in itself. But seen from an evolutionary point of view, each organism is merely, as it were, a 'cross-section' of a developing stream. Common to all structures which carry evolution forward—all animals and all plants— is the requirement that they must absorb more energy than this effort itself costs. Wherever this condition is not fulfilled, evolution, or 'life', is extinguished. The picture (above) shows the juvenile form of a marine angel fish (pomacanthodes).

To compare a fish with a shoemaker's workshop or an industrial concern would seem to us absurd—but merely because of an ingrained mode of thinking. The fact is that it is not the naked human body that achieves a positive energy balance, but the 'occupational bodies' and 'organizations' developed by us. They represent, therefore, the continuation of animal and plant evolution: Man is merely the creative and controlling germ cell. Whether we are dealing with a coral fish or with General Motors, the space-time structure which carries evolution forward must always be so adapted to an existing energy source as to utilize it.

Above: *Wrasse* (Coris gaimardi); *below it a red mullet (mullidae).*

Right: *Curlyfins (cirrhitidae).*

We shall put one of these boats at your disposal, so you can be right in the thick of the hunt. Whether you will feel like getting into the water I would rather doubt.'

'You don't use harpoon guns?' I asked.

'No. The whales have disappeared off the Portuguese coast since they've been using guns. We don't want to drive them away from here as well. Whaling, as you will see and hear, is still done exactly as it was 300 years ago. Even the specially built catcher boats are still the same. A pity you didn't come sooner. We had a good season. But if you are patient you'll still see whales now.'

We organized a dinghy service to the ship. A boy was to notify us the moment any whales were reported. Jimmy Hodges and I got everything ready for underwater photography. Our first attempt was to be made by the two of us alone; later, if it was not too dangerous, Lotte was to dive with us. Tschet was to film the whaling from above water. The remaining members of the expedition would investigate the coasts and familiarize themselves with the diving equipment.

Only the fifth alarm proved genuine. In a hired car we raced to La Capelas and then galloped down the steep path to the beach, carrying our equipment. One of the motor boats was waiting for us, the other had gone ahead with the catchers and was already out of sight. A single large bull about fifty feet long had been sighted to the north-east. Whereas the sperm whale cows and their calves swim in schools, the big bulls are nearly always on their own.

Through wind and spindrift we raced towards the open sea. The sky was cloudless and conditions seemed promising. I could not have had a better diver with me than Jimmy. During the war he had trained the British frogmen and later specialized as an underwater cameraman. He had been the first to inspect the *Truculent*, the British submarine that had sunk in the Thames estuary; he had dived on his own off Zanzibar for a film company, and he had dived in the China Sea during the war. He was calmness and assurance personified. We could not suspect that he would die before our expedition was over—and while doing a perfectly safe dive.

'The question is,' Jimmy was saying, 'whether the fellow will take us for an octopus or not. We must not stick our arms or legs out too far, otherwise he might take them for tentacles and swallow us.'

After twelve miles the boats came into view. They were drifting quite calmly on the water, at considerable distances from each other, and the motor boat was likewise hove to. We were told the whale had already been hit by one harpoon and had dived. We quickly transferred our equipment into the catcher intended for us and had ourselves rowed towards the area where it would surface again.

191

We had intended to swim up towards an as yet uninjured whale. Now that it was held by a line the situation was changed. True, it only had one hook in its blubber, but the restraint this imposed on it might have irritated it. So what were we to do?

We waited. Our boatmen were looking inquisitively at our fins and at our small spears. They laughed and lit cigarettes. Suddenly there was shouting across the water. Half a mile off, fountains of spray were rising at an oblique angle. The whale had surfaced. The boat which had hooked it was moving off, being towed by the long line. A few other boats swiftly raised their sails and headed into the wind towards the whale. They all tried to block its path. In the bow of each boat, like a figurehead, stood a harpooner.

. Our crew was rowing till the oars bent. No Oxford eight could have displayed more enthusiasm. Whaling was more than just a job to these simple types. Their eyes were shining and they seemed to have completely forgotten our presence.

Suddenly they stopped. One of them straightened up and they were all talking at us at the same time. The whale had turned and was making straight for us. We saw a huge black back curving out of the water.

Picture a large locomotive moving just below the surface of the water, hunching its back now and again and surfacing. That was, roughly, what this whale looked like. Whenever it surfaced it blew a jet of spray into the air, just like a railway engine releasing a puff of steam.

Jimmy and I exchanged glances. Without further reflection I jumped overboard with my camera.

As fast as I could I swam away from the boat to get into the creature's path. Every second counted. The whale was barely fifty yards away when its back curved up once more. I rapidly dived to twenty-five feet and waited. I was right in its path. I just about had time to check the camera setting, then the beast was upon me. It looked quite different from what I had expected. A plump mass, several feet thick, was coming straight at me, wriggling with the ease of a tadpole. It was square and broad, without any shape or articulation— but the enormous thing was alive. The broad transversal tail was beating effortlessly and this motion vibrated through the whole vast fleshy colossus. Like some supernatural apparition the monster was racing towards me. Life was here embodied in a mass of incredible shapelessness.

I clicked the shutter, wound on the film, clicked once more—and the whale heard the faint sound of the shutter. Its whole massive body reacted to it. If one may say of a house that it gives a start, then this colossus just gave a start. It dived obliquely downwards. The whale had done nothing to harm me, but the click of my camera had frightened it. The rope on which it was hanging shot past me, and the last thing I saw was the great tail fin flicking up and down.

On the surface I was greeted with confused shouting. The boat, dragged by the whale, was coming straight at me through the spray. I dived quickly and saw it pass above me like a dark bird. Then, at last, I was able to breathe. I climbed back into the boat and told Jimmy what I had seen.

It was only afterwards that I realized what had been so uncanny about this creature. I had not seen an eye or a mouth. But without an eye an animal is no animal. One views a sea urchin or a starfish as a strange living ornament—but only when a creature turns its eye on us does it become a creature in our mind. It is in its eye that we see its individuality, its soul, its essence. Even when an animal attacks us we look not at its mouth or its paws but at its eyes.

What I had not myself seen was subsequently revealed by my photographs. The eyes of the sperm whale are quite minute and are located ten to thirteen feet down the side of its head. With them the sperm whale can see a short distance to either side of it, but it cannot see what lies ahead. Melville in his immortal novel *Moby Dick* has wondered about the whale's mental perception. Man is intellectually the most highly developed creature, but even so he can only focus his attention on a single point. How then does the whale orientate itself when it perceives two totally different images? Melville thought that the whale had to do some switching—either its attention was focused towards its left or it was focused towards its right. He thought this was the reason for the panicky behaviour of sperm whales when attacked simultaneously from different sides.

The motor boat came up, took us in tow and conveyed us back to the battlefield. The whale had meanwhile been hit by a second harpoon. It was now towing two boats behind it and surfaced far more often. The other motor boat cut off its path and the whale started swimming in a circle as if in a circus. When it came close to us we saw that instead of white, frothy spray it was now blowing a blood-red fountain into the air. The creature had been hit in the lung and, as the whalers put it, had 'hoisted the red flag'.

It was such a horrible sight that we did not feel like getting into the water. But on its next circuit we both went in nevertheless. The huge mass was now clearly betraying fear and pain. The creature which a short while ago had seemed so alien now aroused our understanding and compassion.

Left: *In 1970, after an absence of eighteen years, I once more went diving on the Great Barrier Reef with Lotte. On our first visit—our honeymoon—we had decided to repeat Captain Cook's historic voyage to the northern tip of Australia, lonely Cape York. We did not suspect then that we would next time be accompanied by a grown-up daughter, herself a keen diver. We were delighted to find that the Great Barrier Reef—apart from the areas where there are tourist centres—was as rich in fish as ever.*

The colossus was pitifully helpless. Lack of air forced it to surface again and again, and its tormentors were waiting for it, ready to strike at it with their spears. In spite of its condition it saw us and avoided us. It certainly did not suspect that we belonged to its pursuers. Trailing a broad dark streamer of blood it came close to us and then turned away as if trying not to hurt us with its bulk.

A sperm whale can never know what its enemy looks like, the enemy threatening it from above. Probably it regards the boats themselves as its enemy. It may think of them as thin sharp creatures, with vicious stings which they fire off above water, stings which lodge in its flesh and pull it back.

Although our sympathy was with the whale we could not but admire the men. Like swift arrows their boats skimmed over the waves, which were growing higher under the freshening wind. Skilfully they avoided its tail whenever the whale thrashed about in desperation. By incredibly clever manoeuvring they prevented anyone being caught by an uncoiling rope and dragged into the water. Boldly they rowed their boats straight on to the broad back in order to sink their flattened twelve-foot spears through the blubber. In doing so they chose the vital spots with the care of surgeons. Laughing, they straightened their bent spears against the gunwales. They were all sweating and excited. Each boat was an entity, an organized death-dealing creature which did not let go until the enemy was overcome.

The whale broke out of the circle and the hunt continued in a straight line for many miles. Drawing on some mysterious reserve of strength, it was now keeping under water for longer periods. One of the motor boats took over the two ropes and had itself pulled along by the whale. We shouted and waved, but the second motor boat totally forgot our existence. So we were left to our own devices for a while, while the wild chase disappeared over the horizon. Half an hour later it returned. The whale was still alive. Still vigorous, it was pulling the heavy motor boat without apparently noticing when the engine was put to full speed astern in order to apply a brake.

The struggle continued for four hours. The sun was considerably lower, the wind had freshened a great deal. Slowly, very slowly, the whale was tiring. More and more frequently it flung its great tail fin into the air in order to dive. It could barely manage two minutes under water now. Its body was shaking and twisting. A brilliant red circle of blood was spreading around it. The hunters now moved in from all sides, trying to deal it the *coup de grâce*. Once more it rose convulsively, and its tail swept wearily over the water. Then it rolled over and its broad pectoral fin appeared on the surface. The whale was dead.

'Over there—look!' Jimmy suddenly exclaimed.

Close below our boat several sharks were swimming straight towards the circle of blood. They had white fin tips, and each was accompanied by a dozen small pilot fish. As the whale was being towed away and the water cleared we saw the sharks biting chunks of blubber out of the whale's body. We felt no desire to watch them under water.

A week later we witnessed another hunt; this time the prey was a herd of sperm whale cows. They were only half the size of the males and died very much more quickly. The longest struggle lasted half an hour, the shortest a mere seven minutes. Altogether four cows and calves were killed.

This time we stayed in the water when the sharks appeared. They came up from the deep sea, pounced on the bleeding whales and tore pieces out of their flesh. I had always regarded sharks as beautiful, but here we came to know them as beasts. They acted as if they wanted to drink the blood. They were interested in nothing but the wound.

These sharks were exceedingly impertinent. They were scarcely longer than six or eight feet, and they came quite close to us like inquisitive dogs and would not be driven away either by shouting or by our spears. As they only appeared when there was a great deal of blood in the water, I had the impression that this species was attracted not by the sound of struggling but by the smell. Hence perhaps also their total insensitivity to screaming.

What struck us was the large number of pilot fish which surrounded each of them like a cloud. Lotte had come into the water with us when some of these pilot fish detached themselves from a sizeable shark and, in a purposeful squadron, made for us over a distance of twenty yards. They sniffed around us and sped back to their shark again in tight formation. This kind of behaviour may be responsible for the legend that pilot fish lead the shark to its prey. But in fact these sharks were so overpopulated with pilot fish that they probably came over to us to discover if we were not also sharks and perhaps still in need of pilot fish.

We were approaching a harpooned cow when, to our surprise, we sighted two further whales. One of them was a calf which evidently belonged to the wounded cow, but the other was a fully grown whale which for no obvious reason remained faithful to the harpooned animal. This was the only opportunity we had of filming uninjured sperm whales. They allowed us quite close, then they took fright and dived away.

A little later we witnessed an astonishing incident. The dying animal dropped its lower jaw almost by a right-angle and an exceedingly strange sound echoed through the water. It was like the creaking of a huge barn door, moving on rusty hinges. A very low, hard, vibrant note rang through the sea at quite perceptible strength. At first we thought that it had been produced by the opening of the whale's mouth, but we later saw another whale which produced the same sound with its mouth shut.

This call of the sperm whale, which, to the best of my knowledge, we were the first humans to hear, may explain how these creatures find one another. Normally they swim so far apart that they cannot possibly see each other under water. Frequently the bulls are miles away from the cows. How then do the sexes find each other? How do the females stay together in herds, and how do they avoid losing the herds each time they make a deep diving excursion? Dolphins also emit noises, but these sound far more normal and are reminiscent of the squeaking of pigs. The voice of the sperm whale, on the other hand, is as unreal as anything else about this astonishing monster. This very penetrating note must be audible over great distances.

It is not impossible that the whales use this call also for locating octopuses. They may possibly, rather like the dolphins, intercept the echoes with their ears. The sperm whale must certainly have some faculty of this kind since otherwise it could hardly hope to catch the fast-moving molluscs. Swimming through the darkness with its mouth open could hardly be enough.

At San Vincent, at the whalemeat factory, we witnessed the final act of the tragedy. The very animals we had seen alive under water were now dragged ashore with cranes and sliced into pieces with huge knives. The men first severed the head from the body with a long circular incision. Then a crane peeled back the thick layer of blubber from the body, while another team of men split open its head with axes.

The head of the sperm whale accounts for a good third of its total length—that of a large bull is twenty to twenty-four feet long. The strange dome above the forehead, five or six feet high, is hollow inside and divided into several chambers. These contain the valuable sperm oil, a viscous fluid of as yet unknown biological significance. We watched the workmen ladling it out of the whale's head with buckets.

The cross-section through the body clearly showed how whales differ from fishes. Because of their snaking movements their main muscles lie along both sides. But as the fishes crept on to dry land and their fins gradually developed into limbs, the dorsal and ventral muscles became decisive for their locomotion, and those along the sides diminished in importance. This was the heritage to which the marine mammals had to adapt; their tails therefore are not flicked sideways but up and down. The formation of this tail fin was a further problem. In the whales and dolphins it developed from a transversal skin fold unsupported by any kind of skeletal structure and reaching a width of over sixteen feet in large whales. The lobe-shaped frontal fins are transformed forelegs and still contain the wrist bones and finger joints in latent form. The rear legs have disappeared completely with only a small residual trace left of what used to be the pelvis.

The land animals' hair was likewise lost except for a few hairs on the nose. The nose itself became a breathing hole, and it is therefore assumed that the sperm whale has no sense of smell. The ear is closed to the outside and invisible; the skin is so thin that even a light touch will pull it off. This is why the protection of the body was taken over by the thick layer of blubber under the skin. For a shark biting a whale is like biting into a piece of cheese.

Inside one female we found an embryo. It was only three feet long, which meant it was at quite an early stage of development, since young whales are born about twelve feet long. Professor Ankel and Dr Scheer conserved it; it subsequently became the subject of a special investigation. In the whale's stomach we found numerous partially digested octopuses. The late Prince of Monaco, an enthusiastic marine biologist, has described several still unknown deep-sea species of octopuses from specimens found in the stomachs of whales.

One particular surprise was the discovery in the stomach of a fifty-one-foot bull whale of two half-digested sharks, one of them eight feet long and the other just over ten feet. This discovery caused us to view the legend of Jonah in a new light. A large sperm whale might be able to swallow a man in one piece.

When everything had been carved up into pieces and placed into the cauldron, men arrived with brooms and buckets and started to scrub the bloody battlefield. They dragged the saw-shaped lower jaw to a heap behind the factory, where forty or fifty others were already rotting away. They were left there until the forty-two teeth—each one the shape of a blunt cow horn—dropped out by themselves. The teeth were then used to make carved objects.

Two years later, in London, the well-known film director John Huston invited Lotte and me to the Elstree studios where *Moby Dick* was being filmed and showed us the huge models of the legendary white sperm whale. As I looked on the gigantic mechanically-operated mouth which, in the film, bites a catcher-boat in two, I thought of the graveyard behind the factory at San Vincent, where the final remains of these proud and eerie creatures were flung. Until they are extinct they will remain for man the symbol of demonic forces reigning the ocean depths.

The Galapagos Islands

The Galapagos Islands, the 'bewitched islands' as their Spanish discoverers called them, occupy an historic place in natural history and in Man's self-

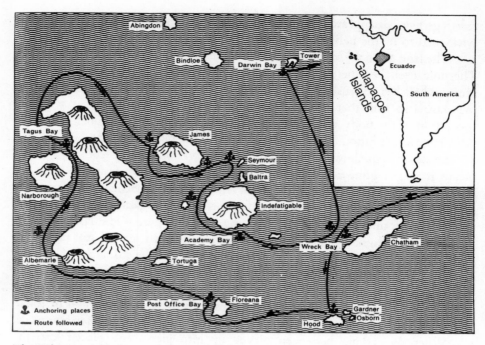

The Galapagos archipelago with the route of the Xarifa. The Humboldt current coming up from the Antarctic here meets warm equatorial currents; as a result, the sea is rough and often murky.

knowledge. It was here that Charles Darwin, on his visit on board the survey ship *Beagle* in 1835, made those observations which led him to develop his teaching of the origin of animals and Man.

We soon discovered why these islands had been called 'bewitched'. We had sighted them at nightfall, we had slowly approached them during the night, and in the morning they were gone. A strong ocean current had displaced us by many miles.

The archipelago, consisting of ten large and numerous small islands, is situated at the exact confluence of the Humboldt current, a cold current moving from Peru in an arc towards the South Sea, and of the Equatorial current which is eight to ten degrees warmer. In consequence one may find oneself diving in cold water off one island, while off another the water may be of a tropical temperature.

The composition of the islands' fauna reflects their strange position. The Equator runs between them, yet there are sea lions here and penguins. At the same time, there are tropical animals, such as large reptiles and tortoises. As we were soon to discover, there are also coral fish. Antarctic and tropical forms of life are combined here within a small space.

Towards 10 a.m. the islands were clearly in sight. The regular slopes of the Chatham and Indefatigable volcanoes rose higher and higher from the sea. Through our binoculars we gazed on scrub-grown lava slopes which we knew, from accounts we had read, to be exceedingly difficult to climb.

At the time Darwin visited the islands there were clearly visible paths running up the slopes through the thorny scrub. The Spanish pirates who called at these islands were familiar with these tracks and knew them to lead to the few water-holes found in the higher parts of the islands. The paths had been made by the giant tortoises after which the archipelago is named. *Galapagos* is Spanish for 'tortoises'. Darwin encountered large numbers of these creatures, moving uphill and downhill along their tracks. But since the crews of passing ships caught them in their hundreds, taking them on board as live food supplies, they are now near extinction.

In Darwin's day some specimens were so big that six or eight men were needed to lift them. The creatures were deaf. If Darwin approached them from behind they noticed him only when he was upon them. They then uttered a hissing noise and let themselves drop as if dead. If he stepped on their back and tapped the rear end of their armour they would stand up again and carry him along.

Large specimens yielded up to 220 pounds of flesh and their fat produced a clear oil. The hunters used to make incisions into the skin near the creature's tail to examine if there was enough fat underneath the shell. If they were not satisfied they let the creature go free again and it is claimed that they recovered from this strange operation.

At Kicker Rock, a picturesque cliff rising vertically from the sea to some 460 feet, we came quite close to Chatham. The water was a milky green and totally opaque. We then entered Wreck Bay and our anchors rattled down.

The Ecuadorian Commandant in person came on board. He invited us to the Military Casino for a drink and, towards the evening, we all went ashore in the launch. The colourless dusty beach was lined with some fifty depressing shacks. They were knocked together from boards and sheets of tin. Progreso, the main town with 500 inhabitants, lies higher up the mountain in the more humid regions.

We bought a few pineapples, which were cultivated there, and paid our respects to the neatly fenced-in Darwin Memorial. The Commandant then took us to the pleasantly furnished Casino and showed us his record-player. Outside our crew were strolling about gloomily. They had seen all there was to see in this desolate spot, and they had bought all there was to buy. As far as the eye could see one looked upon dirty sand and black lava detritus covered with thorny leafless scrub with a few birds piping in it.

The following morning Chatham was behind us and we were approaching Hood Island, which Beebe had described as the most beautiful of the Galapagos Islands. We were being escorted by numerous boobies and terns. Dolphins and large mackerel were leaping and a lonely shark fin was sailing along at some distance. After the depressing Wreck Bay we were breathing more happily in this magnificent untouched solitude. We sailed to the small island between Gardner and Hood which Beebe had christened Osborn. It rises rather like a 150-foot-high rock garden. Among creviced-riven boulders of lava spouted cacti, flowering shrubs and colourful moss, with white and pitch-black birds circling overhead.

'See them?' Dr Eibl called excitedly. Through his binoculars he was watching the flat tip of land on the southern side of the island. There were brown patches among the black rocks. Occasional sounds of bleating were coming across on the wind. Sea lions!

As soon as the *Xarifa* was anchored and the boats were in the water we rowed ashore. There was a considerable swell and landing was not easy. A sea lion, a bull at least six feet long which was ceaselessly swimming up and down in the shallow water, gave us a very unfriendly roar.

We jumped ashore with our numerous photographic and cine-cameras. A few female sea lions, which had been dozing in the sun, sat up in surprise but made no effort to move. In the shallow pools whiskered pups were playing and fighting. Barely ten paces away a buzzard was perched on a tall block of lava, watching us with interest. None of the creatures betrayed any fear.

This phenomenon had been well known ever since the islands were discovered. As there are no land predators on these islands, the animals have developed only a very slight escape reaction. Almost any bird can be approached to within a couple of yards, and the same is true of sea lions and all other creatures. Only the goats, pigs and cattle, introduced here by pirates and whalers, and which on some of the islands have greatly increased, are the exception. Now that they have lost their veneer of domestication they are once more displaying the normal flight reactions of their wild ancestors.

They are indeed bewitched islands. Wild beasts here are tame, and the tame animals introduced by Man have become wild.

If we were walking upright the sea lions let us approach only up to a certain point; but if we crawled on all fours and bleated at the same time we were actually able to touch them. While Tschet was getting his film camera in position, Dr Eibl got to work with his notepad. He established first of all that all the creatures on the western side of the headland belonged to one herd which was subject to the roaring bull in the shallow water. There were twenty-one females, each with one pup, and three pupless ones. A short distance away a smaller bull was sitting on a rock, longingly gazing on the old tyrant's harem. He was alone. He looked as if he were waiting his chance.

We soon made contact with the old gentleman. We saw a few females playing in the water and, armed with spears and underwater cameras, swam out to observe them perform their swimming tricks. The sea was cloudy, and the bottom consisted of black lava with sparse growth. We thought we were close to the female sea lions when suddenly the fat bull came at us under water. From its behaviour it was clear that it was not joking. With bared fangs it made straight for us. I prodded it with my harpoon, it roared under water, blew bubbles, about-turned and made for Lotte. I struck it again, and once more I could see that I had produced a visible bump on it. It now kept at a distance, looking rather offended. Its whole attitude suggested that it had been affronted while pursuing its proper duties. It realized that it was no match for my spear. But this spear was a weapon not admissible under the sea lions' code of honour.

Wringing his hands, Eibl implored us not to disturb the colony. We therefore took what sequences we needed for our film and left the field to him. During the next few days he was hardly ever on board. He was a disciple of Konrad Lorenz and there were no half-measures about his observations. We had to send his meals across to him by boat, as well as a flysheet and blankets, since he had decided to sleep among the sea lions. In this way he was able to observe the entire daily routine of these creatures.

In the morning, at sunrise, the bull was the first to move. It slithered into the water, swam up and down for a while and uttered its hoarse roar. It roared particularly loudly on the boundaries of its territory, where the young bull had its sleeping place. In this manner it informed all and sundry that this strip of land, complete with all the ladies on it, belonged to the old bull.

Now the females began to stir and moved into the sea. They hunted for a while, amused themselves by flinging stones into the air, and generally enjoyed themselves. Whenever they encountered the bull they rocked their heads in salutation and allowed themselves to be sniffed. A few of them went further and bit the bull in the nape of his neck. But the bull was not in the mood for pleasantries. Whenever a female swam out too far he immediately drove it back.

Meanwhile the pups had also woken up and were playing in the pools. Their mothers returned, sniffed them, each looking for its own in order to suckle it. In doing so, as Eibl observed, they made sure that the pups greeted the adults politely by bleating and rocking their heads. If a pup mistook its mother it was chased away. As it got warmer, the females and the pups lay down in the sun and slept. Sprawling in the most curious postures they scratched themselves pleasurably. Even the patrolling bull forgot his duty, fell asleep while swimming, and from time to time put his head out of the water, eyes closed, to draw breath. Whenever a current carried him towards a rock he would avoid it without waking up. When he did wake up he roared vigorously.

There was some squabbling among the ladies and some angry hissing at each other. In lesser quarrels they confined themselves to calls of 'Ek-ek'; whenever they became more violent they roared 'Oyuy, oyuy, oyuy!' Immediately the bull would hurry ashore and call them to order. 'Ow, ow, ow!' he declared. The young bull was watching wistfully and longingly from afar. He called 'Oa, oa, oa!'

Not until nightfall did the females bestir themselves again. Just before sundown they went hunting once more, and then wearily climbed ashore, the conscientious bull last of all. The pups wandered from one female to another, sniffing them, each looking for its mother. If they did not find her they would utter a pitiful 'berr'. Gradually all fell silent. At first the bull looked around every fifteen to twenty minutes—especially towards the young bull. Then he too fell asleep. And so did Dr Eibl.

We sailed across to the east coast of Gardner Island, where we saw several other colonies of sea lions. The water was again dirty, but a short distance offshore it was crystal clear. It was there that Jimmy, Lotte and I swam about on the surface with our diving equipment, trying to attract the females of the sea lions. In one colony we saw the bull lying on a rock, fast asleep. Invitingly and longingly we bleeted our 'Oa, oa, oa!'

At once the ladies pricked up their ears. They cast one glance at their sleeping master and wriggled into the sea.

We dived down to the bottom, in just under forty feet of water, and waited. Almost at once the young ladies appeared. We had never seen anything more elegant or graceful than these supple creatures. As if there were no such thing as gravity, they seemed to enjoy the water and its resistance on every inch of their skin. Their whole bodies vibrated in graceful motion. Their frontal fins served them both as paddles and for steering.

Lotte and I were standing next to each other on the bottom while Jimmy with the film camera was about fifteen yards away. As we heard the creatures squeaking, Lotte and I squeaked too. The sea lions approached quite close, circled us at a distance of barely three feet and gazed upon us with their large brown eyes which on land had seemed so dull and short-sighted but now, under water, were flashing with curiosity and intelligence. One of the females halted next to me, blew bubbles and squeaked. That was something I could do too. I blew even prettier bubbles and put the most seductive notes into my voice. The young female moved her nose right up to my extended hand. With quiet pleasure I acknowledged a simultaneous steady purr in the water—Jimmy's film camera was running.

Then the young lady shot up to the surface in a pleasurable movement, breathed in and returned in a graceful arc. A second animal brought its delicately whiskered snout almost up against our masks and inquisitively peered through the glass. A quick turn—and both of them were speeding over to Jimmy who was filming ceaselessly. They skimmed close over his camera, circled him and hurriedly swam back towards the shore. Jimmy was performing a kind of St Vitus' dance on the sea bed. Judging by his gestures he had just filmed the sequence of a lifetime.

We next dived in a strong current off the eastern point of Gardner, where a large lava cliff lies off the coast proper. What we saw here below water was almost incredible. The flat sandy bottom, sixty feet deep and lined with large boulders, was virtually covered with fish as if with a blanket. Groupers of ten to twenty pounds approached us from all directions as if offering themselves for lunch.

Behind a wall formed by stone blocks Lotte discovered a sleeping sting-ray. She roused it with her harpoon, and it was so dazed that it bumped into a stone and dislodged it. At the same moment Jimmy prodded me in the ribs. No fewer than sixteen large eagle rays were coming towards us in close formation.

Jimmy was working his camera with British sang-froid. The massive creatures slowly sailed over our heads like prehistoric winged reptiles. Suddenly the sea lions returned and again circled us. A moment later, glancing casually into a crevice in the lava, I discovered there no fewer than twelve large crayfish. As if sitting in theatre seats, they were arranged in a perfect row next to one another, stretching their long antennae before them.

We summoned the boat and Xenophon passed me one spear after another In barely five minutes I brought them all up—altogether thirty-eight pounds of them. They were magnificently patterned red and blue. Two of them had just cast off their armour and still had a soft, not yet calcareous, skin.

We also visited the minute island east of Osborn and named it Xarifa. Here the sea was positively seething with fish. Since warm and cold currents meet all round the Galapagos Islands, millions of minute suspended plankton die here, and this attracts thousands of millions of fish, which in turn are followed by the great predators.

We also saw a number of sharks, some of them of impressive size, but they displayed little interest in us. In view of their richly laden tables they probably did not think it worth their while to tackle some strange new creature.

A week had passed before we even realized it. We dived, made observations, collected specimens and took photographs. Then the current changed and the water turned opaque. On the eve of our departure we picnicked on the beach. We had shot a few wild goats and we roasted them over an open fire. The sea lions watched us from the distance. Among them an important change had taken place—the old bull had been dethroned.

One morning Eibel noticed that the young bull had taken over command. Now it was the old one that was sitting away from the herd, where the young one used to sit. Perhaps I was even indirectly responsible for the change. Perhaps I had humbled his pride by prodding him with my spear. I remembered his eyes. Something new, something superior had entered his life. Perhaps this had given the young bull the chance he needed, the chance to replace his rival.

A fortnight later, on Seymour Island, we saw a giant colony of several hundred animals. In a small, clearly defined area, a few old, half-blind bulls were sitting, waiting for death like the inmates of an old people's home. They had been defeated and cast out. They were old and weary, and were now living alongside the dried-up corpses of some which had already died. They were probably dreaming of the days when they were strong and masterful, swimming up and down their strips of the foreshore, with attractive females fussing about them and biting them in the napes of their necks. Their day had gone and no one cared about them any more. Nature, which promotes all that is young and strong and ruthlessly sweeps aside all that is old and weak, had assigned to them, as a special favour, a small patch of ground on which to die.

On Floreana Island we visited the tomb of the famous Dr Ritter, whose fate had once figured so prominently in the world's press. His patch of land had reverted to nature and nothing was left of his house. In a thicket, now totally overgrown, I found the small stone seat on which he used to sit and meditate.

He had come to the Galapagos Islands in 1929 in order to lead there a healthy life and meditate quietly about the world. Perhaps his model had been Nietzsche who had been inspired to write his *Zarathustra* among the lonely rocks of Rapallo. But things worked out differently for Ritter. The first two years were exceedingly difficult for him and his companion, Frau Dora Strauch. They had read Beebe's book about the Galapagos Islands and had not realized that Beebe, as a zoologist, had seen the islands through rose-coloured spectacles. The arid, dusty reality was terrifying. On an elevated part of the island Ritter found water, but it was a long time before they succeeded in wresting any food from the dry soil.

On the other hand, rich Americans soon began to arrive in their yachts, curious about the man who roamed naked about the place and intended to reach an age of 140. They left him various articles of daily use and tinned food. Then, attracted by newspaper reports, an Austrian baroness arrived with three young men and settled nearby. She proclaimed herself Queen of Floreana. When more yachts arrived with presents a quarrel developed between the two groups.

Two years later everything was over. The baroness and one of the young men disappeared without trace. The second returned home and the third was soon found on a sandbank, decomposed. Dr Ritter, a vegetarian, surprisingly died of meat poisoning.

In the bay below, the Wittmer family were still living. They were not pursuing any grand plans but were working hard laying out a plantation and fishing. Frau Wittmer hospitably invited us to her attractive house. The last ship calling under a German flag had been Count Luckner's *Seeteufel*—the very ship I subsequently acquired and lost again at the end of the war. Frau Wittmer had a grown-up son and daughter; a second boy had been drowned while fishing. Apart from their cruel loneliness they were reasonably happy.

Our next stop was at Albemarle Island, the largest of the archipelago. Here there had been violent volcanic eruptions quite recently, and there was one crater next to another. From the exceedingly dirty water—because of the stirred-up lava dust it is never clear—numerous large devil rays surfaced close alongside the *Xarifa*. The strong currents around the islands made great demands on our officers. We sailed along the ravine-riven lava coast and dropped anchor in Tagus Bay, a small flooded crater on the walls of which numerous ships had recorded their visits in white lettering.

There were flashing fish in the opaque water—except that they were not fish but penguins merrily diving and surfacing. The dark cliffs along the coast were covered everywhere with large dirty-green lizards—the famous swimming marine lizards of the Galapagos Islands.

These iguanas grow to a length of up to five feet and look like antediluvian dragons. On their heads they have numerous bumps. The males are considerably larger than the females and have a much taller crest. Just like the sea lions, each male iguana has its harem of females and a well-defined territory which it vigorously defends against any intruder. As we approached them the creatures showed no fear whatever. The males looked at us menacingly, nodding their heads.

That is their challenge to a duel. Whenever a male wants to invade another's territory the two creatures face each other on the boundary, nodding their heads. Suddenly one of them pounces on the other and their armoured heads crash together. Each tries to push the other away. With a few pauses such a duel may last up to two hours. If one of the contestants surrenders, it lies down flat on its belly, in a posture of submission. After that it is no longer attacked and can crawl away defeated. The creatures never use their sharp teeth.

On the totally desert island of Narborough, a tall crater which we visited from Tagus Bay, we found the slopes covered with hundreds of these marine lizards. They clung to the rock, motionless, and as we approached all the males started nodding their heads. We were able to walk right up to them and lift them by their long tails. In the surf zone we saw them feed on algae, and a few of them swam a hundred yards or so out to sea.

While Tschet was busily filming and Scheer was observing his birds, Eibl tried to transplant some male iguanas into the territory of others. Immediately a far more serious fight developed. Since the intruder had not approached the boundary in the customary manner, nodding its head, it was now mercilessly bitten. Besides, it clearly felt unsure of itself and tried to return to its own territory. When it had done so—and it would invariably find the spot from as far as thirty yards away—it fully recovered its courage. Here it was prepared to fight. Here it was in the right. Here it was at home.

In addition to numerous pelicans which rested in the mangroves and penguins which sat on the volcanic rocks like porcelain figures, we also observed the flightless cormorants, whose wings have become atrophied into stumps. Only here, on an island without predators, could such a regression survive. Elsewhere these cormorants would have been exterminated long ago.

Unfortunately, because of the complete opacity of the sea, we did not succeed in observing a penguin under water as Beebe had done. Later, when we put into Academy Bay in order to buy potatoes and meat from the settlers there, we saw a captive penguin which was being kept in the kitchen and looked very sad. We bought it and called it Benny; soon it became the undisputed ruler on board. Mouche, our cat, humped its back and scrambled up the mast in terror. Benny, invariably good-tempered, wobbled confidently about the decks. He was everybody's delight, with the exception of our officers who liked to see the deck spick and span, and of the cabin boy who had to clean up in Benny's track.

From Albemarle we sailed to Seymour Island, where there had been a large American depot during the war, and then on to Indefatigable, from where we visited the picturesque Guy Fawkes Rocks. We dived in a great many places, collected specimens and photographed the submarine world, but nowhere found such clear water as off Hood.

Our last stopping place was the large Darwin Bay of Tower Island into which we sailed the *Xarifa* in spite of the tricky passage. Among the picturesque rock faces of this ancient crater thousands of boobies and frigate birds were nesting in the bushes and trees, and among the cliffs we encountered the rare Southern fur seal which had long been thought to be extinct. Dr Eibl made an excursion to the Arcturus Crater Lake, which had been discovered by Beebe, and there found a number of still unknown forms of plankton. Dr Scheer, as elsewhere on our voyage, not only conducted his ornithological researches but also performed geophysical measurements which yielded interesting results concerning the brightness of the twilight on tropical islands.

We felt sad when Tower eventually dropped behind us. Time, which had been at our disposal, had run out. In addition to a live pig, two large tortoises and a penguin we now also had numerous large marine lizards on board. Captain Diebitsch patiently watched us opening our cages and feeding the animals on deck. In the delicate pink of a magnificent sunset we watched the 'bewitched islands' disappear behind us.

We had no sooner returned from our expedition than we were confronted by the question: What now? Should we discharge our crew? Where was the ship to lie? How were we to ensure and finance the necessary service and maintenance? The members of the expedition all went off home, content with what they had seen and experienced, and looking forward to publishing the results of their various researches in scientific journals. My very first task was to finish the film. But what was to become of the *Xarifa*? There was no possible hope of another expedition for the next eighteen months or two years. Should the organism I had created be immobilized during that period? And if so, where and how?

We paid off the crew and berthed the ship in the yacht harbour of Genoa, where Xenophon continued to live on board, looking after her. It turned out that considerable overhaul and repair jobs were necessary. My mind had always been merely on the realization of my project of a floating research station and I somehow assumed that the rest would take care of itself. Now I had achieved my aim—but the rest was by no means looking after itself.

It seemed a good idea to hire out the *Xarifa* in the meantime. But to whom? For private people the ship was too large and not sufficiently luxurious. We publicized the offer among film companies. An Italian production group showed interest but lacked the money. If I could get them a contract with a German distributor for their film project they would gladly use my ship. I approached the distributor of my own film and got him to agree in principle.

'But I'll only do business with you,' he said. 'I have no confidence at all in Italian productions. You'll answer to me for the whole business—in other words, you are the German co-producer. Two of the principal actors must be German stars, that's my condition—as for the rest, I'll leave that to you. But I don't want to have any dealings with the Italians.'

The exciting plot of this film was about the salvage of Rommel's treasure. Before I really knew what had happened to me I found myself the co-producer of a feature film. But at least the *Xarifa* had been hired out for a considerable sum for a number of weeks, for filming off the island of Ponza. The main part of the film was shot in Alexandria and Cairo, the rest chiefly in Rome and, of course, off Ponza. I was frequently reminded of Anton Dohrn. In order to set up his Zoological Station at Naples he had travelled from one country to another to persuade their governments to underwrite research places. He too had found himself moving further and further away from his real zoological interests. Now, for the sake of this ship, I had turned into a manager whose business was getting further and further away from my real sphere of interest. But I was not prepared to let go of what I had started.

Soon our own film began to make further demands on us. For the sake of appropriate publicity it became a matter of course for us to be seen at film balls, to appear on the title pages of glossy magazines and to be generally engulfed in a publicity campaign which was not greatly to our taste and even less to that of my fellow scientists. As the Italian firm remained the only one in the film industry to show any interest in our ship we tried another tack. Jointly with the Kuoni travel agency in Zürich we organized 'underwater safaris' in the Red Sea. To this end we equipped the cabins a little more comfortably, engaged a new crew, and as a publicity exercise I invited a whole shipload of V.I.P.s and journalists for the first voyage at our own expense. Nowadays there are a number of enterprises of this kind which all do very well, but in those days we were ahead of our time. Very few genuine paying guests came forward, and these were disappointed when they found they were not received in the same way as in a luxury hotel and could not meet charming strangers at the bar. Horrified, I watched my life increasingly moving away from what I had hoped to achieve. To the public we became the darlings of providence, and I was seen as an underwater playboy who had cunningly arranged for himself a life among millionaires.

I thought a little enviously of Cousteau who had been relieved of all his worries by the French Navy and the State. Critics, initially well disposed, increasingly turned against me. The playboy, the darling of fate, was arousing envy, and a research worker ceased to be a research worker once he stopped publishing. I got tired of all this and confided to Eibl, with whom I had become close friends, that I was determined to give up and sell the *Xarifa*. I felt sure I could achieve a lot more with modest means by travelling to some place and by diving on my own.

'You mustn't on any account do that. The ship has been a tremendous success and you've got to hold out. The zoologists are on your side—you can believe me. We simply have to tackle things the right way. Leave it to me. We'll form a committee, and we'll find some way of financing the ship. German research needs such a ship.'

All future projects must go entirely to the credit of Eibl's initiative and powers of persuasion. We spent weeks driving all over the country in a Volkswagen, calling on nearly every biologist of repute, and Eibl succeeded in interesting nearly all of them in our project. The *Xarifa* was to be permanently active in the tropical seas and six working places were to be made available to zoologists for six-month voyages. Each workplace was to cost 22,500 marks and the places were to be taken up—in much the same way as at the Zoological Station in Naples—by scientific institutions of different countries. We planned to make our first two voyages to the Indian Ocean, to the Maldive and Sunda Islands. After that the ship was to be stationed off Port Darwin, on the north Australian coast, from where voyages were to be made to the Arafura Sea, to the Solomon Islands and to other regions. Otto Koehler, Konrad Lorenz, Erich von Holst, Karl von Frisch, Bernhard Rensch, A. Remane, E. Stresemann and eighteen other leading biologists supported our project in extensive scientific testimonials. At the annual meeting of the German Zoological Society an application was tabled for finance from scientific associations. The German Research Community in fact promised to take three of the workplaces provided that the Max Planck Society and other bodies underwrote the remaining places. The Max Planck Society did in fact underwrite one place, and so did the State of North Rhine-Westphalia. I myself was prepared to finance the sixth place. However, the German Research Community let us down; one reason may have been the fact that the construction of a German research vessel was being planned at the time and certain interests therefore opposed us. What was particularly hurtful was the arrogance with which the refusal was made and the fact that it was delayed so long that it only reached us when the expedition had long been on its way and the *Xarifa* was already in the Red Sea.

In order to save the project I had approached German Television and the BBC, and had contracted to produce twenty-six half-hour films. In this way the first year's programme was saved. Four of the research places had thus again been financed by me by way of my filming activities.

'Once we have enough results to show they won't be able to turn us down any longer,' Eibl comforted me. 'The *Xarifa* must be saved for research. Just wait—all will turn out well.' Unfortunately he was to be proved wrong.

ON BOARD THE XARIFA TO THE MALDIVE ISLANDS

Prelude

In our new project we were faced with particularly difficult problems. In the Maldive Islands we would be cut off from the world for months on end and would therefore have to be equipped to cope with any situation. For our eleven most vital engines, pumps and assemblies, all possible spares had to be taken along, or else we had to be in a position to manufacture any replacement parts ourselves. Foodstuffs and fuel, according to nautical handbooks, were either not obtainable in the Maldives, or only with difficulty, and fresh water was a further problem. The *Xarifa* had a fresh-water capacity of twenty-two tons, which was enough for cooking and drinking but left little over for washing, especially for the rinsing of the diving equipment, which is attacked by salt water. True, whenever it rained we might collect water on deck or with our sails, but we could not rely on that. According to the map there were a few freshwater lakes on some of the islands, but because of the reefs the *Xarifa* would not be able to get sufficiently close inshore. We therefore procured a hose several hundred yards long, complete with pump.

Through the good offices of the British Commonwealth Relations Office I received a general permit for our work from the Maldives Government. But we were unable to get any reliable information on the currencies to take with us. On the islands a local coinage was in circulation which was not available in any bank, but it was thought that Ceylon rupees and U.S. dollars would be accepted. For bartering and as presents we chose practical items, such as axes, fish hooks, linen, cloth and jewellery.

Meanwhile it was discovered at the shipyard in Genoa that the *Xarifa*'s rudder had to be renewed—at a cost of 500,000 lire. The deck had to be resealed—100,000 lire. Six work benches for the scientists—400,000 lire. A new ship's battery—about 5,000 Swiss francs. A modern self-inflating rubber life raft—2,700 German marks. The list went on and on.

Another major problem was the galley. Propane gas, which we had hitherto used for cooking on board, must not be stored below deck for safety reasons as it is heavier than air. On the other hand, we could not rely on having our cylinders refilled in port since every country used its own different connection threads and had different testing regulations. We therefore equipped ourselves for a possible switch-over of cooker and oven to petroleum. Rye bread or wholemeal bread in tins was not obtainable in Italy. So we ordered it from Germany.

For Dr Franzisket our bathroom on board was converted into a physiological laboratory. Dr Gerlach, who needed the most light for his microscope work, was given a workplace in the deck saloon, as was Prof. Luther. Eibl was away on a Galapagos expedition and would not join us until we reached Aden; there he would take over from Prof. Luther. Dr Klausewitz and Dr Scheer shared a cabin equipped as a laboratory. Other workrooms were assigned to Hirschel for his photographic and mechanical work and to Klaus Wissel for the diving, hunting and trapping gear. We had intended to take a third assistant with us, Herr Noack from Berlin, to preserve our specimens, but for economy reasons we had to put him off. Dr Kost, our doctor, informed me that most of the firms approached had made the necessary medical supplies available to us free of charge. In a circular letter we advised all participants of our expedition to have their teeth thoroughly seen to before departure. They also had to submit medical certificates concerning their general health, lungs and eardrums; they had to have their blood group established and supply proof of all the prescribed immunizations as well as immunization against tetanus.

A particular cause of worry was the fact that, as with any ship, nearly all the expenses had to be met before departure, whereas I had merely received advances from the television companies and the approved sums from Göttingen and Düsseldorf only arrived during the last week. Fortunately my bank in Liechtenstein obligingly granted me a long-term credit. Another problem was customs. No fewer than eighty crates of equipment were arriving from various countries and this led to insuperable formalities in Genoa. Since these matters were simpler in France we moved the *Xarifa* to Cannes a fortnight before our departure.

We had to keep to 15th October as our final sailing date because we needed six weeks for the voyage through the Red Sea and for our programme there, and during the second half of November wind conditions begin to be very unfavourable in the southern part of the Red Sea. Moreover, the best time for our work in the Maldives was from December to April. Everything was in a state of chaos—but we made it. The participants arrived punctually, and crates and curious spectators were jamming the waterside. Our engineer fell in love with a French girl and we were afraid he might run away at the last moment. The BBC and the South German radio turned up to say goodbye, and so did the French pioneer diver, Commandant le Prieur.

In the golden afternoon light Cannes and the façades of its magnificent hotels slowly disappeared astern. Our sails went up, the ship's engines purred reassuringly. We were standing on deck, looking forward and back. Our yesterdays gradually dropped away; our tomorrow had begun.

The crew of a ship like the *Xarifa* presents a problem. Sailing ships have become rare and the crews of present-day yachts are frequently better suited to the gay life in port than to a voyage into the unknown. Herr Heinrich Becker, who had been the second officer on our Galapagos expedition, had in the meantime got his master's ticket. He had sailed a great deal in small ships and was a man who lent a hand wherever and whenever necessary. He told me that if I entrusted the ship to him he would not let me down.

I agreed. This left open the question of a first officer. But as we had to save wherever possible, Becker declared himself ready to sail with only our Yugoslav boatswain Adamo. The members of the expedition would have to take their turns on watch duty, and, if necessary, I could always deputize for Becker, acting in accordance with his instructions. He also took on the duties of honorary paymaster and mess officer. Captain Becker's performance on this voyage was outstanding. With a boatswain and four sailors he took the *Xarifa* wherever we wanted and simultaneously overhauled her so thoroughly that at the end of our voyage, in Singapore, she was in better shape than when we left Cannes.

As engineer we first had the Greek Manoli and later the excellent Herr Wilhelm Jauch, whom we had summoned from Germany. A cook and a cabin boy completed the crew. For electrical matters we had the help of Dr Scheer, and in the case of repairs that of the engineer Hirschel. He had proved his exceptional technical skill on our Galapagos expedition and this time he tackled repairs to the ship's engines and the refrigeration plant with the same virtuosity as those to the radio equipment and our underwater television outfit. At the same time he was my indefatigable and skilful assistant cameraman.

Whereas the Captain's quarters were astern, the crew were accommodated aforeships. The same food was cooked for everybody on board, which caused a few problems since sailors are used to heavy meals whereas divers need an easily digestible diet. A further problem was the chain of command. As the captain assigned to his crew an exact schedule of jobs, it was not possible for members of the expedition to give the sailors any major tasks of their own; all such requests had to go through me and the captain.

The news of the sinking of the *Pamir* reached us before we left Genoa. Captain Diebitsch, who was in charge of the training ship on this tragic voyage, had been our Captain on the Galapagos expedition. He was then almost sixty-five and had told us that that would be his last major voyage. But subsequently he had been unable to resist the tempting offer. 'At the end of this month,' he wrote to me, 'I take over command of the *Pamir* for a voyage to Buenos Aires. When I cross the course of the *Xarifa* I shan't omit to spit into the sea and give it your regards.'

The spot where the *Pamir* perished in a hurricane was barely fifty miles from the spot where the *Xarifa* had also been caught in a violent storm. That time Diebitsch had dodged it by changing course for the Canary Islands. This time he had left his canvas up and tried to run before the hurricane. That proved to be the ship's doom.

In the Strait of Gubal

At Bluff Point we took the members of our expedition under water for the first time, with schnorkel and breathing apparatus. Thus they were introduced straight away to one of the most beautiful coral reefs of the northern Red Sea.

Scheer, Hirschel and Wissel were experienced divers; Franzisket, Klausewitz, Gerlach and Prof. Luther had their first lesson. The important thing for beginners is to get them confident and assured in a strange environment. With diving equipment one should not, to begin with, descend to more than twenty feet and one should swim about as little as possible. The best thing is to sit down on the bottom and look about at leisure. Then, gradually, one can start exploring one's closer surroundings and one's own mobility. Scientists make good pupils. They become so absorbed by what they see around them that they soon forget about themselves and their own nervousness.

As a diver one has no gravity and must therefore learn to move where one wants to move. The refraction of the light makes everything appear closer and larger than in fact it is; whenever one tries to reach for something one finds oneself missing it at first. To catch fish with a net or a harpoon is by no means easy. If water penetrates into one's mask this can be expelled again by blowing in air. For safety two divers should always stay together. In deeper dives the rate of ascent has to be watched. And during ascent one must not hold one's breath because otherwise the lung vessels suffer damage from the expanding air.

On this expedition we used chiefly compressed air. Our cylinders could be charged to a pressure of 200 atmospheres, which gave us a diving time of over an hour.

On his second day I took Wissel to the sixty-year-old wreck which was lying barely a hundred yards north of Bluff Point. There were considerable currents at that spot and diving was not without danger. The old steel skeleton, lying in sixty-five to 130 feet of water, was magnificently overgrown with corals. Wissel had a photographic camera with him and I watched him choosing his subjects calmly and carefully. To dive in these tropical waters was for him the fulfilment of a lifelong wish. I did not suspect that he was to have only a few more dives before him.

When a ship sinks to the bottom of the sea it stays there as a kind of milestone in time. It arrives there one day as a large, disturbing foreign body, and from then onwards the creatures of the sea take possession of it. The coral researcher will find valuable data on the varying rate of growth of different species of coral. We found these differences to be quite considerable. Whereas the delicately ramified acropora form colonies up to five feet in diameter in a mere fifteen years, the compact brain coral and porites barely reach a diameter of eight to 10 inches.

Since, moreover, a submerged ship is an invitation to virtually any larva which swims past to remain and establish a colony, rare species are often found on ships which do not occur elsewhere on neighbouring reefs. The same is true of sponges, snails, shells, hydropolyps, leathery corals, moss animals, crabs, squids, etc. That is why a visit to a wreck is not only an exceedingly thrilling and exciting experience but also an excursion into a submarine zoological garden where wonderful discoveries can be made.

Settlement frequently varies a great deal according to the position and nature of the various parts of a ship. The greatest variety of life is usually found among the former superstructures, presumably because these provide the best hide-outs and because the currents ensure a steady supply of fresh water rich in plankton. On the bare steel plates of the ship's flanks, on the other hand, only a few robust species of coral ever settle. As these parts provide no hiding place they are usually avoided by freely mobile creatures.

A different fauna is encountered on the dark underside and in the ship's interior. Here the water contains little oxygen and is poor in nutriment. But even these conditions have their 'specialists'. On the ceilings of what used to be cabins, frequently in the remotest corners, we found the most magnificent scallops and thorny oysters. Their graceful and artistically perfect shape raises the question of why nature should produce such striking beauty in the remotest darkness. The answer surely is that what seems beautiful to us fulfils a very practical and vital task. The dove-tailed shape of the shells and the sharp spikes are an effective protection against the principal enemy of all clams, the starfish, which climbs on top of them, clings to them firmly with its suction cups and forcibly opens them.

In order to finance our expedition I had undertaken to produce twenty-six television programmes of thirty minutes each. That meant about thirteen hours of film or the equivalent of eight full-length documentaries. In terms of footage, allowing for a two-thirds cutting rate, this meant roughly 115,000 feet of 16 mm. film.

An even greater problem was the necessary creative effort. The main difficulty about any such production taken from real life is the need to shape it artistically at the very same time as this real life is being filmed. It is by no means enough to make as good a film as possible of what seems interesting at the time. One has got to film what will seem interesting to the spectator at a future date—and that is a very different matter. One is still immersed in the reality of air and fragrance, with time running at a normal rate, and already one has to think about reshaping it artificially in the spectators' imagination by one's camera work, cutting and commentary.

Besides, television has its own requirements. Long panoramic shots are not effective on the small screen; one's tendency must be towards close-ups. The television film, moreover, is shown to a small circle of people in their homes; in consequence, one's tone of address is more intimate and the internal pace is different. The spectators at a cinema have paid for their tickets and will remain in their seats for better or worse. On television, on the other hand, you only need one overlong sequence and the viewer will switch off or switch over to a rival programme. Every single theme, therefore, must be interesting and, if possible, comprehensible even to those who have only switched on half-way through.

In a big task such as this the most important thing is an orderly system. Each reel was numbered, and the sequence on it was noted down in word and sketch. Under water I always carried an aluminium plate on my left wrist on which I jotted down my notes with a pencil. Immediately afterwards, in the boat, while my recollection was still fresh, I dictated further details on to a Minifon tape recorder. On board the *Xarifa* I then transferred my sketches and recorded notes into a book.

In a second note book I tried to make a start with arranging the sequences. Whenever I had filmed an interesting event I would reflect how I could develop my shots into a self-contained film story and what sequences I still needed to supplement this story. I then planned these additional sequences in my mind, and, if they were underwater scenes, wrote them on the back of my aluminium disc and subsequently tried to find these scenes in real life.

Our research work provided the main theme for the general plot. This time, fortunately, I did not have to fit everything together into a single dramatic structure as in earlier films, but was able to construct self-contained episodes from our experiences. Each of these programmes, though, had to have a length of exactly thirty minutes. It happened therefore that I would move individual episodes, like the pieces in a jigsaw puzzle, from one programme to another, in order to achieve the correct length. I could not tie myself too rigidly to any particular line but according to what our cameras happened to catch I had to be ever ready to rearrange and change.

I am not sure that film critics watching our work from the comfort of a cinema seat have always made allowance for these difficulties. There is a very considerable difference between thinking up a film plot in advance, as a scenario, and shooting it—as happens with feature films and indeed with most documentaries—and, on the other hand, trying, or being compelled, to let real life itself become the author of the scenario, and nevertheless producing films which would satisfy a modern taste pampered by the dazzling products of fantasy.

Wissel's Death

After a short visit to Mukawwar Island we reached the reef area of Shaab Anbar in the central Red Sea on the afternoon of 6th November and with some difficulty dropped anchor inside an enclosed lagoon. The following morning we went diving in two groups. While Klausewitz and Dr Kost were being led down by Wissel and Scheer, I dived on the other side with Franzisket and Prof. Luther.

Towards noon, just as we were surfacing from a dive, the other boat with Scheer was noisily racing towards us. We were to come to the *Xarifa* at once: Wissel had met with an accident and was probably dead. He had first dived with the two scientists and had subsequently swum over into shallow water to photograph a fish there. When Scheer had looked for him a little while later he had found him hanging lifeless in water only eight feet deep. His breathing tube had no longer been in his mouth and the camera had been lying on the corals a few yards away. They had got him into the boat and Dr Kost had immediately tried to resuscitate him.

We hurried across to the *Xarifa*. Kost meanwhile had administered heart and circulation stimulants—but in vain. We continued our resuscitation efforts until the appearance of rigor, but Wissel had clearly been dead by the time Scheer found him. His diving apparatus was in order; the cylinder still contained forty atmospheres of oxygen. As Wissel had a congenital compensated heart condition, Dr Kost assumed acute heart failure with subsequent pulmonary oedema.

216

Wissel had informed me of his heart condition shortly before our departure and had accepted full responsibility for anything that might happen. Two Munich doctors had told him that his condition could kill him any day but that he was just as likely to live until he was ninety. Now perhaps the hot climate and the effort involved in photography in shallow but choppy water had tipped the scales. The accident was the more tragic as Wissel, undoubtedly the best German skindiver, had already made a name for himself by his exceptional dives in the Mediterranean. It seemed a bitter irony of fate that he should now have met his death in eight feet of water.

The clouds had piled up even further and a rainstorm was imminent. Captain Becker declared that it was impossible in this weather to sail out of the reef ring. I regarded this as a favourable turn of events. Unless a dead body can be taken into port within twenty-four hours the law permits burial at sea. We knew that Wissel's wife was expecting a baby that week. If we buried him at sea—which would certainly have been his wish—we need not inform the authorities until we called at our next port, which was Aden, in about a fortnight's time. It would surely be better for Frau Wissel not to receive the terrible news until then.

We were all stunned by the blow. Wissel had not only been a good companion but had been universally respected for his great ability. He was a typical Berliner—enterprising, hard-working, highly intelligent, and a gifted cameraman and writer. Our scientists, who had just gained some assurance in diving, were deeply shocked by the disaster.

We laid out his body in the mess and held a brief ceremony. During the night Captain Becker sewed the body up in a coarse sail canvas, in accordance with ancient sailing-ship tradition, and fastened the German flag to it. Early in the morning we took the body out of the reef ring in the boat, through storm and gusty rain, and committed it to the deep. His diving mask and fins followed.

Everybody was now anxious to leave Shaab Anbar as quickly as possible. As soon as the weather permitted we therefore sailed on towards the south and as our next working place chose two elongated islands in the Farasan group because these offered a good sheltered anchorage between them.

The next two weeks passed calmly and satisfactorily for everyone. The water was not very clear but the reefs were beautiful. There were also submarine forests of sargassum weed along the coast, and there we encountered an entirely different biological community. Enormous shoals of young fish were streaming to and fro. The islands themselves, Sarso and Sarad Sarso, though totally bare and deserted, were nevertheless of considerable interest to the zoologist. Our daily routine and the use of our boats now followed a regular pattern. Meanwhile the deck crew were overhauling the rigging and the sails, and our engineer performed a few necessary repairs. Gradually we got over our shock. After Wissel's death we had all moved closer together and we were increasingly becoming a close-knit team of colleagues and friends.

Some variety was introduced into our lives by a peregrine falcon which settled on our yard-arm while we were sailing from Shaab Anbar to Sarso and was captured during the night. Dr Kost was an expert on falconry and wanted to be the first man ever to have trained a falcon on board ship. With remarkable foresight he had brought along hoods, glove and lure, and now, quoting from a book written by the Emperor Frederick II, he explained to us how the bird must be trained to perch on his fist for feeding at a whistled command and how, upon another command, it must return to his fist.

Sinbad, as we called the falcon, was a noble and intelligent bird. Within a week it came down to Kost's hand from ten yards away. Every morning Kost washed it expertly by filling his mouth with water and blowing it over the bird. During the day Sinbad would sit over the deckhouse door, watching our activities with interest and a little disdain.

We had some difficulty making our exit from the Red Sea. Our first two attempts against a gale, the current and heavy seas were unsuccessful. Only after returning to Massawa, where we bunkered and where Prof. Luther had to leave us, did we succeed in passing through the notorious Bab el Mandeb, the 'Gate of Mourning'.

At Aden we were met by Eibl who had successfully concluded his Galapagos expedition. We learned from him that Frau Wissel had given birth to a girl and that I, too, had become the father of a girl. We also learned that the German Research Community had at last come to a decision on our application and that this decision was negative.

The Eastern Tip of Africa

We were lying off Abd al-Kuri, a lonely, rocky island off the easternmost point of the African continent.

After a hurried breakfast we sailed both our boats across into a sunlit bay which was picturesquely framed by dark hillsides. A group of scantily clad Arabs was sitting motionless on the shell-strewn sand. We clambered up the beach, which was dotted everywhere with ancient pieces of wreckage half-buried by the sand. One part of a ship was lying on the waterline, licked by the frothy waves, while washed up a little higher were the exposed ribs of one side of the hull, terminating in an elaborately carved bow. One of the sleepy figures who were inquisitively following us repeatedly uttered the incomprehensible word 'Pompai'. Suwitt, our galley boy hired in Aden, likewise repeated 'Pompai', accompanying this with a sweeping gesture across the mountain. Eventually we understood that the timber vessel which had foundered here had come from Bombay. Eibl and Klausewitz were turning over stones, looking for giant geckos. Higher up the slope we saw Franzisket; now and again we could hear the report of a shotgun.

Together with Hirschel I filmed a few ancient graves before sailing across to the headland on the eastern side of the bay, where we had seen a white line just above the water—the remains of calcareous algae. There was a heavy swell. I dropped anchor near some cliffs and it rattled down to a depth of sixty feet. The current spun our boat round and pushed her stern close to the rocks.

Suwitt rolled his eyes frantically. I calmed him by telling him that I would myself move the anchor. I wanted to take the camera down with me but speed was now more important. I slipped on my diving equipment and clambered into the water. I had hardly descended six feet when I began to regret having left the camera behind.

Below me, in the choppy bluish-green water, appeared steep cliffs. On them grew waving yellow algae, like the tufts of hair of a giant sleeping on the sea bed. All round, from every direction, fish were appearing. The anchor rope led down a rock face through a crack as wide as an arm. A greenish shark, about eight feet long and with white fin tips, was slowly swimming past the anchor. It paid no attention to me but it had probably been attracted by the rattle of the anchor. Slowly and massively it swam about the bottom, not always clearly visible because of the countless fish which interposed themselves between it and me.

The fauna was strange and almost incredible. A Mediterranean landscape with algal vegetation like that at Sydney and with tame shoals of fish like those along the black cliffs of the Galapagos Islands. Two blue angel fish of a species I had never seen before were approaching with dancing movements like the heralds of an inquisitive world of fish, turning this way and that like vain young girls in front of a mirror. The crack in which the rope was held led down obliquely between two rocks and the water was gurgling up and down it. At least thirty fish were flicking their tails close to one another, forming a slanting column in the narrow crack. I dived down close to the rock and pulled out the rope and with it some fish. At the bottom a spacious grotto opened out. I peered into it. On its dark ceiling, like neatly arranged flowers, two dragon fish were pressed close to the rock, their backs and heads downwards. A short distance behind, the long white antennae of crayfish appeared from the shadows. Next to them a massive, flattened grouper turned in alarm and swam out into deep water.

I swam right down to the anchor and looked about me in case other sharks appeared. Yard by yard I dragged the anchor over the crumbled rock and wedged it into a suitable crevice. All around me the dance of the fish was in full swing. There were countless large and small parrot fish, some strikingly large barbels with dark transversal stripes and long moustache-like bristles, unicorn fish, butterfly fish, groupers, angel fish, wrasses—there was no end to the procession. I hurried to the surface.

Suwitt pointed to the observation box. He had been watching the shark closely from the surface. My rating had clearly gone up in his eyes.

. Hirschel handed me the Bolex and himself took the Rolleimarin. Now began a filming feast without parallel—I took 2,000 feet of fish sequences that day.

This was a heavenly spot. As on the Galapagos Islands the fish here displayed no fear at all. All I had to do was to sit quietly on a rock and press the button—and a never-ending stream of fishes would inquisitively swim to and fro in front of my lens. Under a boulder the head of a moray eel appeared: I estimated its length at eight feet. Its body was some ten to twelve inches thick. Above its wide, viciously opened mouth its skin hung in slack folds; another sign of its old age was its greatly bulging nostrils.

In each of the dark grottos we peered into there were dragon fish hovering by the roof, and large and small crayfish in the lateral niches. I also saw two particularly long antennae with another two appearing between them forked about half way. Later I discovered the creature belonging to them. Compared with the length of its antennae it was a dwarf: a prettily patterned black and white crayfish which we preserved in formalin for later identification.

After the first hour's diving we sat in the sun to stock up with heat. We were in walkie-talkie communication with the *Xarifa*, where Captain Becker always responded promptly. We heard that Franzisket and Gerlach were back on board and asked them to bring us some of our close-up lenses as well as a hand net and a bucket for catching the dragon fish.

They turned up.

'Do you know that Gerlach was very nearly killed?' Franzisket cheerfully greeted us. Gerlach was grinning a little sheepishly. We tied up the boat and listened to his story.

'You really ought to try filming these mudskippers,' Franzisket said. 'A few years ago there was a fascinating paper about these little creatures. A man named Harms, if I remember rightly, injected them with pituitary hormones and thereby produced changes in entire organ complexes in the direction of adaptation to terrestrial existence. Even their eyes changed, from a slightly short-sighted fish eye to the slightly long-sighted eye of an air-breathing animal. The conclusion was that the mutation of a single gene affecting only the output of the pituitary gland changes a whole complex of organs in a way which enables the creature to exist more effectively on dry land. They were also able to stay below water longer than the normal periophthalmus.'

'And what did these creatures do to Gerlach?'

'They didn't do anything to me,' Gerlach said, 'except lure me to them.'

'What happened,' Franzisket continued, 'was that he rather carelessly held on with his hand to a vertical rock about five feet high, which suddenly cracked along its length and fell on him.'

'The whole block?'

'Yes. About three by three feet, and maybe sixteen inches thick. A smooth slab. Certainly weighed a ton. The same kind of granite which forms those fine stratifications up on the summit. It first bounced down a short way and then tipped over straight on to him. It knocked his feet from under him and the block fell on top of him. You know the short dry smacking sound when rock hits rock. Fortunately Gerlach had fallen into a crevice so that his legs and abdomen fitted into it and the rock then covered him.'

'His whole body?'

'Up to his chest. His back was in the water and he could not move. You can imagine my fright. I tried to lift the slab but that was out of the question. It didn't budge by as much as an inch.'

'And what did Gerlach say?'

Gerlach grinned. 'I said, "You'd better run and get some help before the tide rises and drowns me." '

'Every now and again a wave would come and wash over him. So I raced off, stumbling over the shingle, and eventually decided to run along the waterline where it was firmer and smooth. I trotted along with my tongue hanging out and my belly flopping, and yelled. I could see Eibl climbing about the rocks a few hundred feet above me, but he couldn't hear me—the wind was against us. Then I met the Arabs. One of them immediately understood my urgent sign language. He sent his people off while I raced on to the boat. Boris heard me call for help but couldn't see me. He ran off a short distance in my direction and then remembered that he had to keep watch by the boat and ran back again. More than once. What behaviourists call a conflict situation. When I got to the boat I used the walkie-talkie and gave Becker the alarm, telling him to get crowbars and stone-breaking tools and also a schnorkel and a compressed air set. If Gerlach had found himself under water from the rising tide we would have laid on an air supply for him.'

'Twenty inches can make a lot of difference,' said Gerlach.

'Well, finally we also shouldered an oar and I trotted back with Boris—I must have lost a good five pounds. I had a shock when I got there because I saw the Arabs standing about without apparently making any effort to free him. I thought he must be dead. But in fact that cunning Arab had quickly sized up the situation, reached under the stone and taken Gerlach's shoe off—and lo and behold, he was free. He was able to slip out.'

'And you're not hurt at all?'

'Not in the least. I just fitted into that cavity.'

'I saw a beautiful shark,' I told them.

'In that case we'd better get back,' the two declared.

While they were leaving we reloaded our cameras and went under water once more. Towards 2 p.m. the small boat reappeared with Klausewitz, Eibl, Gerlach and Kost. Time was beginning to run out. I was anxious to take at least three films of close-ups of fishes, and Klausewitz wanted one live specimen of each for identification.

Hirschel got the dynamite holder ready in the boat, I dived, held the cartridge near the fish, pressed the trigger and collected the stunned fish in the net. Eibl took the holder from me and I went on filming. Just as I was rewinding Eibl came into my field of vision, signalling me to surface. I followed him.

'Hirschel and Kost have been injured,' he said. 'The cartridge went off in Hirschel's hand.'

'And the safety catch?'

'Didn't work.'

Hirschel was standing in the boat, his whole body spattered with blood. His arms were hanging down limply and blood was dripping from his fingers. One of his little fingers seemed to be missing.

'You haven't lost a finger?' I shouted.

'No, no—it only looks like that,' he replied. 'But my hands are in a bit of a mess. Full of splinters.'

Dr Kost also had a lot of blood on him. As I clambered into the boat he wordlessly showed me his diving mask. Because of his short-sightedness he had glued his spectacle lenses to the inside of his mask visor with transparent putty. Just above these two lenses the visor had three deep dents.

'If I hadn't been wearing this I would have been blinded in at least one eye,' he said softly.

'Haven't we got a first-aid pack here?'

'No. When we cleared out the boat we left them behind. I didn't realize it. But we don't need one now anyway.'

Gerlach rowed the two back to the *Xarifa*. Eibl and I dived again. But I was so jittery that I simply did not see any subjects any more. Besides, there were fewer fish about. The sea had gone noticeably murky and countless small flakes were floating in the water like falling snow.

It was odd that most of the large transversally-striped barbels had settled down to rest on the rocks. They were lying on their bellies in small suitable hollows, rubbing about a little as if they were going to spawn. I was able to get quite close with the camera and with my telescopic lens filled the frame with eyes and mouth.

When we got back to the *Xarifa* Kost had already bandaged Hirschel's fingers.

'There's no point in trying to dig out the splinters. In fact, it wouldn't be possible,' he said to me. 'Two of them went clean through his nail right to the bone. We'll leave them where they are. They'll get encapsulated and will heal up.'

'They'll fester their way out of my skin all right,' Hirschel remarked with equanimity.

'Not necessarily,' Eibl objected. 'After all, they are beautifully sterile. They must have been red hot during the explosion. You'll find they'll get overgrown with tissue and stay where they are.'

'I've got a few dozen in my face myself,' Franzisket said. He had been a fighter pilot in the war. 'I once had an X-ray made of my face. A very pretty picture, I can assure you. They've certainly never worried me.'

We were sailing across the wide Indian Ocean. In order to save fuel—to make sure our supply lasted for the four months in the Maldives—we were using only our sails. During the first two days we averaged 4.3 and 5.4 m.p.h. respectively, and subsequently, probably thanks to a favourable current, we achieved an average of 6.7 m.p.h.

There is wonderful quiet on a ship without engines. The sea was murmuring its lullaby for us, the sun rose, and the moon, and most members of the expedition lay on their bunks reading thrillers. It takes a great deal of practice to do anything on a rocking boat other than hold on to the rail or lie on one's bunk. For our meals we made our way to the galley, where hot-pot was issued to everybody. With our full plates we tacked back to the after-deck, sat down around the wheel and ate our pea soup with pork or sausage, lentils and potatoes.

Two people had to do watch duty for stretches of four hours at a time, except for the afternoon watch, which was six hours to enable people to take turns. As the sailors had plenty of other things to do the scientists all helped—Gerlach, a sailing enthusiast, with particular pleasure. Captain Becker took the whole night watch and slept during the day, except when taking bearings.

Bearings were taken three times every twenty-four hours. The most accurate were the ones at dawn and dusk, by observation of the stars. In the morning Becker observed the elevation of the sun and subsequently, to complete his noon observation, he would 'shoot the sun'. If the sky was overcast navigation had to be done by the log, allowing for our drift. Our navigational equipment consisted of two sextants, one chronometer, one navigator's compass and one azimuth compass, one sonic depth finder with recorder, one patent log and a radio telephone. We had no radar, but among the Maldives, where every island is surrounded by innumerable coral reefs, it would not have been much use anyway.

The *Xarifa* was insured with Lloyds at an annual cost of about 22,000 Swiss francs. All our participants and their equipment were insured, and I had also taken out a general liability policy to the amount of 1,000,000 Swiss francs. For whatever happens on board the ship's owner is always liable.

After crossing the fifth degree of latitude the swell diminished noticeably. On 15th December the wind had almost dropped and we restarted our engine. During the morning of 16th December there was a terrible crash. One derrick had broken and the mainsail boom had crashed on to the deckhouse. Adamo had let the sail drop before the second derrick had been secured. Across the deck came a roar of sailor's language. Shortly afterwards there was another bang and the gaff crashed down, narrowly missing Suwitt and Ante. The steel drum of the sail winch had come off and dropped on Hirschel's foot. 'The two lads might have been killed,' I noted in my diary. 'Our guardian angel is working overtime.' To restore morale the cook issued beer at lunchtime.

On 18th December the sky was totally overcast and there was not a breath of air. The sea was a leaden grey and completely smooth. Only a few small whales with white-flecked heads bobbed up through the surface. We were sailing parallel to the Equator at $1\frac{1}{2}°$, but the air was fresh and it soon started to rain. On 19th December we captured another hawk, our first having flown off at Massawa. Sinbad II was smaller and looked like a prematurely aged professor.

On 20th December we staged the traditional crossing-the-line ceremonies and had a hilarious time. The following morning, at first light, the dark cloud bank ahead opened and we were gazing on a long string of rich green palm-trees rising straight from the sea behind a white barrier of foam.

We had reached our first destination.

Secrets of the Indian Ocean

Afif Didi, headman or judge of Hitaddu, was waiting for us as we stepped ashore. He wore a light sarong and a pale grey upper garment with a rolled handkerchief in his breast pocket. He first took us to his house. It was one of the biggest, neatly built of white coral rock. In the garden were banana trees, a well, and at the back a shed with a large bellows and iron tools. From a side wing of the servants' house the inquisitive eyes of women and children were peering at us. We were invited into a large room in the middle of which stood a kind of writing desk and along the walls were lined up a number of dignified chairs. Hanging on the walls were a pendulum clock, several Arab maps and tablets of unknown meaning, and between them a calendar from a Swiss watch manufacturer, open at a picture of the Matterhorn.

He had prepared breakfast for us. We stepped into the next room which contained a large heavy wooden table, probably brought here from Ceylon, as well as a cupboard and a chest. The attractive china—I looked underneath—was marked Grindley, England. We were served tea. In front of each cup stood four small bowls. In the first was a kind of sliced pancake, made of rice, coconut milk and eggs; in the second sliced coconut; in the third dried Maldive fish; and in the fourth *bodihalwa*, a kind of sweet pastry cut in slices. Finally there were bananas.

Afif gave us an interpreter and we strolled through the village of friendly dreamy people. In front of the airy houses of woven palm leaves stood graceful hammock beds, and the garden paths were all neatly covered with white gravel. No one was importunate or begged; the natives took no particular notice of our presence. Our first visit was to a weaving shop. Everything here was minute, toy-like, made of ancient carved wood. The loom was set in motion for us; it was home-made. I filmed a young girl at a spinning wheel; she looked like seven and was thirteen. Of marriageable age, the interpreter assured me. A small fragile creature with South Sea eyes, utterly still and serious and feminine like a lake, her small swift fingers were turning the bobbin. I filmed her through the wheel and she gazed calmly and reverently into the camera. We tried in vain to make her smile.

'Nice girl,' I said to the interpreter.

'Yes, nice,' he said. And without hesitation, anxious to please and anxious to do business, he continued in the same voice, 'Do you want her?'

On the adjoining flat of land adjoining the palm-tree a young fellow was crouching. He was fixing a hollowed-out coconut to the hacked-off stalk to get toddy. Each palm-tree produces three coconuts full per day. I tried it. It tasted like excellent lemonade and not at all like coconut. The goldsmith whom we next visited fuelled his fire with charcoal made from coconut shells. Schoolchildren walked past, their lessons painted on wooden boards which they carried on their backs. Some of the small children, running about naked, wore a hand-knotted silver rope round their bellies or a gold chain around their necks. Later we also saw noble ladies hung with magnificent gold jewellery. We were told that for each item of jewellery a special licence from the Sultan was necessary. We looked into a kitchen. It was a dark hole with three large cauldrons simmering on an open fire. In the afternoon Afif himself accompanied us. He told us that the land was allotted by the mosque whose head he was, at a charge of one to two rupees per annum. Marriage customs had not changed at all. Admittedly there was now a law which prohibited a man from marrying the same woman more than three times. If a man wanted to do this all the same an intermediary had to be found. 'Some of the older people in Male,' Afif Didi said with a smirk, 'have been married a good seventy or eighty times.'

The fascination of skindiving is in the fear which one experiences of the deep and in the sense of power one gains by overcoming that fear. Added to this is the charm of experiencing a still untouched natural world in which nothing at all has changed in spite of Man, civilization and progress.

At first, one still sees the surface with waves passing along it like clouds in the sky. Then infinite nothingness spreads overhead and the friendly familiar world of air, sunlight, fragrance and sound is left behind. A cold silent solitude opens before one. A tomb without bounds, without mercy, without friendly rules. A vastness into which one enters, into which one glides, which receives one impassively and yet gently. Here one does not have to push up from the ground as one does on dry land. Here one is just as free and as lonely as a comet sailing through space.

At some of the outer reefs we dived to a depth of 260 feet. This requires special precautions. The light of understanding, of reflection and thought is gradually dimmed at increasing depth. Reason gives way to a calm, fearless sense of well-being. Off the Florida coast a diver once tried to set up a new deep-diving record and swam down into the tempting all-embracing vastness. Up in a boat a sonar instrument was tracing the depth of the slowly descending body. It stopped. It continued to descend, beyond the greatest depths ever

Ari Atoll in the Maldive archipelago. The huge ring is formed by reefs which are themselves ring-shaped. Along its outer sides the large atoll drops steeply to great depths.

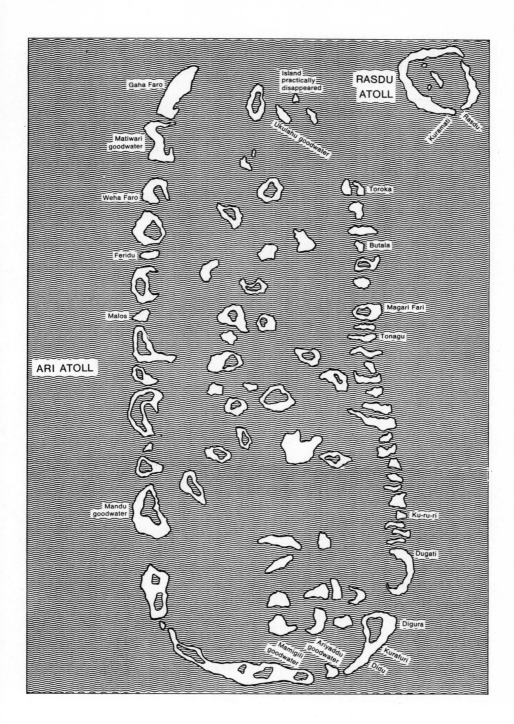

Gaha Faro

Island
practically
disappeared

RASDU
ATOLL

Matiwari
goodwater

Ukulahu goodwater

Kuramati
Rasdu

Weha Faro

Toroka

Feridu

Butala

Malos

Magari Fari

Tonagu

ARI ATOLL

Mandu
goodwater

Ku-ru-ri

Dugati

Digura

Mamigili
goodwater

Ariyaddu
goodwater

Kurafuri

Didu

reached by a swimmer, and still it descended. It went on descending. It vanished into eternity which received it as its own.

Below a depth of 160 feet what is known as deep-sea intoxication occurs. Under a pressure of six atmospheres one loses all misgivings and inhibitions. The abyss below one becomes a pleasant walk. Why not? A little bit further— why not? And then suddenly comes the end, without one's even being aware of it. Death catches the diver in a butterfly net whose mesh is so soft that it closes in on him unnoticed.

I was wearing an aluminium plate on my left wrist: on it I had written down exactly what I had to do. First I had to take a photograph of the slope and its vegetation. Second, I had to break loose some specimens of the corals growing at this depth and put them in my collecting net. Third, I had to note down what else I could see below me. Fourth, and finally, I had to ascend again after no more than five minutes. I photographed . . . I broke off the corals and stowed them away in my net . . . I observed and noted . . . and slowly I swam up again.

The feeling of returning to life, to fear and reality is something like a consciously experienced and explosively unfolding new birth. Pressure and cold and fog dissolve. A burning, tingling, throbbing feeling spreads through you. The air bubbles which accompany you burst apart, dancing and reeling drunkenly upwards towards the light. One of these intoxicated bubbles is yourself. Everything expands. Everything gets brighter and warmer. Life, suddenly regained, becomes almost painfully delicious. The slope with its plants and animals glides down before you like a dropping curtain. It closes over a receding dream, over a danger one has escaped, a danger not from outside but from within oneself.

One floats towards the light, towards warmth, back into the air. The air one breathes from the bottle on one's back has become stale and dry, a machine product. The air up above smells of wind, of palm-trees and hot sand. In between lies a breath of decomposition, the basis of new life, a breath of perfume, a symbol of the delusion of our senses. Stop. Placed neatly among the corals there is a breathing apparatus. One's return to the world above must not be too sudden. I slip off my breathing equipment, take the mouth-piece out of my mouth, insert the other, and breathe . . . and wait.

Other fish-men are coming down, circling me, peering into my mask. What was it like below? I lift my thumb. It was O.K. The dream seems a long way back. One's skin hurts with pleasure at the recommencement of life. Not far away, obliquely above, the dark hull of the boat is bobbing, a friendly plump mother receiving us all. I have to stay where I am for another thirty minutes; I must ascend slowly, a little at a time. Then the quarantine is over and the world to which I belong receives me back.

It was getting on for nine o'clock in the evening. We were lying off Gem Island, the southernmost of the Maldives. A rain squall had passed over the ship and had driven us with our record-player below deck. We were playing Smetana's *Vltava* and Tchaikovsky's *Pathétique*. Gerlach and Franzisket were writing. Eibl and I were smoking our pipes. Suddenly Captain Becker appeared in the door.

'I don't know if you want to come and look. There are some large creatures in the water.'

We left the brightly lit saloon and hurried over to the dark after-deck. There was a new moon and the sky was overcast, so it was totally dark. From ashore shone the lights of the RAF station and the officers' mess. Most of them were white, but a few were red and green. These were left-over Christmas decorations.

'You'll see them best from here.'

I leapt up on the stern apron. Below us, dimly outlined, our two boats were rocking. All round the boats and spread out over the black surface of the sea bright patches were flashing regularly. These could not be reflections of the stars—for one thing no stars were visible, and for another they would not have turned their lights on and off in the same rhythm. I made sure they were not reflections from our portholes. But there was no light in any of the portholes. Nor did the flashing lights have anything to do with the faint reflection of the distant lights ashore.

'Quick, over here!' I called excitedly.

The light sources were below the water. There were about a hundred bright circular patches, each about three feet across, flashing and vanishing again in a regular rhythm. The patches were ten to twelve feet apart. The whole sea astern was filled with these regular beacons, arranged in several fields of about 130 to 200 feet across. The incredible thing was that all the patches within one field flared up and went out again absolutely simultaneously, just as if they were all on the same electric circuit. Whatever creatures these were, they were moving, or rather flashing, in perfect step. They were singing their mysterious inaudible marching song in perfect rhythm.

'They are medusas!'

'They look like flying saucers!'

'Over here, Klausewitz; come round here. Call the others—this is something quite unique!'

'We must time the rhythm. Who's got a stop-watch?'

'Couldn't we dive with a pocket torch?'

'We could get down into the boat.'

229

'Herr Becker, Herr Becker, can you pull the boat forward? I'm getting my mask.'

'No need—we've got the observation box in the boat.'

'Someone take the bow lamp off!'

'The interval is about one and a half seconds.'

We stared down through the observation box. The lights were small and circular. They were floating about thirty feet below us. They had a perfectly well defined edge, but because of the reflection of the waves the light sources had looked from above like patches three feet across. The flashes lasted something less than a second, after which they were switched off for one and a half seconds. Within a field they were all completely synchronized, but adjacent fields were fractions of a second ahead or behind. We were faced here with a miracle. From the cold silent depths of the night there glowed a harmony, an organized friendly calm, a regular pulsating of sentient beings.

Franzisket had meanwhile got his pocket torch and was flashing it out of time with the floating creatures. Whether it was his doing or from some other cause the harmony was lost. The fields moved away, there were a few sporadic flashes, and then everything was as dark as before.

We were not able to establish whether they had been medusas or perhaps worms or other luminous creatures. Presumably the signals were a preparation for the act of procreation. The creatures stimulated one another optically until their excitement was synchronized, producing a simultaneous emission of male and female propagation products. Franzisket told me that Professor Rensch had observed luminous beetles in India which synchronized their flashing signals in a similar manner and rhythm.

In the autumn of 1939, when I was diving in the Caribbean with Jörg Böhler and Alfred von Wurzian, we had encountered a strange jelly creature off the steep coast of Curaçao in conditions of considerable wind and waves. It was a completely transparent tube about six feet long and a good twelve inches across. It floated, ephemeral and exceedingly fragile, close below the surface. Since scientists assume that all life on our globe originated in the oceans, it has often been thought that somewhere in the deep sea there might still exist some exceedingly primitive and primordial form of life, a kind of primal slime. It had looked at that time as if we might be face to face with the earliest of our ancestors.

I published the picture in a book and we also showed it to a number of scientists. But none of them was able to tell us definitely what it was. As the coast at that point dropped steeply to great depths I assumed that it was a deep-sea form that had been washed up by a current.

Now, nineteen years later, in the Addu atoll, from aboard the *Xarifa* I suddenly caught sight of just such a jelly tube. I have rarely been overboard with a camera more quickly. While the ship sailed on and Hirschel was getting ready to follow me with a bucket I did what, to my annoyance, I had failed to do eighteen years before—I observed the structure closely, filmed it from all sides and touched it.

Here I had a surprise. This was no tube but an entirely compact jelly sausage. But because it was totally transparent all that showed was the spiral structure of its outer surface. On closer examination this structure proved to be an endless thread which circled the jelly in neatly touching spirals and on which, as though on a string of pearls, countless minute globules were arranged next to one another.

What fascinated me in particular was a kind of independent rotation that I had noticed even off Curaçao. This sausage-shaped primal slime was rotating. The movement started at any point on the roughly six-foot-long creature and was continued along its entire body. Today I know that my observation must have been at fault. What I saw was evidently not an independent motion but the result of currents and eddies below the surface. For it is hardly to be assumed that a structure of eggs—and that is what it proved to be—could perform a movement of its own.

Hirschel was swimming up with the bucket and tried to slip the tube into it. It was obstinate, elastic and slippery. Only by our joint efforts did we succeed in forcing it into the bucket and a short while later we were examining it on board.

Under the microscope it was obvious that the globules arranged on the thread were eggs. The embryos enclosed in them, now nearing maturity, could be clearly made out. They were ten-tentacle squids. This huge set of eggs probably came from one of those giant octopuses living in the open sea at a depth of many hundreds of feet, the kind the sperm whales dive down for. Judging by the tentacle stumps discovered in the stomachs of sperm whales they reach a length of more than thirty feet. The set of eggs presumably rises by itself since the young creatures enjoy better living conditions in shallow water. Here it had obviously been washed into the atoll by the high tide.

The solid jelly offers the eggs good protection. We did not see bite marks of fish anywhere, and indeed it could not be easy to bite through such a firm, slippery and elastic substance. The young inside the eggs were turning and twisting in all directions.

Once more our microfilming equipment installed in the mess proved exceedingly useful. It enabled us at any time to film captured specimens instantly under considerable magnification. The tentacle stumps on the forward end of the embryos' bodies were clearly recognizable, and so were the almost fully developed large eyes and the sack-like body covered with pigmentation cells.

The next day the first of them hatched. They looked exceedingly dainty and showed considerable differences from each other in their reaction to their first day of life. Some were shy and instantly contracted when colliding with others. Others were inquisitive and go-getting, and tried to make contact. Yet others were *joie-de-vivre* personified. They took no notice of anything and gyrated in a kind of exuberant waltz.

Outside, in nature, this first day of life more often than not ends tragically. Of a hundred young hatched ninety are certain to be eaten by fish. There are no hiding places in the open water. They are thus at the mercy of chance, even though their own skill in evading attack plays a considerable part.

We were particularly interested to find the contracting and expanding pigmentation cells already present in the young creatures. To the fully grown squids they offer the opportunity of an exact colour matching the environment. But this change of colour also reflects the creature's mood. In these embryos, which were excitedly swimming into their new life, the pigmentation cells were continually changing their size.

It is generally believed that fishes are mute. If my supposition is right they are able with their lateral line system to perceive the fin movements of other fish so that a kind of communication is achieved in this way. But even if I am right this is not a real language. Eibl, on the other hand, observed incidents of fish conducting a kind of dialogue with questions and answers.

He had made his first observations on our voyage through the Caribbean. There he had found coral clumps which were regularly visited by sizeable fish. They would swim to the clumps, take up their position above them, motionless, open their mouth and open their gills. In fish language they were saying, 'Here I am; I want to be cleaned.'

The other group, to whom this invitation was addressed, were small slim fishes belonging to various families but practising the same trade. In response to the invitation they instantly appeared from the coral clump which served them as a home and hiding place, swam over to the caller requiring to be cleaned and busily began to search him for parasites.

Eibl observed that it was chiefly small copepods which had got a hold on the fish's skin. During the cleaning operation he saw them frantically escaping along the body of the large fish. They were ruthlessly pursued, and in the course of this pursuit the zealous cleaners would slip into the open gill slits and reappear through the fish's open mouth, re-enter its mouth and emerge again from its gills—in short, they felt completely at home about and inside the larger fish.

Eibl was able to observe clearly that the big fish would hold its breath for up to thirty seconds in order not to disturb the little ones. Its whole body would go rigid and frequently it would even begin to keel over. When we are in the dentist's chair we similarly hold our breath and likewise go rigid—except that to the fish being cleaned is clearly a pleasurable experience.

When the cleaned fish has had enough it makes two more signals. First it briefly closes its mouth, though not completely, and immediately opens it again to enable the cleaners to get out. Then it shakes its body and swims off. The first signal clearly means, 'Thanks very much, that will do'; and the second could mean, 'Well done today. I'll be back soon.'

An interesting fact observed by Eibl is that with most species it is only the young that work as cleaners—a parallel perhaps to the human young earning their first money by delivering newspapers.

In the Indian Ocean also we found mouth-cleaners but these belonged to different genera and were differently coloured. I was able to film this cleaning procedure in great detail with groupers and tiger fish. When the big fish opened their mouths and the cleaners slipped in it looked just as if they were eating spaghetti.

The day before our departure from Addu atoll we were diving in the channel off Gan Island which leads out to the open sea. The bottom there was at fifty to eighty feet and polished smooth by the fierce current. In the middle of it, above a solitary block of coral over twenty-five feet in diameter, we saw no fewer than eight large devil rays circling.

We dived down and filmed them at leisure. The creatures took fright when they saw us and fluttered away like giant birds, but presently, as if held by a rubber band, they invariably returned to the rock.

Not until the next day, when I was filming there once more with my telescopic lens, did I discover what attracted them to this spot. The large block was the abode of several hundred mouth-cleaners—a kind of large-scale de-infestation centre. The devil rays, too, are a favourite hunting ground of troublesome parasites. These rays also know the signal, they too had command of the secret language.

They placed themselves three to six feet above the coral, gills wide open, and remained hovering there like clouds. Whole battalions of cleaners appeared to decontaminate them. Whereas one lot spread over their undersides and there hunted for parasites, the rest wriggled into the not over-wide gill slits, dis-appeared in them, and subsequently emerged from the creatures' huge mouths.

The extent to which devil rays suffer from ectoparasites is shown by the fact that they sometimes leap up into the air and let themselves fall flat on the water, producing a thunderous smack. At other times they will take the anchor chain of ships between their head lobes and rub along it. With small ships— as I have mentioned before—the result can be that the anchor is dislodged and caught in the devil ray's head, so that the creature then tows the whole cutter behind it.

Eibl and I were swimming over a sandy bottom, at a depth of about sixty feet, when our attention was caught by a kind of meadow whose blades of grass were worms sticking some eight inches out of the sand. They were waving to and fro and twisting like cobras. As we approached them they withdrew into the sand, and they did so in a beautifully staggered manner. Those closest to us disappeared first, while the ones behind them were still showing their heads, and the ones further back were each standing a little higher than the ones in front of them, just like organ pipes. Eventually they all disappeared, leaving only holes in the sand.

Because of some reefs we could not anchor the *Xarifa* near enough to get our soundless television camera into position in front of these mysterious holes. But there was a small island nearby. So we established a television centre there, powered by a portable generator, and installed our tele-recording equipment in a tent. Soon we saw and filmed what came out of those holes.

The first things to appear were small heads with large inquisitive eyes peering around in all directions. They looked at the eye of the TV camera and disappeared. Then they reappeared and once more disappeared. Eventually they emerged a little further. They were not worms but eels. The tail part of their body was in a vertical tube which, as we subsequently established, they themselves produced by the excretion of a fast-hardening slime. They fed on minute creatures drifting past them. In doing so they twisted and coiled, and this gave them their snake-like appearance.

Eibl dived down and with a pipette he injected an intoxicant into some of the holes. Soon afterwards the creatures were reeling out and Eibl seized them with his hand. The moment he released them they wriggled back to the sand and, tail first, dug themselves in. Eibl held one of the creatures close to the camera for identification. The smooth body bore a regular pattern as well as three pairs of sizeable patches. Eyes and mouth were much larger and more crudely shaped than with normal eels.

We discovered subsequently that similar creatures had been captured off California in 1923 and off the Philippines in 1930, in both cases in very shallow water. The 'tube eels' discovered by us in the Indian Ocean and closely studied with the television camera live at a depth of sixty-five to 160 feet and differ from those discovered elsewhere by essential features of their anatomy. As

Klausewitz established, they were not only a previously unknown species but even an unknown genus. He honoured our ship and me by naming the new creature *Xarifania Hassi*. Among the numerous fishes which have adapted to a variety of habitats these tube eels occupy a special place. They are the only ones with an almost non-locomotive plant-like mode of life.

We never, however, saw any young creatures of this species. We were to observe tube eels at several more places in the Maldives and later encountered a closely related species in the Nicobars, but invariably the waving, snaking field consisted of fully grown specimens. It may well be that the young still lead a fully fish-like, freely mobile life and only adopt their more comfortable stationary mode of life at a more advanced age. The formation of colonies is probably an adaptation which provides more efficient defence against enemies.

With great patience Eibl succeeded in doing what initially only the television camera had succeeded in doing. As the television picture had only a limited resolution and definition he lay down motionless in front of some of the holes with his Rolleimarin ready for action and thus remained lying on the sea bed, without moving, for half an hour. His self-discipline was the more admirable as a few small crabs moving about the sand were nibbling at him. Only when our eels had got used to his presence and the whole waving meadow had risen up again to its full height in front of him did he press the shutter.

A deputation of Maldive natives who happened to be visiting us at that time also inspected our tent. None of them had seen a film before and their astonishment at the television picture was all the greater. They assured us with gestures that our sand eels were totally unknown to them. Because of their hidden mode of life they had never yet been caught in nets or with rod and line. Only when Eibl caught one of the tube eels in front of the camera and brought it to the surface did the Maldivians believe what they had seen, and they left us with much cheerful shaking of heads.

The Shark Wreck

Thinking back to our experiences at Gaha-Faro I ask myself whether Eibl and I were really in our right minds during those four days. Before leaving we had both promised our wives that we would not forget that we were family men. I certainly had no intention whatever of taking any chances such as those on my early voyages. But then we got swept away by a kind of intoxication. If I had not recorded everything in great detail on film I would even hesitate to speak about it. After all, a diver can tell virtually any story he likes. Who can check whether he is telling the truth?

Entering the Gaha-Faro lagoon was difficult. We arrived later in the day than we had planned and the sun was already low over the horizon as we sailed along the long white surf-line of the reefs, on the look-out for the narrow entrance into the lagoon which was marked on our chart. Becker was perched in the crow's nest, giving his commands by signals. When we at last discovered the narrow forked passage, just before dusk, I jumped overboard and swam ahead of the ship.

From the mast it was almost impossible to tell how deep the channel was and which of the two passages led into the lagoon. Swimming in the dark water, with its strong currents, I guided the *Xarifa* through the narrow gap. The following morning we sailed on to the stretch of coast, where according to the Maldive natives, there were two sunken ships. We found them both. One was small, totally smashed and uninteresting. But the other, which we soon christened the 'shark wreck', was one of the most beautiful I had ever seen.

The ship had run on to the reef plateau over her whole length but the waves had only smashed her bows. Her stern was still intact and projected a good thirty feet over the steep slope of the reef face. According to the natives this ship had foundered sixty years ago. Parts of her machinery were level with the surface so that we were able to make fast our boat to part of it. The stern was fifty to a hundred feet below water and was picturesquely overgrown with corals which had spread over it like creepers.

There we encountered the first shark. Admittedly this was a harmless nurse shark which was having a mid-day snooze in the hollow of what used to be the hull. I handed the camera to Hirschel and he filmed me waking the shark. As I was pursuing it over the ship's rail, a larger well-shaped shark passed close by me.

We first explored the still intact cabins in the stern, where huge shoals of fish were hiding. Next we investigated the reef slope below the ship. It dropped to 160 feet, where the bottom then sloped less steeply. During our descent we caught sight in the distance of a dark object slowly approaching us.

It was a giant turtle. Calmly and full of dignity it paddled towards us and then passed us. About a dozen exceptionally large barnacles were clinging to its shell. A moment later another creature sidled past us—a magnificent large sting-ray.

We let it pass below and followed it. I was filming it. After some forty or fifty yards we came to a cavity in the rock, and this the ray entered, evidently on a routine call. The cavity was flat and extended a good way into the rock; its floor was covered with sand in which the ray was digging. Eibl swam in and chased it out again. Alarmed, the ray fluttered against a coral, very nearly bumped into my purring camera, and hurriedly made off.

Meanwhile three sharks had come into sight. None of them was longer than six feet. They were swimming in deep water, eyeing us with interest. While I was filming one of them, Eibl swam on a little distance over the slope. Suddenly I heard a clang in the water and saw a sizeable fish wriggling on his harpoon.

I remember thinking that it was rather reckless to harpoon fish off this steep slope, with so many sharks about. Already the first of them was approaching. This was a different one, a larger one, which had been attracted by the wriggling fish. With the wonderfully effortless movement of these creatures it charged towards us like a missile, close to Eibl, circled him, took fright and swam off obliquely downwards. Eibl's eyes flashed with pleasure as we met again. We swam closer to the wreck. There Eibl drew his knife and boldly drew it across the now dead fish, so that a cloud of blood began to spread. We were both very elated and, keeping the sharks continually in sight, swam on a little distance, wedged the bleeding fish body under a coral and hurried back to the wreck where a big rent in the hull offered an absolutely ideal hide-out.

We waited. About two minutes passed before the first shark sensed the smell of blood. Then the quiet scene was abruptly transformed. At about twice its normal speed, the shark made for the bait. Two other sharks turned and just as fast raced after the first. Barely fifteen feet away they excitedly circled the spot like aircraft about to land. After several vain attempts the larger shark thrust its nose among the corals, seized the dead fish by its tail, lifted it, jerked its own head to get a better grip and vigorously shook its prey, which was evidently too large for it. Part of it dropped down and the other two sharks pounced on it. In wild pursuit the three of them disappeared in an oblique dive.

Eibl and I were electrified. With our backs covered by the wreck we were here able to establish how quickly sharks can perceive the smell of blood and also how they behave towards man when there is blood in the water. This second point would be of exceptional importance for the shipwrecked. During the next feed we no longer hid in the wreck. The sharks' interest was so clearly focused on the bleeding baits, and on these only, that our presence did not seem to matter to them at all. The moment blood began to spread in the water a wave of excitement rose throughout the sea. These otherwise royally arrogant creatures totally lost their self-control and performed the most astonishing charges, contortions and capers. Eventually we were crouching in the open

237

on a slope offering no cover, with the bait barely six feet away from us, either in front of or between us, and up to eight sharks carcharhinus were circling us simultaneously.

Eibl, who was engaged in the bloody business of harpooning and chopping up the fish, was in greater danger than me. His hands and arms were smeared with blood. But somehow we both felt increasingly secure. What Eibl had started on an exuberant impulse of the moment had now become an exceedingly interesting and important piece of research.

In Australia, where fatal accidents are caused by sharks every year, it has also been observed that persons hurrying to the aid of victims are never bitten themselves. The sharks invariably try to take further bites from the person already wounded (Coppleson 1950). I used to think that nothing was more dangerous than to be among sharks when the scent of blood was spreading, but I now revised my opinion. On the contrary: the bleeding object positively protected us. Whenever we got in the sharks' way they avoided us just as if we were some annoying coral obstacle. All that interested them was the bleeding bait. Only when this had been swallowed or carried away by one of the sharks did the others again show any interest in our movements.

This is a valuable hint for shipwrecked persons. For those who have suffered injury, of course, it is not reassuring, since with open wounds they are indeed in serious danger when sharks are about. But those uninjured, no matter what is happening all round them, need not despair. Although sharks are highly excited whenever there is blood in the water, their interest is entirely focused on the object from which the blood comes.

On our second and third day there were even more sharks about than on the first. Word had evidently got around. At one point, while I was filming, Eibl suddenly pointed downwards. A little lower down on the slope, not far from us, a sixteen-foot tiger shark was calmly swimming along. We held our breath and it passed by. By coincidence, another giant visited us barely ten minutes later—this time it was a hammerhead shark, likewise sixteen feet long. It, too, paid no attention to us but swam on calmly along the slope. Our knees were still shaking a little when we got back into the boat. But the following day we nevertheless continued our investigation.

During the war the US Air Force tried to find a way of protecting bailed-out airmen against attack by sharks. They came up with a 'shark repellent', which was in fact copper acetate. We had taken a few pounds of this with us in order to test it. Now was our chance. We poured about 100 grammes each into small cotton bags and took them with us under water.

To start with, the effect of the dissolving chemical was very good. The sharks, which had hitherto invariably shown up whenever we dived under the wreck, stayed away. Two which came into our field of vision slowly swam off again. Eibl next killed a fish and cut it up. Within two minutes the first sharks appeared. They seemed a little irritated but very soon found the bait and devoured it.

Eibl then thrust a bag of copper acetate directly into the mouth of a speared perch. Again the sharks came. The smell of blood totally eliminated the effect of the copper acetate. Not until one of the sharks was holding the fish in its mouth and shaking it did the bag slip out and drop among the corals. Otherwise it would probably have swallowed it.

After our dives we crouched in the boat, lay in the sun, reloaded our cameras and again and again exchanged our impressions. The ship, the others, their work—all these had become a secondary affair. I had long shot enough film to support our scientific findings and for our television programmes. Nevertheless, to make doubly sure, we reloaded our cameras and made further descents.

Cousteau and his men made a film, from inside a steel cage, of a whale which had been rammed and killed by their ship and which was being torn to pieces by sharks. His shots showed clearly how the sharks cut chunks of blubber from the huge body by means of a shaking movement of their head. Exactly the same movements were made by our sharks whenever a piece was too large for them to swallow it whole. In this way the shark uses his rows of sharp teeth like a saw, leaving a smooth clean cut.

The next day we fastened our bait to a strong hook and tied the other end of the line to a projecting piece of metal on the wreck. Then, admittedly, we took cover. Presently a shark came and swallowed the hook. It swam off but was abruptly halted by the rope, reeled, and thrashed about wildly. Instantly six other sharks were all around it. There was a furious commotion, then the hook tore out and the sharks disappeared down the abyss. That night Eibl wrote to his wife, 'Re-runs are not planned—just to reassure you. I shall now paddle about in the shallow water and take pictures of fish. After that we shall go walking about the Malaysian archipelago.' Nevertheless, this last day had its after-effects. We had spent nearly four hours at a depth of 130 to 150 feet and in the excitement had been careless about our rate of ascent. Deep diving, however, produces a cumulative affect. We both had pains in our limbs and, whether we liked it or not, had to go down again for a slow decompression. The sun was plunging below the horizon as we lowered ourselves to a depth of sixty feet by a rope from the *Xarifa*. We had to take a whole hour over our gradual ascent.

The sea turned a deep blue and night was falling. We had not been afraid of the sharks raging all around us. But to be hanging in the dark open water now was exceedingly unpleasant.

While the ship remained at Colombo for eight weeks and the members of our expedition amused themselves as best they could, I had to fly to England and finish both the German and English versions of the first six television film programmes with the BBC in Bristol. Under the terms of my contract I had to deliver the programmes before getting the money I needed to continue the enterprise.

I would be presenting a distorted picture of my life were I to describe myself as too much of a martyr to a malevolent fate. Certainly, my zoological ambitions were not being fulfilled. There was Gerlach lying in his hammock, puffing at his cigar, and turning again to the study of the worms which interested him. There were Eibl, Scheer, Franzisket and Klausewitz all happily working on the problems which occupied them, and indeed their work later brought them much well-earned praise. And here was I, the only person on board the *Xarifa* who was prevented from following his real profession. That was a fact. On the other hand, I was fascinated by my film work, and the sense of producing something which no one else had ever produced before in the same way very largely made up for what I was missing. My life was full of unique experiences. Whenever we entered a new port we were treated like royalty. The governor or whoever the local leading figure was almost invariably came on board. Our work received recognition, and we were everywhere welcomed with open arms and supported in every way. What every skindiver had always dreamed about came true for us. The world was before us. I explained to the captain where we wanted to go, and next morning, when we opened our eyes, we had anchored in just this bay or along that reef. We had all comforts on board, we had all the equipment we needed, we had good food—except on the cook's off-days—and we had every conceivable technical aid. When we returned from our dives we were able to lie down on a soft bed and sip iced drinks. We formed a pleasant community and got on well with one another. We were extremely fortunate.

I arrived in Bristol, fresh and with a ferocious determination which caused some consternation there. People were accustomed to working in the comfortable manner of English gentlemen, to trooping down to the canteen for a tea break every two hours, to ending the working day sooner rather than later, and to keeping the week-end sacred. The savage Teuton—who knew exactly how much each day cost him in ship and crew maintenance—and his works were regarded with some alarm. My cutter was a Pakistani, named Paul Kahn, with whom I got on splendidly. He loved food and I respected this by taking him to the best restaurants. In return he worked with me virtually day and night—only occasionally, on a Sunday, did he take half a day off.

Somehow we actually managed the job in eight weeks. Absurdly, the German version of the films eventually caused me the greatest difficulties. I had been speaking English all the time and had tried to adjust myself to English tastes. Now that I was to record the German commentaries, surrounded by nothing but Englishmen, I discovered that I had acquired an English accent—not of course in my pronunciation but in my rhythm of speaking. Moreover, I was so run down that for some time past I had only been able to sleep with the aid of sedatives. When I returned to Colombo everybody there was wonderfully rested and raring to go again. I did not get even half a day's rest. The moment I arrived I was swamped with all those problems which had been saved up for me to decide in person—both technical and human problems. They were solved. Lotte was again with me and would take part in the second half of our voyage; our little daughter was being looked after by her grandmother.

Because of the tense situation in Indonesia the ship insurance rate for that area had become exorbitant. I therefore decided on the spur of the moment to make the Nicobars our next destination. We had no permit to visit the island group, but that did not worry me much. The islands, until recently an English possession and now Indian, would certainly be of considerable interest to us. In 1899 they had been visited by a German research vessel, the *Valdivia*. In contrast to the Maldive Islands, the Nicobars were mountainous with impenetrable primeval forests. The natives there were rather primitive and of great anthropological interest. I settled all our obligations and debts at Colombo and we moved off without further delay.

It was a slightly unusual situation for a ship with specialized scientists, whose trip was largely financed from official quarters, to be sailing to a group of islands for which no entry or work permit had been obtained. But I was past worrying about such things. Together with Lotte I sat in Captain Becker's cabin and we all reflected at great length where we would be safest from Indian police barges. Our choice eventually was the small island of Kondul, where the *Novara* had anchored almost exactly a hundred years ago. At that time natives had been seen on the island; fifty-nine years ago, when the German research vessel *Valdivia* called, none had been seen. This remote spot seemed particularly suited to our research activities.

We dropped anchor there in the morning. The primeval forest landscape was of breath-taking beauty. Shortly after lunch a busily paddled dug-out canoe approached us: in addition to a number of natives it contained three Indians with submachine guns. We told them blandly that unfortunately we had engine trouble and had to perform a repair here. After a long palaver, first on board and then at the near-by police station, we moved the *Xarifa* into the bay of Great Nicobar which we had declared to be the only sheltered spot but which in fact had the great advantage of being so far from the police station that it could be reached only after several hours of paddling. The Indians had no motor boat.

In this bay we worked undisturbed and most productively for three weeks. Then an Indian hospital ship arrived and our excuse of a defective engine could no longer be kept up. We invited all the Indians to a farewell party and told them that to our great regret we had to leave this beautiful spot in order to continue our oceanographic work in the open sea towards the south. The Indians, who had been extremely friendly and had merely been worried about their own position and their duty, watched us sail off with tears in their eyes but with great relief. As soon as it was dark we altered course and, by a round-about route, made for the island of Tillanchong. Close questioning of the natives and of the Indians had elicited the information that this island was totally uninhabited and that we need therefore not fear any further disturbance there.

I dwell on these details with so much pleasure because this final stage on board the *Xarifa* was really the best and most successful. Both for our scientific work and for our films we found here whatever we needed. I have summed up the result of the *Xarifa* expedition to the Maldives and Nicobars in my book *Expedition into the Unknown* (Hutchinson, 1965). Eibl-Eibesfeldt described his experiences as a behaviourist in his very readable book *Land of a Thousand Atolls* (MacGibbon and Kee, 1965). Tillanchong is nine and a half miles long and the shape of an exceedingly graceful long riding boot. Near its heel we anchored in Castle Bay, a sheltered spot. Close to us, above the shaft of the boot, several steep jungle-covered mountains rose to over 1,000 feet.

By good chance we succeeded here in filming the love play of various species of fish and also of sharks. With the latter—at least the species which we filmed—the males get the females ready for mating by tenderly nibbling their gills. One female which I got in front of my camera had three suitors, and her gills were completely in tatters. A short distance away we discovered the wreck of a British warship; its lamp room in the fo'c's'le was still intact. We spent several days sitting on deck, all of us, cleaning up some beautiful brass lamps which had been under the sea for thirty-five years and which now are as bright and sparkling in our homes as they once were on board. Eibl and Klausewitz captured so many species of fish, some by harpoon and others with poison and nets, that the scientific processing of the material is still not completed to this day, fifteen years later. In the bay where we were anchored there also lived a crocodile which made excursions into the sea at night, but in spite of all our efforts we never saw anything beyond its unmistakable footprints in the sand. On the far side of a small isthmus was a sandy beach fringed with coconut palms, and I doubt if in the whole world there can be another as beautiful. One day we experienced here the strange spectacle of a moon rainbow. Captain Becker and I shot pigeons and wild boar in the jungle. On the sandy bottom directly underneath our ship I discovered a clam between whose slightly opened halves two inquisitive eyes were showing. When I approached the clam closed. I took it on board and we placed it in our aquarium. Presently the shells opened again—and between them, instead of the original mollusc, sat a small octopus which operated it just as the mollusc had done. This octopus presently found itself under regular siege from various crabs which likewise inhabited our aquarium. A hermit crab eventually succeeded in so annoying the octopus that it left its hiding place to pounce on the hermit crab. Now we saw that it was a female which had laid its eggs inside the empty clam. I shot a whole film of this mother and her squabbles with the rest of the aquarium tenants. We even succeeded in filming the young hatching out of their eggs. Presently the whole basin was filled with pinhead-sized baby octopuses bobbing about everywhere. The mother octopus began to jerk and died in pitiful agony. Her life's purpose was fulfilled—and so she died.

Among those spots which I would like to see once more before I die Tillanchong heads the list. One day there was engine noise overhead: an Indian aircraft was circling above. We had been spotted. Sadly we took our leave. I was subsequently told that a small Indian naval vessel had been no more than a day's voyage away from us. Whether it presently arrived at Tillanchong in order to arrest the *Xarifa* for breaking the law I do not know. We preferred not to take any chances. We weighed anchor and transferred our activities— by now in their final phase—to the waters off Malaya.

BACK UNDER THE SEA

Deep-Sea Research on dry Land

In Singapore one phase of my life came to an end. We were cordially received there by the British Navy who undertook to look after the *Xarifa* free of charge until I myself was again in a position to dispose of her. That took nearly two years. I completed all the films I had contracted to do and once more I approached the German Research Community. I was prepared to assign the *Xarifa* free of charge to any scientific institution provided it undertook to meet the costs of current research. No such institution could be found—I am tempted to say: fortunately. Otherwise I would have been condemned to continue as a manager whereas now I felt entitled to sell the ship and live on the proceeds.

It was by no means easy to find a buyer. Then, suddenly, two people evinced an interest—an American who organized cruises in the Bahamas and an Italian who had fallen in love with the idea of owning such a ship. I personally preferred the ship to remain domiciled in Europe. Signor Traglio, who owned Coca Cola and other firms in Italy, agreed to my terms; I was merely to arrange for the ship to be brought back to Europe. I suggested that he should go to Singapore and have a look at her first. This he considered unnecessary. I thereupon sent out a crew to sail her back. On this last voyage everything went according to plan—the *Xarifa* arrived in Cannes harbour two days ahead of schedule. Signor Traglio arrived early and looked for her everywhere without finding her. That enormous and rather dishevelled ship in the middle of the harbour had not caught his attention at all. Then he realized what he had bought. We spent nearly a whole week transferring her to him. We accompanied him and his charming wife to nightclubs, but he was pensive. Gradually he revealed to us his intention of selling his house in Monaco and his racing stables. He had begun to realize what he had let himself in for. He subsequently transformed the *Xarifa* into a luxury yacht, which no doubt consumed a small fortune. Lotte, who had so many memories of the *Xarifa*, did not want to see her ever again. I disagreed. I was delighted to see her two years later, brilliantly beautiful and in spotless condition. Carlo invited me on board. The work rooms and laboratories had disappeared. The ship now had exceedingly luxurious passenger cabins, a new deck saloon, and three elegant bathrooms. Eventually Lotte was persuaded, and we accepted Carlo's invitation to cruise on board the *Xarifa* as his guests. This time I reclined in a deckchair, carefree, waited upon. Of course the sale hurt me too. It was as if I had cut off part of myself, as though an organ which had belonged to me had now become part of someone else's body. On the other hand, I was relieved of a tremendous burden which I had borne for eight years. I was free again. The proceeds of the sale enabled me to devote myself for the next few years to my neglected interests. I had come to realize, in the meantime, that my real interest was not the sea proper or its denizens. It had taken me years to realize this, but now at last I understood myself. What I was ultimately interested in lay behind and beyond the visible phenomena. In the unexplored sea I had come a little closer to it than elsewhere, but it was not really fishes or crabs or corals. What ultimately fascinated me was the secret of nature itself. That 'nature' which offers itself to our senses in such various shapes and forms, and of which we are ourselves a part.

On our tiny planet, on this grain of dust in space and time, a process began about 2,000 to 3,000 million years ago which we call 'life'. It spread like wildfire and was passed on by a variety of shapes which we call 'living creatures'. To begin with, this process developed in the sea and subsequently spread to dry land; 'plants' marked its beginning and 'animals' followed. An astonishing variety of forms emerged, and in view of the totally different environmental conditions these 'organisms' were different from those in the sea. And among this wealth of forms one form of life emerged, a 'living creature' which, as it were, burst all previous chains—'Man'. Of all organisms this is the one we find most difficult to assess and understand, simply because we ourselves are this unit of life. The human mind is trying to judge itself, to comprehend itself. Is this form of assessment correct, complete, sober, unprejudiced? This unit 'Man' enlarges the power and capacity of his genetically produced body by attaching to himself artificial organs through which he enlarges his effective body— such as clothes, tools, weapons, but gradually also larger units—houses, machines and, woven into his own effective structure, other 'serving' humans. To this day these additional units are regarded as something separate from our genetic bodies, as our 'products', as something linked to ourselves merely by right of ownership or contracts.

From the point of view of the development of life, however, these are just as much functional units, just as much organs, as are our liver, our toe-nails or our eyes. Their origins and their materials are different, certainly, but functionally that is of little importance. Indeed, some animals show of how little importance this is. It makes no difference whether an armour has been formed from a substance exuded from the body itself or 'artificially' from material found in the environment. What matters is the effect and the overall balance, the ratio between energy absorbed and emitted. Herein lies the real key to everything we call life. All units promoting life must meet the condition of absorbing more energy than they give off; unless this condition is met the process is automatically extinguished.

If, however, we look at things in this light then it is not the human body, as hitherto assumed, that continues animal and plant evolution, but instead the effective bodies created by us—or let us call them 'occupational bodies'—which Man forms and within whose structure he remains merely the control unit. The transition from monocellular to multi-cell organisms took place because some single-cell creatures were so designed that they no longer separated by cell division but formed multiplicities of cells resulting in a division of labour among the daughter cells. If my idea was correct, then evolution had reached a significant point for the second time in Man's evolution. In a manner similar to the germ cells of multi-cell organisms, we too develop systems of a higher order. It is not Man who corresponds to animals and plants, but the superior structures created by us from additional units, the 'occupational bodies', 'economic organizations' and indeed 'states'—these are the units carrying evolution forward.

The conclusions arising from this idea are so diametrically opposed to the self-assessment that has been drilled into us for thousands of years that one can hardly utter them without appearing hopelessly ridiculous. If it is correct, however, then we must shed a third great illusion. The first such illusion was the belief that our earth, inhabited by Man, was the centre of the universe, that everything rotated around us and indeed existed for our benefit. This illusion had to be abandoned. The second illusion was the belief that Man, though not the centre of the universe, was at least its final achievement, the culmination of an evolution taking place on our planet, that we were something fundamentally different from other organisms, from animals and plants, that we were the special objects of divine interest and that the rest of nature was created more or less to serve our needs. This second illusion was also shattered. As we know today, we too are part of evolution. Man developed from the animal kingdom. But we continue to regard ourselves as the ultimate accomplishment, the culmination of this development. If, on the other hand, my idea was correct then this belief, too, had to be discarded. In that case we were merely part of an evolutionary development which had long gone beyond us; Man, seen from the evolutionary point of view, and his 'will', were not the decisive or specific element at all. What advanced the evolutionary process was our economic and

246

luxury structures in which the life process was being continued with the necessary positive energy balance.

This alarming—and in terms of accepted criteria humiliating—idea had never been put forward before, as far as I could find out. Everything else had been questioned, but not this point, simply because it contradicts our sensory impressions and the manner in which we interpret them. But if my idea was correct then it meant that the economic structures created by us—occupational structures, industrial organizations, states—were directly comparable to animal and plant bodies. These thoughts now mapped out my future course. Proceeding from biology, I had to examine those bodies which had hitherto been investigated not by natural science but by the totally separate sciences of management and economic theory. I had to study even political science, and above all I had to try to arrive at some common basic concepts. Because these 'bodies', merely because they are not solidly grown together, had been viewed as something basically different from animals and plants, each of the sciences dealing with them had evolved its own specialized language and produced its own concepts and problems. This then was the road my future researches would take.

I gave up diving and soon found my friends writing me off as a bad loss. Instead of making enjoyable films I had set myself an object which no one cared about. I could not, of course, foresee that these activities would engage me for more than ten years. But the deeper I tunnelled into this mountain of problems the higher rose the ranges before me.

At last I reached the objective I had set myself and published my results, though not with much hope of arousing interest. I would certainly not recommend anyone who enjoyed my books or films about my deep-sea activities to read this book of mine—indeed I would warn them against reading it. What I reported from the depths of the oceans was apt to arouse pleasure and interest, and communicated experiences which many readers might wish to share though they were in fact unable to do so. What I reported from the sea fitted into the framework of present-day life. My more recent field of work cannot make any claim of this kind. What I have to say now is certainly not pleasant or stimulating, rather the opposite, because it basically questions our accepted system of thinking in which we are comfortably featherbedded. What I have to say now runs counter to our thinking as dictated by our sensory perceptions and forces us to adopt a way of looking at things which results in totally different and unaccustomed value judgments. The only people to whom my new field of work has anything to offer are those who are not simply content with our way of looking upon the world but anxious to discover the truth no matter what it will look like.

In these researches an important question was that of the extent to which human behaviour is still 'genetically' determined. If, in the final analysis, we are germ cells building larger living structures then it is vital to know to what extent our modes of action are 'free' and to what extent directives for our actions are instilled into us by upbringing and tradition. In the germ cell of every multi-cell organism there are innate modes of behaviour which are passed on to the daughter cells and which then cause these, instead of developing an independent life of their own, to participate in the formation of an eye, a toe-nail or a flower petal.

I racked my brain to discover a way of breaking free from our accepted mode of viewing things, to force my brain to see Man for once as something unknown, strange and fundamentally new. How would a visitor from another star, who knew nothing of our judgment of ourselves, judge us? It occurred to me that film techniques might help here. In order to get an unprejudiced record of human behaviour I would have to do my filming unobserved. That much was obvious. But beyond this I wanted to get away from the stranglehold of our sensory perceptions. I experimented with filming people through mirrors and simultaneously altering the film speed. I took slow-motion and rapid-motion sequences and thus changed the time scale one way or the other. The results were interesting. They did in fact compel the mind to view and register even everyday occurrences as something new. Our mind is clearly adjusted to the time scale normal to us—a time scale resulting from the number of impressions per second that our ganglion cells can process. That this is not an absolute figure and that 'time' is not an absolute concept has already been suspected by a number of biologists. Insects are able to process more impressions per second, and therefore, compared with us, all processes must appear to them in slow motion. Other animals, such as cattle or snails, may act more slowly— to them, Man must move at a rapid tempo.

I used this film technique first in Europe and then in Samoa and India. The results were received with particular interest by Konrad Lorenz and his circle. I was interested mainly in the objectivization of Man, but Lorenz's group of scientists also discovered in my sequences many phenomena of interest to behaviour researchers. Eibl enthusiastically joined my new endeavours. Together we made journeys to all five continents and filmed humans in every conceivable activity—always unobserved, through mirrors, and always with a changed time scale.

I made a film series and published a book about this work—both with a moderate response. People had got accustomed to linking my name with sharks and coral reefs and regarded this unexpected new activity as something of a regrettable deviation. I was beginning to understand how hopeless the prospects for my real efforts were. Eibl, on the other hand, adopted the technique with success and we founded another institute in Liechtenstein. It was the first institution concerned with a biological examination of human behaviour, in other words human ethology. Subsequently, thanks to Eibl's persistence, the Max Planck Society authorized the establishment of a bigger institute of which Eibl is now the director. Thus the technique developed by me on the basis of a totally different point of view has found a fruitful field of application in behaviourist research and is being extensively developed in that field.

At the same time, out of the corner of my eye, as it were, I noticed how my former field of activity was becoming more and more fashionable every year, how increasingly large numbers of skindiving enthusiasts were swarming about the depths of our native and tropical seas. My nostalgia for the sea returned. I decided that, once my publication was out, I would join the large number of my own followers and enjoy myself diving again—not for the sake of any definite research but in a naïve and uncomplicated search for adventure, just as I had in the beginning.

Harold Holt's mysterious Death

I was reclining in the seat of a Qantas airliner. My destination was a lonely bay not far from Melbourne. There the Prime Minister of Australia, an enthusiastic skindiver, had disappeared in the sea. His body had never been found. What had happened to him?

I was accompanied by my son from my first marriage. Hans, now twenty-three and with quite a reputation as a pop singer and composer, was to help me with the camera and sound recording work. When the television people heard that I was once more going to put on my fins they suggested I should make a film about it at the same time. This then was my intention. At Sydney airport we were welcomed by Jim Fitzpatrick, the chief cameraman of the News and Information Bureau; the Australian Government had attached him to us as technical consultant. His broad smile was the same as on my last arrival in Australia, nearly twenty years before.

'Welcome to Australia,' he said. And because he is a nice chap he added, 'You haven't changed much.'

That remained to be seen. After all, I was fifty-one and had not dived for the past twelve years.

We were taken into a room where some forty journalists and photographers were assembled. Spotlights sprang up from all sides; even our entrance was filmed. During the bombardment by questions which now followed I realized that I had made a basic error. The death of Harold Holt was clearly not just a skindiving problem, as I had assumed. We soon discovered that there were a number of theories on this point. Quite a few people seemed to think that their Prime Minister had committed suicide; others believed that an enemy agent had shot him or that frogmen had abducted him.

It took us two days to get used to the time difference. Hans went off to take trial shots on Bondi Beach and came back with two girls. I felt as if I once more was with Jörg and Alfred. I once more belonged to a gay, simple and uncomplicated life.

Jim was in charge of our programme. He had introduced us to several of the most experienced divers—two of them had started skindiving after reading my first books. He next telephoned the Premier's widow. She would be delighted to see us. Harold Holt's week-end house at Port Sea, which I was anxious to visit, had remained unchanged.

We flew to Canberra. Jim thought it proper for us to make the acquaintance of the official in charge of fisheries, and subsequently we called on the State Secretary who had been a close friend of Harold Holt. Hans taped what he told me. He utterly ruled out the theory of heart failure. Holt had been in good health. Of course he had been overworked, but there was nothing unusual about his going into the sea in spite of fatigue and high waves. Cheviot Bay had been his great relaxation; all through the week he would look forward to skindiving there. There he was able to unwind completely. And once he had made up his mind about something nothing would make him change it. That had been his way in politics and also in his life. There was certainly no mystery about his death and any such rumours were a lot of silly gossip. He wished us the best of luck.

We drove all the way down to the coast in an official car. The landscape was pleasant—fields and woods, not unlike Europe. Nowhere a kangaroo. Dame Zarah, the former First Lady, had married again—a member of parliament who appeared to be something of an eccentric. Jim explained to us that this man, Jeffrey Baines, owned a small and somewhat ramshackle farm. There he made cheese.

We arrived. No one was there to receive us. The slightly shabby wooden house was by the coast; tall waves were crashing against the rocks. A few cows and sheep eyed us inquisitively. After a good deal of ringing a servant appeared. Dame Zarah had clearly forgotten about our visit. Half an hour later we were facing her in a room whose walls and ceiling were covered with a slightly way-out French tapestry. A mosaic of nude women, a fireplace with two stuffed pheasants over it, some magnificent vases with huge flowers, and soft music.

Dame Zarah told us about her first husband and his passion for skindiving. I discovered that I myself was not entirely free from blame. One of their sons, Sam, had got my first book as a school prize. This had induced him and his twin brother Andrew to start diving. And the two of them had then persuaded their father to join them and he, in fact, had soon become far more addicted to the sport than the boys.

'He was totally mad. Often he would swim about in the waves for a couple of hours, right out of sight.' When they had visitors his greatest pleasure would be to vanish in the sea and then return with several speared fish and crayfish. These he would personally grill on the spit. Dame Zarah was a charming, vivacious woman. Without beating about the bush she offered us the use of the house. 'Over the week-end my three sons usually come down with their friends, but the rest of the time it just stands empty.' I could see Jim smirking. He had clearly hoped for this invitation.

A few days later we stood in front of this week-end house. It was near the sea in an attractive garden. Port Sea lies on a spit of land which encloses the Gulf of Melbourne against the open sea. The house overlooks the Gulf, while Cheviot Bay is about four miles away, on the open sea. It was a Defence Zone and we had received special passes for it in Melbourne.

But where was the key? Dame Zarah had told us she had hidden it under one of the doors. She had described the exact spot to Hans, with whom she had had a lengthy conversation—but now we were unable to find it. There were no fewer than five doors to the house, each with some steps in front, but no key. The next-door neighbour, Harry, received us with open arms. Of course he had a spare key, but we must first listen to his new stereo set and have a few whiskies with him. He rushed to the telephone and drummed up some friends. In no time Hans was again surrounded by pretty girls. I was tired: I would have liked to unpack and go to bed. But is was no use. Harry had the key and it was two o'clock in the morning before he produced it.

Cheviot Bay: not a soul in sight, not a house, not a boat. A wild rocky circle with a broad reef plateau pierced in many places. It was low tide and the plateau was dry. Everywhere there were small lakes and pools, deep blue, while the reefs were covered with green algae. It was in these pools that Harold Holt used to dive. Jim had often joined him. Holt would collect abalones, spear fish, and extract crayfish from their holes with his gloved hand. He never used diving equipment. He was not really a strong swimmer, and because of a damaged shoulder could not do the crawl. But he had been a skilled and experienced skindiver.

'That Sunday the tide was in and he didn't want to dive at all but merely to cool himself. The surf was over thirty feet high. Together with Mrs Gillespie,

Allan Stuart, Mrs Gillespie's daughter Vane and her boy-friend, a student, he was strolling along the beach. Allan went into the water but felt a strong current and immediately came out again. Harold swam about a little—out there over the white sand which is now dry. He got out a little too far and was seized by a current. After that there was no help for him. You can see those reef channels forming a V over there. All the water thrown into the bay by the breakers collects there and flows back into the sea through the channel at the point of the V. At high tide the current there runs at about eight knots. The waves caught him and flung him against the reefs. By the time help arrived there was nothing to be done. For two days the whole area was searched by helicopters. Never before and never since has there been a similar search operation—the whole of Australia was in a flap.'

We were staying at the Prime Minister's house and I filmed the pictures and photographs on the walls. We were getting to know this man who had so abruptly vanished in the sea. He had been both gifted and popular, both lovable and stubborn. The neighbours told us their stories—some of them rather strange. We talked to Mrs Gillespie, a very charming woman. She had not yet got over that terrible shock. The Holts had been close friends and she had watched Holt disappearing in the waves. He had not called for help, he had not signalled. This had been most heroic as he must have known what was happening. But he also knew that no one could help him out there. If he had signalled then the two young men would have had to follow him and would have likewise met their death.

Mrs. Gillespie accompanied us to Cheviot Bay and showed us the rock from which she and Allan had looked for the head that had disappeared in the water.

Wearing breathing apparatus we roamed the reef pools, filming algae and fish. It was a dark sinister world: everything was vibrating and moving. Some of the kelp was a brilliant purple, another kind with huge tentacles groped about like hungry octopuses. This kelp probably was a factor in Harold Holt's death. A skilful diver can manage to dive underneath even very high breakers. One looks for a channel where the water is a little deeper, presses oneself to the bottom and lets the wave wall roar over one. Close to the bottom the water is still and one subsequently gets carried through the channel by the current. Here this technique could not be applied. The outer rocks were all covered with this kelp, the leaves of which were broad and heavy like thick leather and up to twenty feet long. The breakers lift the plant so that one is faced with a green wall and then their whole weight crashes down on one. To dive through underneath the breakers would be impossible here.

There was a fancy dress party at the house of our neighbours. Many of

Holt's friends were present and there was heavy drinking. Ghostly shadows flickered over the walls and over the pictures. At the spot where Harold Holt met his death the Melbourne Underwater Spear Fishermen had erected a memorial tablet. We filmed it at night with spotlights. The shadows there flickered just as spectrally over the motionless algae as they did here over the pictures on the walls.

The press was intensifying its siege of us daily. No doubt they were secretly hoping that we might come up with at least a bone of their Prime Minister. Youth Magazines interviewed me, women's magazines interviewed Hans. The rest interviewed both of us. They even set up Ampex equipment on the beach for live relays—except that it did not function. We calmly went on with our filming while they were busily repairing their equipment.

Then came a day which very nearly was my last. So far we had not been too lucky with the weather but at last the sun came out. Hans and I were alone for once; the time was 5.30 p.m. The tide was in and the scene was beautiful in the late afternoon sunlight. The breakers on the outer cliffs were a good twenty feet high. Six-foot waves were rolling well into the bay. I was saying to Hans, 'We'll never get this chance again. We'll take the shots now of how the waves spin me round.'

'Without a line?' Hans objected. The Melbourne Underwater Spear Fishermen had provided us with a long line and a large buoy in case I intended to investigate the currents at high tide. But we had left them behind.

'But it's quite shallow over the reef plateau,' I said.

Hans erected the tripod on a rock and fitted a telescopic lens to the camera. We agreed our signals. When he raised his hand the camera was ready for action. If he rotated both arms I was to repeat the sequence. If he crossed his arms the sequence was O.K. and done with.

Wearing only beach shoes on my feet I waded through the waves to the reef plateau. I was without fins and mask—just as Holt had been. All we needed for our sequence was my head in the waves. Our difficulty was that we were unable—and also unwilling—to reconstruct the actual occurrence. But at least I wanted to show what happened to a swimmer in these waves. I took note of where the deep water of the reef pools began; the boundary was clearly visible, even in the foam, by the dark blue colour of the reef water. I kept about thirty yards from this edge. Hans raised his arm: he was ready. I was standing with the water to my waist and flung myself into one of the waves and then tried to get out of it sideways—as Holt had probably done. The breaker seized me and spun me round. I let the roar pass over me, rolled over the rock plateau, tried to swim a short distance and stood up again. Hans rotated his arms.

253

We shot four or five takes of similar scenes. A particularly high breaker treated me like a beachball. As I tried to stand up again I suddenly found no ground under my feet. An icy shock passed through me: I could not believe it. A moment ago I had been a good thirty feet away from the edge. Without a mask I could not see much. I dived as fast as I could. I clutched the bottom. A powerful current was dragging me towards the open sea. I waited for the next breaker: I could clearly recognize it by its roar. Quickly I let go. I shot up and let the wave carry me towards the shore. But my calculation went wrong. My eyes were smarting with the salt but I could see clearly that I was not getting any nearer the edge of the reef plateau. I was only thirty feet away but in spite of desperate swimming movements and in spite of the wave motion I could not get any closer. And once again the powerful current dragged me seawards.

I was down at the bottom again, clutching whatever I could clutch. I realized that this was it. Inch by inch I dragged myself from one rock to another, hanging on to seaweed, digging my fingers deep into the sand. I was almost out of air, everything was spinning about me—clearly I was no longer quite as young as I used to be. Now the rock face was ahead of me and I was in the lee of the current. I swam, climbed up, clutched the edge and, straining against the current, managed to drag myself over the top. I was safe. On the beach Hans was crossing his arms: he had not noticed anything.

My knees shook so much I could hardly move. Now, in retrospect, I realized only too clearly how narrowly I had escaped Holt's fate. This was exactly what must have happened to him—he too had obviously been caught by an unexpected current. Would I have got through the breakers? Once these giant waves had got a hold on me and flung me against the cliffs I probably would not have had a hope. And even if I had got through that wall—what then? It would have taken Hans ten minutes to get up to the car and another ten minutes to the entrance of the Cadet College, where there was a telephone. By the time a boat was alerted and came round the headland it would have been night. The water was cold. How long could I have survived out there? Paddling back towards the beach I decided not to reflect on what might have been.

A few days later the waves were again very high but this time I set up the camera with the telescopic lens on the reef plateau. It was low tide. Hans was to climb up on top of one of the inner rocks to provide a scale for the towering wall of breakers behind him. I was setting the aperture when I noticed that Hans had climbed up one of the outer rocks. I pressed the shutter—and saw him abruptly turning and sprinting away. A real monster of a wave was roaring towards the shore and I could see Hans disappearing in a seething vortex. The giant wave flung him straight into a mass of rocks. I ran out over the reef and saw him emerge again. Fortunately he was conscious and I helped him ashore.

His hands and arms were badly cut. A few kind ladies who were just visiting us packed him into their car and took him to a doctor who put a few stitches in his hand. By nightfall we were again attending one of those parties which took place here every evening. We gradually came to know the pattern of Holt's life. As in a mosaic the pieces of his past were taking shape for us.

What had happened to his body? At the entrance to the channels which formed a V was a rock known as the 'Cathedral'. It was totally undercut, and at high tide the water found its way back to the sea through these submarine grottos. It was not far from that spot that Mrs Gillespie had seen him disappear in the waves. I consider it likely that the currents dragged him into the system of grottos and that he might have been caught in there. Crabs, fish, and sharks would have consumed his body very quickly. Some of his bones, crushed by the breakers, may have become part of the sand. Or perhaps some remains might still be found in the grotto. But there are few days when the sea is calm enough for a man to penetrate into them.

There remains the question of why Holt made the mistake of swimming a little too far into deep water. But, as my experience showed, it is very easy to make a mistake there. Holt, his diving companions told us, was fond of out-doing younger men, of showing them how good he was. Allan Stuart had gone into the shallow water with him but had come out again at once. He was an Englishman, it had been his first visit to this bay, and he had not liked the current. Perhaps this fact in itself had called forth a little bravado. Certainly in this lonely and fascinating bay a trivial cause might have very far-reaching consequences.

Threatened Nature

We left Cairns in a small but seaworthy motor yacht and set course for the inner reefs of the Great Barrier Reef. Our first objective was Pixie Reef. Lotte and I were standing in the bows, and with us was Meta, our thirteen-year old daughter. In my mind's eye I could see ourselves sailing these waters on our first journey nearly twenty years ago. Even then the diaries of Captain Cook and the biologist Banks who accompanied him had been our most precious luggage. We decided then that, if ever we had a little time to spare, we would come back and follow the whole of Cook's adventurous voyage as far as Cape York, the northern tip of Australia. What we did not expect was that it would take quite so long or that we would be accompanied by a daughter keen on diving herself. By sheer chance we were now doing this voyage exactly two hundred years to the day after the historic voyage of the great English explorer.

Eibl, too, was once more with us, and I was particularly pleased to be able, after so many joint diving expeditions, to introduce him now to the world's largest and most beautiful reef. He was sitting under the sun awning, reading. For him this voyage was to be his last diving enterprise for some time. On our arrival in Cairns he received a telegram informing him that our planned Institute for Human Ethology—the biological investigation of human behaviour—had at long last been authorized and that he had become the Institute's Director. As soon as we finished our voyage he would fly straight to Johannesburg in order to make some unobserved slow-motion films among the Bushmen. The first major project of his Institute was the investigation of the inborn elements of human mime and gesture—a huge project.

For supper Ray, our skipper, had cooked delicious fish fillets for us, from freshly caught fish. I was browsing through Cook's diary. Not far from the spot where we were he had written: 'Last night, about the middle of the watch, an extraordinary incident took place. Mr Orton, my servant, had taken drink in the evening and a malicious person—or several persons on board—used the opportunity to cut all his clothes off his back. As if this were not enough, they returned once more to his cabin, and whilst he was sleeping, cut a slice from each of his ears. . . .'

Meta's diary was on the table. She had written: 'Tomorrow we shall reach Pixie Reef where I shall make my first dive. When Mummy and Daddy were first here, on their honeymoon, the newspapers were carrying wagers on how long it would be before they were eaten by sharks.'

Banks had written in his diary: 'For dinner we had the bustard I shot yesterday; it proved an exceedingly tasty bird. As it weighed fifteen pounds our meal was not only excellent but also very plentiful.'

The following morning we dived at Pixie Reef—one of the most beautiful reefs I know. It is quite small and covered with stagshorn coral like a tropical palm-house. Meta, guided by Lotte, was enjoying herself with a schnorkel. We investigated the reef at various points but were unable to find a single *Acanthaster planci* anywhere. These are the large multi-branched starfish of which it is said that they are a serious menace to the Great Barrier Reef and other Pacific reefs. They settle on top of the coral, fold their stomachs out, and thus, outside their own body, digest the organic substance of the polyps. All that is left is a snow-white patch—the totally emptied calcareous skeleton.

Until 1960 there had been no reports of a mass invasion of these starfish. After that reports began to come from Guam, where entire sections of reefs had been destroyed, and from other regions of the Pacific. In the area of the Great

Barrier Reef it was Dr Endine of Brisbane University, an enthusiastic skindiver, who brought the first alarming news: some reefs in the central section of the Barrier Reef were smothered with hundreds of thousands and indeed, as he claimed, millions of such starfish. In Guam, Dr Chesher put forward the theory that this had been caused indirectly by human interference. The natural enemies of the starfish, the corals and their larvae, had probably been affected by bombing and blasting. Or else pesticides had accumulated in the bodies of beach organisms, which had then drifted out to sea and had been eaten by the coral polyps. In consequence they had damaged them and thus eliminated a natural enemy of the starfish larvae.

However, explosions could not have caused any damage to the coral growth on the Barrier Reef. Dr Endine put forward a different theory. He held the shell fishers indirectly responsible for the mass infestation by starfish: by collecting the large Pacific triton snails (*Charonia tritonis*), the only real predator feeding on starfish, they had upset the biological balance and thus made it possible for the starfish to multiply explosively. On his insistence the Government prohibited the collecting of these snails.

In America the U.S. State Department authorized considerable sums for the investigation and control of the starfish plague. Divers were employed for their destruction. Using injection harpoons they squirted a 5 per cent formaldehyde solution into the body cavity of the starfish and thereby killed them. The injection harpoon was connected by a hose to a container filled with formaldehyde; according to Chesher, by this method three divers were able to destroy no fewer than 1,500 starfish in under three hours. In Australia Dr Endine found it more difficult to get the necessary finance for research and control. There the Government is less generously disposed towards biology— as shown by the fact that along the entire south coast of Australia, undoubtedly an important coast, there is not a single marine research station. The project of Melbourne University to establish a Harold Holt Memorial Station at Port Sea, a most suitable spot, has still not been realized in spite of repeated attempts. Endine eventually took the matter into his own hands and mobilized the press. A quarter of the Great Barrier Reef, he positively declared, had already been destroyed and another 300 miles would follow over the next five years. This was enough to alarm the whole nation. The Great Barrier Reef is something treasured by every Australian—after all, it is one of the great wonders of the world and of enormous importance to future tourism. Some papers warned that anyone wishing to see the Great Barrier Reef had better hurry up. Others remarked that once the Barrier Reef had died and been washed away by the waves there would be no protection for the coasts behind it.

All this produced an opposition movement. Other Australian biologists declared that there was no threat to the reef as such. The Premier of Queensland, Mr Bjelke-Petersen, declared that 'there was serious doubt as to the competence of those attempting to cause a mood of alarm and despondency'. Nevertheless the Government decided to authorize the necessary money for a Commission of Investigation.

This Commission was interested in facts and figures. The Great Barrier Reef is over a million years old, and each female starfish produces twelve to twenty-four million larvae annually. One adult *Acanthaster planci* destroys one square metre of living coral a month; one triton snail eats one adult starfish per week or a corresponding number of young ones. Dr Endine had seen only a few starfish in twenty minutes of swimming off Fitzroy Island in August 1966; in March 1967 he had counted 930 during the same length of time, and in October a mere two. The Commission investigated thirty-six heavily infested reefs: coral growth there had been destroyed to 90 per cent. On Feather Reef near Innisfall the figure was 94 per cent. Only the elkhorn corals along with gorgonians and sizeable brain corals were spared by the starfish; resettlement was exceedingly slow, amounting to one per cent on Feather Reef. The Commission was unable to decide whether this increase of starfish was due to man. In favour of that theory was the fact that the centres of mass appearance of starfish were usually found near inhabited regions; against it was the fact that such centres were found equally in entirely isolated areas. The question was considered as to whether the starfish might not be controlled by the artificial introduction of triton larvae or whether such a course might result in an epidemic of triton snails with other unforeseen consequences. At any rate, far too little was known about the biology of *Acanthaster planci*, especially its early development, and the Commission therefore recommended further intensive research along those lines.

From the moment of our arrival in Australia we had been dragged into the pros and cons of this argument. At the Max Planck Institute at Seewiesen in Upper Bavaria, where Eibl had worked, it had been discovered by chance that a certain type of shrimp very effectively killed the murderous starfish. The shrimp would stroke the starfish with its claws, lift up its tentacles and thus get at its unprotected middle. It would then kill it and eat it from inside. The press was now discussing whether the Great Barrier Reef might not be cleared of its infestation by the introduction of these crustaceans or their young.

From Pixie Reef we sailed north. We followed the precise route taken by Cook with his *Endeavour*. We dived at Endeavour Reef, where his ship foundered, we visited Cooktown, where he had her pulled ashore to mend the leak, we climbed Lizard Island, from whose summit he looked for a way out from the countless reefs, we dived at Providential Passage, through which a strong current again carried him back to the open sea. There can be few reefs in the world to match this most enormous coral structure. To our delight we found that nowhere over this whole area were starfish present in any numbers, and the wealth of fishes seemed undiminished. Naturally, in the neighbourhood of Cairns and Cooktown the Australian spear fishermen had left their visiting card—but along the outer reefs, especially those north of Lizard Island, every-thing still remained unchanged. On some unforgettable dives we found here an eldorado for the naturalist and underwater photographer.

The northernmost point of Australia, lonely Cape York, is adorned with towers. Some of these are stone, but most of them were built by creatures—termite hills up to sixteen feet high. A little sentimentally we looked for Australia's northernmost tree, her northernmost flower, her northernmost blade of grass. The northernmost land creature turned out to be an insect larva adhering to a bare foreshore rock. The sea bottom in Torres Strait is sandy, with a considerable current running. The Barrier Reef is over ninety miles distant from this point. It runs on in a northerly direction, in a straight line, until it terminates not far from New Guinea.

'One day, when we can spare the time, we'll have a look at its final tip,' Eibl said.

As for the pressing question whether the whole Barrier Reef is seriously threatened by the starfish *Acanthaster planci* and whether immediate counter-measures are called for, we were unable to make a useful contribution. What our voyage made us clearly realize, however, was that coral reefs die also from other causes. Cyclones may cover them with sand or mud and so suffocate them. If there are downpours at low tide—the tide difference may be as much as twenty feet here—the corals are killed by the fresh water. Extensive sections of the Great Barrier Reef are certainly not 'alive'. Very important also is the fact that coral reefs, in spite of their name, are by no means built up entirely of corals, but that calcareous algae play a decisive part. They cement the loose rock, they convert the loose coral detritus into the reef plateau, which in some ways is like a concrete structure. These calcareous algae, however, can thrive only where the corals have died off. Certainly they can turn the most delicate stagshorn coral into a massive block of stone—but only if the coral is dead. For the formation of reefs it may therefore be necessary that these corals should be killed at certain times. Viewed in this light, the cyclic mass appearance of *Acanthaster planci* may be part of the general process of reef formation.

Endine and numerous American biologists have pointed out that there is no mention anywhere in historical records of a mass appearance of starfish. Certainly this is an argument that cannot be lightly dismissed. At the same time it should be remembered that man has only recently equipped himself with watertight masks to invade and observe the submarine regions of tropical seas.

The protection of our environment has only now become a topical problem because human ruthlessness towards the rest of nature has had increasingly far-reaching results owing to Man's technological progress. We have reached a point where we must be aware of possible damage without waiting for it to be caused. I believe that Dr Endine and his circle have somewhat exaggerated the significance of this starfish—no doubt with the best of intentions. The Great Barrier Reef—over a million years old and 1,250 miles long—is certainly not in any immediate danger; the tourist centres on the coast, on the other hand, are quite seriously affected. All means should be used today to convince the various governments of the cardinal importance of biological research. It is extremely short-sighted for Man to regard the rest of nature—which produced him—as his unquestioned property. And it is even more short-sighted for us through our selfish activities to destroy that nature which continues to support us.

A week later I was sitting on a coral reef off the coast of Tahiti. I was shocked by what I saw under the sea—or rather by what I did not see. Nowhere was there a fish more than four inches long. Magnificent coral landscapes in crystal clear water—and not a sign of fish. A lunar landscape under water. I was reminded of my first impressions off the French Riviera—the landscape of Cap d'Antibes, near the island of St Honorat off Cap Miramar, and the underwater rocks of Agay with their vast quantities of fish. A few years ago I revisited all these spots in order to refresh old impressions—and I found the same picture there. Nowhere, much as I looked around, was there a grouper, a red steenbras or a dorado. The grottos were empty—not a single umbrine. No trace of grey mullet playing in the shallow water. Nowhere a sheepshead that was more than four inches long, not one shoal of bogue browsing among the boulders. Nowhere a ray hiding in the sand. Another lunar landscape. A mere two and a half decades had been enough to destroy the once so rich stocks of littoral fishes. Perhaps modern fishing methods have played their part—but probably not the decisive part. The principal blame for this development lies with the underwater fishermen—or more accurately, the weapons they have been using.

In the past I had always been glad to think that my books and films have encouraged so many people to take up this enjoyable pastime. But now I am beginning to see things in a different light.

What is to be done? If things continue as at present it is easy to foresee what the situation will be like along the Great Barrier Reef in ten years' time, and sooner or later along all coasts, no matter whether the water there is warm or cold. Difficulties will not deter the underwater fisherman. What, then, does he get out of it?

No doubt there is, first of all, the excitement of the hunt, of stalking a quarry. A great many of the fish thus killed end up in the cooking pot—but this is not the real purpose of the activity. It is a manifestation, as we realize now, of the hunting urge which Man has inherited from his ancestors, the predatory apes. This urge is more strongly developed in some and less so in others; the act of the hunt provides a release. It comes under the heading of the pursuit of pleasurable experiences.

But now we have a situation where one such tendency interferes with another. If all fish are exterminated, then diving and underwater photography must lose their attraction, and we shall lose the pleasure of observing nature undisturbed.

What is there to be done? I believe that there is only one way out today— a general ban on all mechanical weapons for spear fishing. The continually improved catapults, which fire their arrows over ever greater distances, give the skindiver too much of an advantage. The fish simply stand no chance any longer, especially if the skindiver also wears breathing apparatus.

Already in the U.S.A., in Japan and elsewhere so-called 'submarine parks' have been set up—nature preserves where hunting is prohibited. Certainly this is an important measure, but it is not enough. The original form of spearing —skindiving with a simple spear, without breathing equipment—could be permitted outside such reserves. This certainly is a fair method, and to kill a fish in this manner is exceedingly difficult. Indeed, in this very difficulty lies the particular fascination of this form of hunting. But all kinds of mechanical firearms are a degeneration of underwater hunting—that much I realized at the very start. Present-day spear fishing is no longer fair play.

On land it is possible to ensure sensible hunting quotas by regulations. But it is not possible to licence a man to kill under water, say, two groupers and two umbrines. In the present situation, therefore, I can see no other possibility than a world-wide prohibition of mechanical weapons. Perhaps those who are today still using them will eventually come to agree with my view.

To even greater Depths

At the great Underwater Congress in London in September 1956, Commandant Cousteau provided a sensation. As President of the C.M.A.S. (Confédération Mondiale Activitées Subaquatiques) he gave the inaugural address, and what he had to say gave rise to banner headlines and overshadowed everything else that happened at the Congress. In view of the occasion it is hardly to be assumed that Cousteau was joking.

Cousteau proclaimed the dawn of the era of 'homo aquaticus'. He argued that Man's conquest of the oceans could be divided into five phases, into five lines of advance. One: the skindivers, using no special diving apparatus except perhaps watertight goggles or masks. Two: the helmet divers, scaphander divers and those working from diving bells; these still had a link with the atmospheric world. Three: the independent divers who carried their air with them but still depended on a ship or a floating station. Four: underwater settlers living in underwater houses and producing the gas they needed for breathing by a technological process from the water itself. And finally, five: *Homo aquaticus*, transformed into a marine creature by surgical intervention.

In the field of space research, Cousteau argued, considerable progress has already been made in the direction of branching off the human blood circulation under the left arm and passing it through a regeneration cartridge carried on the belt. In this way the human breathing system could be totally eliminated. Once this had been achieved, the arrangement could equally well be used under water. The only difference was that under water Man's lungs would have to be filled with a non-compressible liquid. But this was feasible, and in that case *homo aquaticus*—as animal experiments had already shown—would be able to withstand even the pressures at depths of 4,000 to 6,500 feet. With or without mechanical aids he would then be able to move from the surface down to these great depths, and without any decompression problems. Cousteau continued: 'This new Man will probably be born down there, the surgical operations will be carried out on him at birth in underwater hospitals which will be filled with water. There will also be theatres down there, and there will also be parliaments under water, and probably new nations.'

I have rarely seen journalists scribbling so furiously. Cousteau continued: 'This category of Man will not be confined to an underwater existence. After the surgical operation he will be perfectly able to move also on land, still with his cartridge which will need renewing from time to time. He will be just as capable of skiing as of living underwater. The birth of this new Man lies in the line of natural evolution.'

Since this statement was made on such an official occasion and with such convincing emphasis I would like to comment on it. The public today has been so intimidated by technological progress over the last fifty years that hardly anyone now dares to contradict prophesies no matter how provocative. As a biologist, however, I must state my belief that the development suggested by Cousteau carries not the slightest degree of probability.

As for the fate of a skier having a bad fall after his blood circulation has been diverted through a cartridge, I would rather not go into details. What Cousteau evidently overlooked was the important circumstance that filling the lungs with a non-compressible liquid would not be enough. The breathing movements would also have to be immobilized by the breathing reflex being surgically eliminated. But the submarine surgeon in his submarine hospital would have to do a great deal more—he would also have to exchange the entire skin of a newly born aquatic human since continuous underwater existence with our natural skin is certainly not possible. The problem of the human eye was not touched upon by Cousteau at all. The question arises of whether aquatic man is expected to lie in his matrimonial bed wearing a diving mask.

It seems to me that in making this prophesy—which he wants to see realized within fifty years—Cousteau was influenced by the pressing problem of our population explosion. The idea that mankind would divide one day into one group enjoying sun and air and another which, voluntarily or not, would live underground was first suggested by H. G. Wells. Thinking on similar lines, Cousteau possibly thought that this population surplus, which could no longer be accommodated on dry land, might one day find a new home in the depths of the oceans. But he disregarded economic facts. The cost per aquatic human—even if the project were realizable—would be so high that only the very wealthy would be able to afford this luxury. And it is just this group which, so long as there are sun and air, will no doubt always prefer Paris or Capri to some city on the muddy sea bed of the Atlantic.

Similarly, the claim that the emergence of such a fish-man lies along the natural line of evolution must be contradicted. The typical feature about man is his intellectual development, which enables him to extend his genetic body by additional functional units, to magnify his potential by artificial exchangeable unattached organs. Man thus becomes a specialist in a great many special fields. In power complexes formed by him he is, from a functional point of view, no more than the creating and controlling centre. No doubt these 'functional organisms' of Man would also progressively conquer the ocean depths—indeed this process has already advanced a good way. But Man himself, the genetic nucleus, will go under water for any length of time only whenever his creative and controlling activity makes this indispensable. To spend a few hours a day roaming the blue depths is most enjoyable—but as for theatrical performances, we shall probably always prefer to watch these from dry seats rather than through murky water. Who wants to swim to an underwater buffet in the interval between acts to eat a salty underwater sandwich?

As long ago as 1942 I stressed in an article ('Colonization of the Sea') how important the exploitation of the oceans was to Man, and what vast quantities

263

of food, raw materials and so on, were still available to us in the ocean depths. Many of these arguments were challenged at the time; today they are probably no longer utopian. The conquest of the seas—and here I agree entirely with Cousteau—is certainly of greater practical importance than that of the planets around us. But this conquest will surely not be along the line of some human dolphin or some human sea lion evolving. Instead we shall extend our body, a body designed for terrestrial life, by means of technological advances; we shall then be able to raise the wealth of the oceans without getting any wetter than is necessary or pleasant.

As I have reported in this book, we started by using recirculation equipment but later the compressed-air devices conquered the world. Nowadays the trend is back towards recirculation equipment. The 'Electrolung' manufactured in the U.S.A. is equipped with a small computer which mixes the correct blend of oxygen, nitrogen and helium for any particular depth. With such devices it would be possible to remain under water for several hours on end and to descend to depths of over 650 feet. It is along such equipment that the real line of natural evolution lies. Step by step Man is succeeding in transferring certain necessary functions to technical organisms. In the case of the 'Electrolung' this function is the correct mixture of respiratory gases for whatever depth the diver is at—in other words an extension of the functions of the central nervous system.

As for the utilization of submarine oil deposits and other mineral wealth, and also for research and 'sea farming', the underwater houses first developed by E. Link will prove valuable. And so, no doubt, will they—unfortunately—for military purposes. There are already up to a hundred different types of special submarine vessels available, capable of reaching depths of many hundreds of feet. Their mechanical arms similarly extend the capacity of the human body. But the human body itself wherever possible remains dry.

Homo futurus will be a specialist in a great many specialized fields. He will be a specialist particularly in the realization of everything that gives us pleasure. Here, and here alone, probably lies the only hope for the flora and fauna of the seas. They will eventually be protected by Man—not out of kindness but out of selfishness. If we destroy them we shall destroy the source not only of our food but also of pleasure. To turn himself permanently into a fish will never suit Man the pleasure seeker. But to turn into a fish temporarily will give him—inquisitive creature that he is—an ever-increasing degree of pleasure.

A new location—Grand Cayman in the Caribbean. Anita and Anton, good friends of ours, had told us of this island and of the great variety of its fish life, of magnificent reefs and delicious crayfish. Now we were there, sitting in a motor boat littered with diving equipment. We had cast anchor and below us lay a tempting reef slope. As we slipped on our apparatus and got our cameras ready, Meta was sitting in a deckchair, munching an apple and with her head in a book.

'I am sorry,' I said to her. 'But it's really too deep here. In a year or two no doubt you'll manage it easily. But here the slope starts at 140 feet—that's too deep.'

Without glancing up from her book Meta said: 'I know all that. I wouldn't want to dive now anyway. My book's much more interesting.'

'Is the camera screwed up?' Anton asked.

Anita rinsed out her mask and sneezed. 'Yes. It's O.K.'

'Is this cylinder valve fully open?' Lotte asked me.

I tried it. 'Yes. All clear.'

'Well, here goes. . . .'

And one after another we let ourselves drop backwards into our familiar element.

NOTES

Anyone interested in present-day trends in skindiving and underwater research will find useful articles in the highly recommended periodical *Delphin* (Hamburg). The leading periodical in the U.S.A., also very good, is *Skin Diver* (Los Angeles). Other underwater periodicals are: in Eastern Germany, *Poseidon* (Berlin); in France *Plongées* and *L'Aventure Sousmarine;* in Italy *Mondo Sommerso;* in England *Triton;* in Spain *Cris;* and in Japan the excellent *Marine Parks Journal* (Tokyo).

Associations of skindiving clubs exist in the Federal Republic of Germany, in Austria and in Switzerland. There are skindiving schools at Nervi, on Elba and Corfu, in Eilat and at numerous holiday camps of the Club Mediterranné.